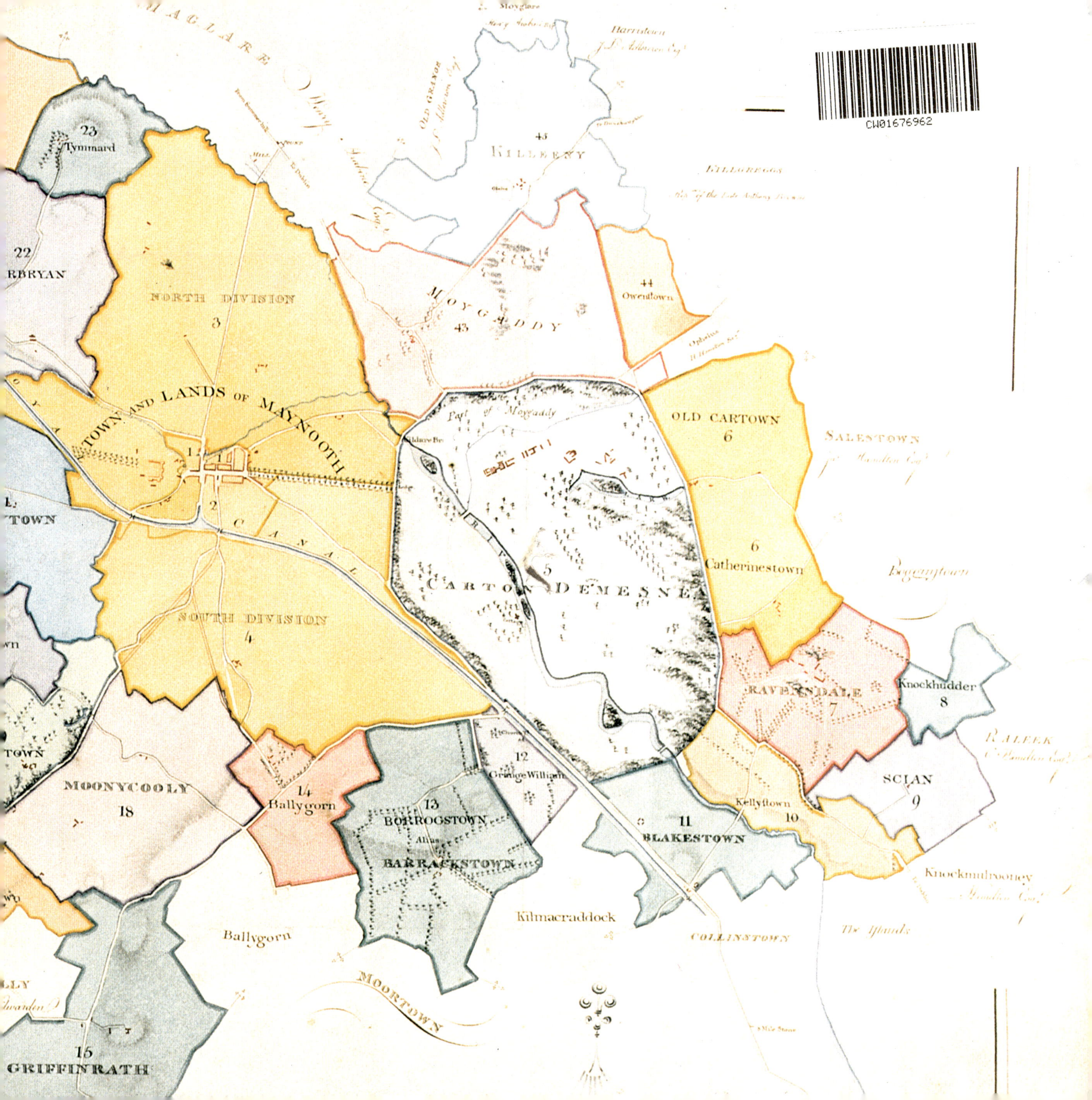
Moyglare
Harristown
OLD GRANGE
45
KILLEENY
KILLGREGGS
23
Tymmard
22
RBRYAN
NORTH DIVISION
3
MOYGADDY
43
44
Owenstown
TOWN AND LANDS OF MAYNOOTH
1
2
CANAL
Part of Moygaddy
OLD CARTOWN
6
SALESTOWN
Catherinestown
5
CARTON DEMESNE
SOUTH DIVISION
4
RAVENSDALE
7
Knockhudder
8
RALEEK
12
Grange William
SCIAN
9
MOONYCOOLY
18
14
Ballygorn
13
BORROGSTOWN
Alias
BARRACKSTOWN
11
BLAKESTOWN
Kellystown
10
Knockmulrooney
Kilmacraddock
Ballygorn
COLLINSTOWN
MOORTOWN
15
GRIFFINRATH

Landscape Design in Eighteenth-Century Ireland

# Landscape Design in Eighteenth-Century Ireland

*Mixing Foreign Trees with the Natives*

Finola O'Kane

CORK cup UNIVERSITY PRESS

First published in 2004 by Cork University Press, Crawford Business Park, Crosses Green, Cork, Ireland.



British Library Cataloguing in Publication data

A CIP catalogue record for this book is available from the British Library.

ISBN 1 85918 362 X

A CIP record for this publication is available from the Library of Congress.

Typeset and designed by Charles Crimmins, Current Visual Communications.

Printed by Butler & Tanner Ltd., Somerset.

www.corkuniversitypress.com

# Contents

# List of Illustrations

# Acknowledgements

Like a garden, a book is made by many people. The initial doctoral thesis was completed with the encouragement of my supervisor, Dr John Olley, and Professor Cathal O'Neill, Professor Dermot O'Connell and Professor Loughlin Kealy of the School of Architecture, University College Dublin. During the early course of my research Terence Reeves-Smyth and Belinda Jupp pointed me in the direction of the Architectural Association's historic landscape conservation community in Bedford Square, London, where Claire Boughey, Elizabeth Lebas, Sir Ferrers Vyvyan and Dr Jan Woudstra shared and encouraged my interest in Ireland's designed landscapes. John Cahill and the Office of Public Works kindly supported my study of the landscape of Castletown House, and the Wingate Foundation awarded me a scholarship to visit relevant gardens in England. Mrs Lena Boylan first alerted me to the information available about the landscape of Castletown and guided me through the documentary material, which was then stored in her house. Dr Edward McParland sparked my interest in Robert Molesworth and his gardens at Breckdenston. Professor Anne Crookshank and Desmond Fitzgerald, the Knight of Glin, directed my interest in eighteenth-century Irish landscape paintings and allowed me to study their exceptional archive. The National University of Ireland awarded me a fellowship, which enabled the thesis to metamorphose into a book.

Dr Toby Barnard persevered in his support for this book and introduced me to the congenial world of Irish eighteenth-century historians. His guidance has always been incisive, instructive and inspiring. Dr Gillian O'Brien painstakingly corrected the thesis from which this book developed and gave generously of her knowledge. Dr Michael Brown and the Knight of Glin read chapters of the thesis while it was being reworked for publication and guided me towards many interesting avenues of enquiry. Others to whom I owe a debt of gratitude include

Julia Barrett, Dr Gary Boyd, Dr Hugh Campbell, Sarah Cremin, Shane de Blacam, Professor Seán de Courcey, Professor James Dooge, Dr Terence Dooley, Professor P.J. Duffy, Professor Tom Dunne, the Hon. Desmond Guinness, Joe Lawrence, John Meagher, the Hon. William Molesworth and Dr Brendan Rooney.

The staff of the National Library of Ireland, in particular Tom Desmond, Sister Frances Lowe and Dr Elizabeth Kirwan helped me to discover the intricacies of that wonderful institution. The staff of the Early Printed Books and Manuscripts departments of the Library of Trinity College Dublin, the Public Record Office of Northern Ireland and the British Library made research both interesting and rewarding. David Griffin, Simon Lincoln and Colum O'Riordan of the Irish Architectural Archive were endlessly patient with my various enquiries, particularly during the book's production. Gerry Hayden and David Davison accompanied me to great houses to photograph their treasures.

My editor Lucy Freeman charmed me through the editing process and Sara Wilbourne never flagged in her ambition to publish this book. Caroline Somers and Mike Collins at Cork University Press brought their expertise and understanding to the project. Charles and Carol Crimmins and Joe Jennings of Current Communications produced designs, which I never had to worry about.

My parents-in-law Catherine and Cathal Crimmins and their extended family provided me with much good food, company and support. The enthusiasm and interest of my parents, Agnes and Philip, my grandparents, Rita and John, and my siblings, Una, Deirdre, Orla and Brian, allowed and inspired me to complete this work. And finally this book is dedicated to my daughters, Aoibh and Ruth, who set many of the production deadlines, and to my husband, Neil, who helped me keep them.

Fig.1. The Castletown obelisk.

# Introduction

Within the walls of the demesne the Anglo-Irish Ascendancy constructed its vision of an Irish Utopia. Ideal landscapes, inspired by the eighteenth century's developing pantheism, were designed and planted out with standard temperate trees and newly introduced exotics from the Americas. Spatial experiments were conducted which were considered entirely alien to the society that lay outside the insistent line of the high demesne wall. Ideal cottages were built, paternalistic estate management structures developed and complex planning and design theories indulged. Here one could build rustic arbours, bathing houses, ornamental dairies and cottages; labyrinthine walks, which space and distance had miraculously enlarged and expanded, confused the traveller's perception. Masques and plays, morally suspect to the strict Protestant code of the time, flourished within the enclosed world of the demesne, 'defined historically as the lands held by the manor for its own use and occupation'.[1] Architects, landscape theorists, practical gardeners, poets, politicians and artists collaborated to produce the villa in its landscape – a great composite work of art, where layered images, frames and views contrived to augment the intellectual and sensual experience. Spatial diversity and innovation developed in a manner that had been banished from the city and town plans of the ever more rational eighteenth century. In the peculiar social and political climate of Ireland at this time, that spatial difference seems to have been even more pronounced than in neighbouring England, whence the majority of the design influence came. Damaged and depleted by the upheavals of the seventeenth century, the surrounding countryside identified the demesne as the exotic in a monochrome environment. The rigid formality of the rectilinear estate town, linked to the estate by the omnipresent avenue, contrasted with the conscious informality of the eighteenth-century landscape garden.

The Castletown obelisk is a pivot for the history of two landscapes. Its prominence in both the Castletown and Carton demesnes orientated the occupants of one house towards the other (Fig. 1).

Katherine Conolly built this great monument on Carton land in 1740.[2] With Castletown's extensive ornamental woodland and the great mass of the house itself, it expressed the Conolly family's extraordinary wealth and power. Katherine's husband, Speaker William Conolly, built Castletown House and was introduced to his architect Alessandro Galilei by Robert Molesworth. A prominent Whig politician and theorist, Molesworth counted the Earl of Shaftesbury and Jonathan Swift among his friends, and this brought Conolly and Castletown into the north Dublin circle of Whig thought. Molesworth had created an ideal model landscape at Breckdenston, Swords, Co. Dublin, to express his own Whig philosophy, and he enriched the moral tone of his improvements with a symbolic and Italianate design vocabulary. He promoted the garden theorist Stephen Switzer's 'farmlike way of gardening', which was well received by the Irish gardening fraternity. He tried conscientiously to balance beauty and utility in his garden design, but luxury and affectation thwarted its successful realization. Together the Breckdenston and Castletown landscapes expressed the force of the Irish Whig ideal. At Castletown, the massive acquisition and expression of wealth and power was stamped vigorously upon the countryside, while at Breckdenston the calm rationale of tempered improvement reinvented the environment with the same conviction. Yet, as Tom Williamson states in his book *Polite Landscapes: Gardens and Society in Eighteenth-Century England*, 'we must be careful not to exaggerate the importance of politics, and especially of one political clique' in the development of the early eighteenth-century landscape garden. What these gardens 'really represented was a new attitude to the relationship between ideas and philosophies on the one hand, and the landscape on the other'.[3] This made it possible for gardens to 'be used as media to vent all sorts of highly personalized views of the world, political or otherwise'.[4]

When Speaker William Conolly died in 1729, his widow Katherine continued to improve the Castletown demesne and its surrounding countryside. She built its great follies and monuments and carefully managed the vast estate lands. In the mid-eighteenth century, the obelisk linked the landscapes of two sisters. Emily Fitzgerald, Duchess of Leinster, and Lady Louisa Conolly collaborated to create complementary environments. Both women elaborated the passage of water through the demesne and found ways to incorporate prosaic activities into the overall design. New theories of management and agricultural production led them to build new farm buildings; leisure pursuits demanded bathing houses, dairies, theatres, kennels and racecourses. They experimented with the English landscape garden style developed by Joseph Addison, Alexander Pope, Stephen Switzer, William Kent and Lancelot (Capability) Brown. The picturesque and exotic influence of Thomas Whately and William Chambers also contributed to the landscape's development. When the sisters' vividly theatrical designs diverged, the identity of the family they each represented was revealed. Louisa Conolly developed a riverside Gothic walk with follies and carefully orchestrated views to express the Whiggish patriotism of the Conolly commoners. Her husband's dexterous ability to buy, borrow and control landscapes that bordered their own continued Speaker Conolly's programme of expansion. Emily Kildare, safe within the aristocratic fortress of Fitzgerald lineage, never employed the strident vocabulary of the nervous arriviste at Carton. She asked the notable gentlemen-gardeners Charles Hamilton, Peter Collinson and Henry Fox to advise her and her husband James, first Duke of Leinster, on the alteration of Carton's landscape. Its early eighteenth-century stylistic loyalty to the Williamite succession was transformed into a fashionable landscape garden, where a variety of influences clamoured for supremacy. The ambiguous tones of the *ferme* and *cottage ornée* were introduced into a garden that had patriotically retained its Dutch topiary until 1750. For these women, landscape design was also a social and environmental responsibility and this concern for health and happiness coincided with their interest in pedagogy. Their design of private space was not only preoccupied with formal and stylistic issues but with the contribution architecture and landscape design could make in the spheres of feminine influence. To advance their particular interests and concerns, women, on occasion, became architects and designers in their own right.

Other Ascendancy gardens spin around the fulcrum of the Conolly obelisk. Neighbouring great houses borrowed its magnificence for their prospects and deferred to its grandiose presence on the horizon. To escape its dominance and the attendant constriction of a great countryside demesne, Emily Kildare and Louisa Conolly also developed alternative villa landscapes at Blackrock, one of Dublin's first maritime suburbs. There they cultivated a more relaxed and informal lifestyle than their city or countryside residences allowed. The theatrical tradition of French gardens influenced the development of Castletown, Carton and Frescati, but when Ascendancy society frowned upon the dangerous power of the theatre, the masque and the festival, demesne design took care to conceal such activity from the eyes of town and tenants. Caught between city and countryside, Dublin's suburbia became an escape, a refuge and a moral enclave for the rich, and an ideal environment for propagating the subversive qualities of the villa, the garden and the park. By asserting its connection with the city and the landscape rather than with the nearby town, suburban Breckdenston sought to balance the questionable luxury of formal design with the wholesome productivity of the farm. The *ferme ornée* developments at Carton, Castletown and Blackrock also questioned and redefined the farm. As the Irish eighteenth century approached the conflagration of the French Revolution and the United Irishmen's rebellion, the landscape ideology which had favoured classical utopianism on its arrival began to adopt more complex, deceptive and insidious iconographies. Some Irish landscape gardens looked to the late eighteenth-century philosophical and political gardens of France to profess their support for the radical enlightenment ideals of the French Revolution. Emily Kildare's garden at Frescati was designed to express Rousseau's controversial pedagogical agenda and to transfer educational and political ideas of a radical cast to her children. One of those children, Lord Edward

Fitzgerald, continued to re-create the Blackrock cottage garden idiom with political intent throughout his life. He drew from the vocabulary of French political gardens and festivals to explore the theme of national identity and individual liberty at his garden in Kildare. As a central figure in the United Irishmen's rebellion of 1798, he eventually transformed his planting schemes into revolutionary action. Valentine Browne Lawless, Lord Cloncurry, Edward's friend and fellow revolutionary, transported the egalitarian ideals of the *ferme ornée* to Lyons demesne, where the great spire of the Conolly obelisk reappears on the northern horizon.

The definition of landscape beauty in Ireland progressed from the beautiful to the picturesque and thence to the romantic and sublime. It was accomplished through the medium of books of views, guide books, memoirs, paintings, tourism and the changing practices of landscape design. The 1790s were a turning-point in demesne landscape design, and in the counter-revolutionary culture of the conservative years of the nineteenth century many eighteenth-century developments were negated. Demesne owners abandoned their dangerous flirtation with the cottage and farmyard lifestyle and began again 'to convince themselves and others that they had been there a long time and that their houses, like so many in England, reflected the vicissitudes of centuries'.[5] The rôle of benevolent landlord was re-established and schools and churches were built on the borders of the demesne to serve the local populace. The harsh history of nineteenth-century Ireland made the rôle a difficult one, however, and the great estate of Carton made only half-hearted efforts to re-embrace its estate town and countryside. With the growing poverty and discontent of the rural populace, a void opened between the environment of the demesne and that of the estate town. The umbilical cord of the benevolent avenue became an uncomfortable reminder of a doomed relationship. Sharply outlined formal gardens then cut out a private space for the noble family from the smooth landscape garden, whose silky transitions from estate to countryside were discarded and destroyed. Romantic landscape,

# Chapter 1

## ‘Securing the Ground and Gardens’[6]
## Robert Molesworth’s Landscape of Breckdenston[7]

*‘The cutting down of our trees displeases me much more than if they had burnt all our houses’*[8]
*Robert Molesworth, 25 March 1690*

Fig. 2
Robert Molesworth, 1st Viscount.
Oil painting after either an original in oils by Thomas Gibson
or a mezzotint by Peter Pelham.

In the latter years of the seventeenth century, Robert Molesworth, a moderately wealthy Anglo-Irish gentleman, lived with his wife and family at Breckdenston, an estate of some 200 acres situated near the small town of Swords, in north Co. Dublin (Fig. 3). Although the estate's area was 'almost all visible from ye house & its apartments', the small demesne had great 'variety within it, of Plain ground, Hills, groves, waterponds & gardens and vallyes and River'. Its proud owner did not 'know anywhere within so small a compass' that could compare with it 'for health, pleasure, convenience and prospect'. Despite its approximate distance of ten miles from Dublin's city centre, it lay 'remote from Highways & from too near neighbours'.[9] Molesworth liked to lie in bed and 'see the fleets of ships pass by to the bay of Dublin'. As Breckdenston was 'above 3 miles from the wild Sea' and 'so much above' sea level 'with a gentle descent all the way to it', he suffered 'no manner of ill influence from it'.[10]

Unlike other Ascendancy families, the Molesworths saw no need to announce their influence within the town of Swords (from which they eventually took the title of Viscount) and were quite happy to include its steeple and round tower as distant prospects for their garden walks. The demesne's principal entrance is situated on the western side of the demesne away from the town. The absence of a formal avenue–main street axis means that the hierarchy of village streets, gates, walls and lodges that characterizes many Irish demesnes did not exist at Breckdenston. Without an estate town to dilute its countryside setting, Breckdenston could remain 'so private and at such a distance from highways',[11] and the demesne's moderate scale rendered it malleable to alteration. Neighbouring houses formed the foci of the garden's avenues and drew the local propertied gentlemen visually together. The softly undulating countryside of north Dublin was considered preferable to the wilds of Wicklow in the early eighteenth century. Robert Molesworth, unconscious of the future impact of the sublime, wondered 'how a good gardener could find matter to work upon and to show his skill in such a mountain as Blessington'.[12] The series of letters written by Robert Molesworth (first Viscount Molesworth of Swords, 1656–1725) to his wife Lettice (née Coote) and others in the years 1690–1723 contains detailed descriptions of how an Irish landscape was improved and embellished at the close of the seventeenth century. Robert Molesworth's lengthy visits both to Parliament in London and to the other family estate of Edlington in Yorkshire compelled him to direct and supervise every aspect of the demesne's design and management by letter, thus bequeathing to posterity a record of his garden. For his particular fascination with the design and engineering of waterworks, he drew inspiration from the most advanced European authorities and created an elaborate water garden.

Molesworth had great confidence in his own taste and ability, proudly stating to his wife: 'My designs have been of many years standing yet with all my Experience and view of the world I find I cannot better them.'[13] Despite this self-confidence, the Molesworths did employ professionals on occasion. The influential contemporary garden designer Stephen Switzer was invited to Ireland by Molesworth in 1719,[14] and a 'Mr. Stewart, the surveyor', completed some drawings for the construction of the canal.[15] Molesworth brought the Italian architect Alessandro Galilei to Ireland from Italy in 1718. Galilei was expected to put his study of 'architecture and the making of

Fig. 3
John Rocque, *Map of the County of Dublin*, 1760.
Detail of Breckdenston.

aqueducts and fountains', his 'knowledge of the architecture of theatres', and his 'great experience, having charge of the fountains of the G.D. (Grand Duke) and those of Florence',[16] to good use. As the British envoy to Turin, Robert Molesworth's eldest son, John, acquired an intimate knowledge of the great Italian gardens, and his father hoped that he would 'improve' his future inheritance with those acquisitions of knowledge, 'especially in gardening and waterworks', he had 'got abroad'.[17] John also sourced books 'relating to Waterworks, fountains &c. or the manner of conveying & collecting water'[18] for his father on the Continent. Molesworth had great respect for the Dutch gardening tradition, and attempted to employ 'a Dutch gardener for fruit flowers and kitchen garden' in 1720. He left the resident native gardener, Nick, with 'his province of setting out works', which Nick liked better than the 'low mechanical direction' of plantsmanship.[19] This suggests that Nick played some part in laying out the great water projects. Robert and Lettice Molesworth treated Nick as a somewhat recalcitrant but gifted child, and his influence on the Breckdenston garden was not insignificant. Many of the Molesworth letters document the variety of plants Robert Molesworth purchased in London and elsewhere for his garden in Swords, and what plants were available in Ireland at this time. Information and plants passed between friends and relations, and the family patronized the great London nurserymen, London and Wise.[20] Molesworth bought and used gardening books and wished that Nick, with whom he had a frequently exasperated relationship, would follow his example. He was also aware that the management of a garden could be improved by the keeping of accurate records. Being equally aware that Nick had no intention of keeping any, he wrote that as 'Mr. Nick (according to his laudable custom of keeping no gardening bookes)' had lost or forgotten to keep them, George (Cartwright, agent) should 'keep a garden book' instead.[21]

The neighbours' landscaping interventions, which were avidly commented on by letter, affected and influenced Breckdenston's development. Molesworth insisted that the 'beauties of Breckdenston do not depend upon what' one neighbour did at the neighbouring estate of Brazeel,[22] but worried if another neighbour had taken 'care to keep all his string of high ponds and decoy ponds as brimfull as possible'.[23] The demesne's riverside views, which bordered both other properties and the public road, were particularly vulnerable to outside influence. Molesworth's hydraulic activities demanded a carefully controlled water pressure and volume, and neighbouring water systems could influence Breckdenston's in a manner infuriatingly beyond his control. Despite such awkward dependence, the interlocking axes and geometric figures of Breckdenston's garden benefited greatly from being able to connect with similar systems in the surrounding countryside.

Fig. 4
View of the old house of Brackenstown, Swords, 1900.

In the sixteenth century the demesne of Breckdenston had been owned 'by the Burnell family; from them it passed to the Nugents who in the reign of James the 1st sold it to one Bysse, whose son became Recorder of Dublin, & subsequently Chief Baron'. Breckdenston came into the Molesworth family through Judith Bysse, 'Chief Baron Bysse's only daughter and heiress',[24] when she married Robert Molesworth's father. The map of Breckdenston that John Rocque drew for his 1760 map of Co. Dublin reveals the general layout of Robert Molesworth's landscape (Fig. 3). It depicted both the seventeenth-century house occupied by Robert's father and his Bysse ancestors, and the early eighteenth-century Palladian house which replaced it (Fig. 4). The Palladian house was destroyed by fire in 1915, and subsequently rebuilt to a different design.

Molesworth identified a '20 Irish acres scope of ground, all one large square with great variety within it' as the core of his demesne. These core 'garden grounds' included the 'Ponds, groves and as much of ye Canal as will be within ye Cherry orchard'. The square also enclosed 'ye new orchard' and his imaginary boundary ended at 'ye south flanker of ye Hall garden'.[25] This description of the central twenty acres at Breckdenston as 'one large square' with a 'south flanker' attached to the 'Hall garden' suggests that the older house formed part of a defensive bawn walled enclosure with several flanker projecting towers at each corner. In the war-torn and suspicious political and cultural climate of late seventeenth-century Ireland, many gardens had been small and practical in emphasis, as defence requirements worked against those of mere pleasure and grandeur. The gardens of Leamaneh Castle, Co. Clare, and Lismore Castle, Co. Waterford, still retain their seventeenth-century flanker towers and terrace walks. The proposed outline of this bawn, the oldest locus of gardening activity at Breckdenston, and the location of the 'south flanker' are shown in Fig. 5. The bawn walls may have been intended as terrace walks from their inception, or they may have become so when no longer required for defensive purposes.

Molesworth demoted the axial approach avenue to the house from Knocksedan in the west by laying out a new curving approach route from the southwest. This intervention increased the privacy of the house and riverside area. The primacy of the new approach route was confirmed by his construction of a lodge 'house by Dublin gate ... as 'tis done in places of 40 times greater resort all about London and Hampton Court'.[26] Curved stone walls set the new Dublin lodge and gates back from the road, and a carefully profiled, curvilinear route revealed views

Fig. 5
Diagram of Robert Molesworth's landscape from John Rocque's *Map of the County of Dublin*, 1760.

a Early eighteenth-century Breckdenston House with curved galleries
b Seventeenth-century Breckdenston House with forecourt and walled enclosures
c Knocksedan House
d Brezeel House (Ned Bolton's)
e Knocksedan Avenue
f Swords church
g Forrest House (James Hand's)
h Dublin Gate & Lodge
i Dublin Gate Avenue
j Diagonal Walk to James Hand's
k South (Great) Avenue
l Diagonal Walk to Tom Cullen's (on axis with promontory)
m Parterre with fountain
n Kitchen Garden / Cherry Orchard
o Clewes Avenue
p Canal
q Water Cistern House
r Great Pond
s Tuckmill
t New Orchard
u Wilderness
v Tuckmill Race
w Bowling Green
x High Walk with south flanker & belvedere
y Long Walk
z Ward River
A Bawn outline
B 20 acre outline

of the new avenues, the new wildernesses, the belvedere walk and eventually the house itself. The new Palladian house was constructed northeast of the older house. When Molesworth decided to focus his new canal on his new house, his son-in-law and agent John Tichborne disapproved. He admired the walled gardens and terraced walks created by Molesworth's grandfather, Chief Baron Bysse. In 1710 Tichborne 'finisht ye walks . . . so that you may go from all ye Lord Chief Baron's walks quite round to ye end of ye Terrace walks and by ye gate going to ye fishponds'. In his 'humble opinion', placing the canal at 'the lower end of ye cherry garden' would have enabled the creation of a much longer axis extending into the parterre garden. The 'walks in ye cherry garden' could then have been made 'parallel to those on either side'[27] of the canal, instead of following the geometry of the house. Tichborne also thought that it 'would look very grand & magnificent' if the canal was terminated by 'fine pallisades with a great gate'. Despite Tichborne's nostalgia, Molesworth proceeded with his 'great many chimerical plans of my own and of others'[28] for the gardens' improvement. He did however retain parts of the seventeenth-century gardens within his new eighteenth-century landscape, and the upper parterre in particular followed the structure of a seventeenth-century walled garden. Two hundred lengths 'of walling . . . necessary for securing the ground and gardens' were built in 1709, despite the growing fashion for opening out the garden to the surrounding landscape. The brick wall from the 'kitchen to the end of ye cherry orchard' became 'ye finest fruit wall in Ireland' with 'Gates and doors in it in convenient places for Dung carts and outlets'.[29]

Free from the unforgiving hydraulic logic which the construction of waterworks demanded, Molesworth delighted in his arboricultural activities; his great *patte-d'oie* (three avenues laid out in the shape of a goose-foot) crowned Breckdenston's lattice of avenues, wildernesses and groves. This feature dominated the estate's southern aspect and terminated the southern garden sequence (Fig. 5). In 1716 Molesworth had described 'Mr. Secretary Johnston's project of carrying forward 2 long diagonal walks from ye middle of ye High Walk towards Tom Cullans' [hill] and Jeremy Hand's [Forrest House]'.[30] The 'new rowes in the long South Avenue towards the forest'[31] were first mentioned in 1712. The older central prong of the *patte d'oie* was lined with '8 rows of trees in ye great avenue towards Hatch Hall, 6 of those are Elms (whereof some are without and some within ye Clipped Hedge)'.[32] Molesworth planted some 'spruce firrs to be put in ye place of some dead and decaying that one saw in ye Great Avenue',[33] in 1714, which suggests that the outer two rows of the eight-row avenue were of spruce. The dark tones of the evergreen would have highlighted the changing hues of the inner elms. The trees marched southwards to meet the undulating landscape of the Forrestgreat townland, which created the desired effect of straight lines moving over a curved and asymmetric plane.

In 1695, Lettice Molesworth was directed to buy as many beech trees as she could to 'make good'[34] the one avenue to Knocksedan then in existence. Molesworth covered the Breckdenston landscape with avenues of trees during the next twenty years. The old beeches of the Knocksedan avenue (or one of its flanking avenues) were replaced with Breckdenston's own elms 'as far as they will go' in 1709.[35] Limes were planted 'in the back avenue going to Swords' because Molesworth had 'no store of Elms for that work',[36] and the new Dublin Gate avenue was also planted with lime trees.[37] The avenues were planted with parallel shelter avenues of hardier and less valuable trees, typically coniferous. These were removed when the avenue trees were mature enough to grow correctly without their protection. Hedges were planted for additional environmental control and their steady horizontal lines acted as a foil for the rhythmic verticals of the young trees. Compound avenues of different tree species and of varied hues and habits were laid out. This created a variety of seasonal effects as the trees alternately bloomed and shed their leaves. A permanent combination of deciduous and coniferous trees was sometimes used (spruce and elm in the great avenue) and this reflected the growing influx and popularity of North American varieties. Fir trees, except the Scotch fir, which Molesworth considered 'one of the ugliest trees', were used in all situations. Their ability to provide shelter for other trees did not preclude their use as specimen or avenue trees. When avenue firs were 'blasted down' by a storm in 1707 Molesworth intended to 'change them for elms' if they did not 'thrive when the shelter trees grew tall enough to protect them'.[38] An old silver fir was saved by 'nothing but ye beauty of it which kept it in that place all this while for it must be owned it stood out in ye way of view & very wrong', by blocking 'ye prospect of ye room into ye Parterre'.[39] This varied use of fir suggests that a hierarchy of tree species, which became a feature of the mid-eighteenth-century garden and which relegated many conifers to the shelterbelts, had not yet crystallized into an appreciable pattern. However, the future supremacy of lime and elm in avenues is suggested by the six rows of elm of the great *patte-d'oie.*

The young avenue trees led a perambulatory existence. 'Every small unsuitable or unthriving tree' in the avenues was to be 'taken away from thence as well as ye dead: or decayed (wch may be replanted in the nursery till they recover & good ones planted in their stead)' in 1716. The ungainly elms of the great avenue were to be 'planted in places of less importance, as on ye hillsides near ye Cherry Orchard and in Rowes', and 'once for all' replaced 'wth ye best trees we have'.[40] Trees which were 'bound about the roots with couch-grass or livery earth' were 'dug about and cleansed from suckers', and the 'earth about such trees . . . made loose and fine for three foot round'.[41] A variety of pruning techniques kept the trees carefully groomed. The awkward habit of elm 'to grow at the top into branches like stags' heads' was amended by 'cutting them off within 6 or 7 inches of the stem' to shoot 'upwards with a round head'.[42] Despite being 'prun'd according to Mr. Bolton's directions as he gave them to Nick', the 'lime trees on ye square pond' aggrieved Molesworth by being 'in shape nearer a pineapple than a pyramidall'.[43] The nurseries grew young trees for the avenues and plantations, and fruit trees for the brick walls of the kitchen garden and orchards.[44] Molesworth concentrated the Breckdenston nurseries together, 'well stockd and Regular: not scattered in small inconsiderable parcells up and down as hitherto but as yr new gardiner has bin used . . . in ye Nurserymen's grounds about London'.[45] The grafting of trees was one of the gardeners' most important activities and they propagated many of the trees required for the avenues, orchards and kitchen gardens. In 1714 Nick was instructed to 'propagate as many Myrtles' as he could and to 'take care of them when he has done'. He was also to 'digg, cleanse and increase all his nurseries' because Molesworth had 'great matters in view as to planting' and wanted 'a fresh supply of all sorts of trees especially elms and limes'.[46] The Molesworths also grew 'oranges and myrtles'[47] on their land at nearby Stormanstown, which became an external nursery for the demesne.

The Breckdenston avenues were incomplete without their accompanying hedges and correctly dressed walks of gravel.[48] Hornbeam hedges screened the less manicured areas from the parterre and these had 'even openings . . . to ye Diagonal walks in order to have a full prospect of those walks'.[49] Concerned with their correct design and maintenance, Molesworth chastised Nick when he allowed the hedges 'both hornbeam and others, to grow too broad'. If greater than two foot broad, they would 'spoil our walks and spoil ye round next them'.[50] His recommended height for 'ye topp of ye high Hornbeam Hedge in ye gravel walk cutt as even as the growth of the Hornbeam will admitt' was 'an equall height' of '20 foot or more'. Molesworth admired some he had seen 'of above 30 foot and very even on the sides and topp',[51] indicating that some of Chief Baron Bysse's hedges had survived Molesworth's improvements. Ungainly mature trees were sometimes concealed behind a hornbeam hedge, which was 'suffered to grow above 4 or 5 foot too broad, on Purpose, to cover and hide the thick bodies of those old Firrs'.[52] The axial effect of an avenue was more intensely appreciated when entered from a densely planted wilderness of 'very narrow and close' winding walks, 'yet the principal ones a little broader than the others'.[53] Despite its complex formality of twisting paths and geometric clearings, the wilderness was considered to be the most informal and natural part of the early eighteenth-century garden, where nature made its most determined assault upon art. Its complex patterning was thought to represent nature, a portrayal that may have more in common with the late twentieth-century understanding of its processes than with the intervening theories of the romantic and the sublime. An unidentified designer was employed to lay out the wildernesses at Breckdenston and Molesworth asked for 'rounds or ovals in the middle of each for a basin and also near the corners for four small ones'.[54] John Molesworth thought that the centres of the wilderness clearings should be occupied by 'figures of shepherds and shepherdesses', if no 'Termini are to be had ready made', and lead statues could also be melted down to 'yield something in case the figure chance to be spoilt' during the passage from London.[55] The wildernesses were 'dug and cleansed' in spring to 'make all ye trees thrive exceedingly',[56] and Nick had to be regularly reminded to 'clip his yew hedges and his wildernesses'.[57]

Robert Molesworth enhanced and enjoyed his new landscape by extending the house. The south wall was inhabited to allow 'ye prospect from ye room into ye Parterre'[58] to stretch from the parterre's central fountain to a belvedere and then to the great south avenue. 'The new gallery between ye house and ye new kitchen ceiled and ye walls well plaistered'[59] provided an interior space from which to enjoy the gardens. Twelve foot in height, it had 'ye best south wall and ye warmest for fruit'[60] and it may have resembled an orangery or other early variant of the greenhouse, as it lay adjacent to the kitchen garden and the cherry orchard. When the roof leaked, Molesworth worried that Galilei would insist he 'pull it all down again'.[61] Rocque's map was produced some thirty-six years after

Fig. 6
Present-day photograph of the belvedere walk.

the death of Robert Molesworth when the family profile had diminished. The numerous geometric water-basins and fountains, fishponds and decoys described in the letters are not drawn by Rocque, but his map still provides an informative, if incomplete, picture of Robert Molesworth's landscape. Fig. 5 correlates the garden buildings and landscape features mentioned in the text with John Rocque's map.

Due south of Breckdenston House a great retaining wall enclosed and elevated a parterre of grass *plats,* statues and flower-filled borders. At the centre of this wall a semi-circular belvedere punctured the enclosed seventeenth-century gardens and established a focus for Molesworth's *patte-d'oie* of three avenues (Fig. 6). Framed views of the surrounding landscape were introduced into the calm environs of the seventeenth-century gardens, and the elevated vantage-point allowed the strict geometrical lines of the 'new orchard' to be appreciated. The new parterre occupied the compartment nearest the house, and quadrants closest to the house were more intricately designed for pleasurable viewing from the upper storeys. The eastern prospect from the parterre extended towards the cherry orchard and the kitchen garden, and the western prospect projected as far as the great water-basin in the sixteen acres.

The upper parterre was laid out in the English style of simple and meticulously manicured grass *plats* with a fountain and basin at the centre, to look 'well from the Parlour door'.[62] The 'large grass plots all of a piece, or cut a little' of the typical parterre *à l'anglaise* were 'surrounded by a border with flowers',[63] and Molesworth planted pinks on 'the edge of all the borders as thick as they can stand'.[64] Breckdenston's gardens were 'filled as full of flowers as they can stick' in 1712, with flowers 'grown to be the chief ornament' of a garden. 'Great multitudes of flowers without being overchoice in the kinds' were planted, with 'as much roots as earth in every border'.[65] The parterre's enclosing walls to the north and west were peopled by statues housed in niches, and statues were also placed at the centres of the grass *plats*. John Molesworth supposed that they would 'be fauns and satyrs' or 'pastoral figures of shepherds and shepherdesses'. He thought that 'Venus, or any other graceful statue, will best stand in the middle of grass plots'.[66] Fruit trees covered the parterre walls, and the Bergamot pear tree was particularly favoured, with '2 or 3 very good sorts against our Walls, some in the Bowling green and some in ye parterre'.[67]

The Molesworths delighted in varying the tints, habits and textures of their plant material. The natural undergrowth of a grove or informal plantation of trees was considered unseemly and was generally replaced by 'sodding ye grove'[68] with turf, which demanded a great deal of maintenance. The fountain under the house was placed in a 'gloomy grove, authorising an air of mystery',[69] and the grove on the 'Hillside under ye French house' was 'planted as thick of trees and shrubbs as they can stand . . . a medley of all sorts for shade, firrs and all'.[70] Flowers were planted with abandon throughout the demesnes. 'Carnation seed, a box of . . . not ordinary pinks' and 'a box of tulip and other roots'[71] were sent to Swords in 1695 and 1696. Areas of the garden were set apart for the particular cultivation of flowers in 1710, when Lettice was supposed to be 'busy making and finishing' her 'flower gardens'.[72] The gardens lacked the distinction of 'several other sorts of common flowers in abundance' in 1714, when there was no 'store of lily of the valley (which ought to be scattered everywhere, even all over the hill's sides and bottom)'.[73]

The walled kitchen garden that Molesworth built was situated to guard against the action of the prevailing southwestern winds. Unlike the late eighteenth-century kitchen garden, which was separated distinctly from the rest of the demesne, the Breckdenston kitchen garden was not hidden from other parts of the landscape. It was located beside the great prospect to Swords and close enough to the house to be visible from its principal rooms. Decorative and pleasurable features were accommodated into its design to make the boundary between the aesthetic and the practical ambiguous. The varied scales and densities of the planting contributed towards creating a productive microclimate and the different varieties of trees, flowers and shrubs, and the insects they attracted, prospered together. Later, less inclusive gardening styles may not have achieved similar success in such an exposed location. Stephen Switzer, Molesworth's favourite garden writer, described his ideal kitchen garden in his 1727 book *The Practical Kitchen Gardiner*. 'A row of limes or elms . . . about ten or twelve foot distance from the wall . . . cut fan-ways, and kept cut at the top to fifteen or sixteen foot high' broke 'the winds from coming into the garden', as did 'the espalier hedges on the inside'. The borders immediately within the brick walls were 'about four feet wide and . . . designed for espaliered fruit'. Sloped ground beyond the borders was planted with 'little bunches of green yew or holly . . . to break the career of the wind', and these slopes were 'of greatest use for strawberries'.[74] Switzer's design for 'The Plan of a Kitchen Garden on three Levels with a Canal at bottom', like that at Breckdenston, has six sub-sections (Fig. 7). In 1707 Molesworth similarly instructed the gardeners to dig and plant 'ye borders and ground' with 'great quantities of Strawberries of all sorts especially ye White'.[75] In 1710 the 'walks through ye new kitching garden' were made 'five foot broader and designed to have handsome borders on both sides for strawberrys, gooseberrys and currants'.[76]

Fig. 7
Plate: 'The Plan of a Kitchen Garden on three Levels with a Canal at bottom' from Stephen Switzer, *The Practical Kitchen Gardiner* (London, 1727).

Robert Molesworth added elements to the Breckdenston landscape that were both formal gestures and utilitarian projects. The avenues grew trees for profit and the waterworks held fish. The plantations, however, contained trees planted primarily for material gain, and these were situated far from the house and the principal routes of leisurely perambulation. In a manner which foreshadowed the later landscape garden, they were cultivated at the boundaries of the demesne, and their aesthetic input into the design was generally limited to the effect of their distant hue and habit from a central vantage-point. For ease of cultivation and harvesting, they were generally of one species and situated beyond the mixed, exotic and decorative planting of the groves and wildernesses. Molesworth greatly increased the number and variety of Breckdenston's plantations, bringing mulberry, acacia and plane trees to Swords, some possibly for the first time. Nick transported 'over some vines, Yewes and other trees' from London in 1709, when 'Peaches and nectarines . . . as good'[77] as those in London could be bought in Ireland. The gardens were used as test sites for many new species of trees, flowers and foodstuffs, and their preferred soil condition was observed and then accommodated. When a tree did not prosper in a particular location, it was transplanted to another. The acorn park plantation was planted 'round with walnut trees . . . the best place to preserve them . . . for timber and the fruit is of great profit'.[78] This also improved the infrastructure of the field hedgerows, and Molesworth never planted 'a quickset hedge' without putting 'in an oak plant every 4 or 6 foot', a practice which had made 'such stately timber hedgerows as may be seen at Edlington & most parts of this country [England]'.[79] The estate was stocked with 'mutton, lamb, veal, ducks, turkeys and pigs . . . plenty of each kind',[80] and Lettice took care of her 'Pheasants, swans and ducks' and 'ye good red trouts'.[81] A pigeon-house was 'placed as handsomely as any thing of that sort in Ireland' to make 'a fine show yet . . . not in the way of any of the Avenues'.[82] Molesworth concerned himself with such mundane matters as selling 'ye great furrs by Tom Cullanes', instructing Lettice to 'begin with an acre' and to sell also 'yr faggots & brush wood that are cut off ye hedges we cutt this year'.[83] The older landscaping interventions of orchards, fish ponds and decoys retained their practical, material and recreational functions within Robert Molesworth's landscape. As a model improving landlord, Molesworth concerned himself with all the workings of his demesne.

R A T H B E A L
S W O
A 554 R 2 P 7
M O O R E T O W N
A 309 R 3 P 32
Glasmore Abbey
OUTLANDS
A 79 R 2 P 0
PART OF
KILLOSSERY
BRAZIL
Brazil House in Ruins
A 216 R 2 P 29
Part of NEWTOWN
A 15 R 1 P 29
WINDMILL LA
A 159 R 0
Wind Mill Stump
Cottage
Flour Mill
Moat
Old Pond
Embankment
Brackenstown Ho.
Gravel Pit
Gate Lodge
Knocksedan Ho.
BRACKENSTOWN
A 221 R 3 P 0
Summer Ho.
HILLTOWN
A 221 R 2 P 28
KNOCKSEDAN
A 98 R 3 P 25
FORRESTFIEL
A 92 R 3 P 17
Gate Lodge
Family Grave Yard
Old Quarry
RATHINGLE
A 113 R 0 P 5
Rathingle Ho.
Old Quarry
FOSTERSTOWN NO

## Design, Engineering and Hydraulics at Breckdenston

*I have the noblest prospect of the main ocean, of the harbour of Malahide, and the sand downs beyond it of several rising rocks and islands (such as Lambay, Howth, Irelands Eye, Feltrim Hill, Malahide Hill, with many castles & Churches & Windmills & c.), that I myself who have been so long used to it am charmed with it.* [84]

Molesworth was convinced that there was 'no seat in Ireland to all parts of which water may be with more ease and plenty be brought than Breckdenston',[85] and this conviction led him to create an elaborate terraced water garden which exploited his exceptional prospect. 'All this water on the very top of a hill, with the sea, ships and rocks & steeples beyond it in view, would be such a sight' that he doubted 'whether the world would afford the like'.[86] Molesworth also saw the potential of the Ward river, which runs west–east through the northern part of the demesne, and developed the river valley in stylistic counterpoint to the controlled geometry of the parterres and avenues. Its natural topography demanded a more 'natural' style of gardening, and the interest Molesworth lavished on the unruly river promoted the principle of the *genius loci* above that of the elaborate axial earthwork. Although the river lay hard against the northern edge of the demesne, Molesworth had gardens on both riverbanks. Walks and designed vistas were laid out on the northern bank, and their adjacency to the neighbouring estate of Brazeel once provoked a 'possible dispute with Ned Bolton [the owner of Brazeel] concerning opening springs on his hillside'.[87] Traces of these diagonal paths remain today. The greater portion of the demesne, however, lay south of the river and had proportionally the greater degree of attention lavished upon it. The design of the water features, and the hydraulic devices which supported them by transporting water up from the river valley to the gardens and cultivated areas concentrated around the house, occupied Molesworth for many years.

Molesworth realized that nothing could be 'so beneficiall to our trees & garden stuff as large and effectuall draining everywhere',[88] and the waterworks both inspired and disguised the imposition of the drainage infrastructure upon the landscape. The watercourse and its surrounding water table were central to the supply and control of the hydraulic system. Breckdenston's undulating topography and the steep slopes of the river valley meant that water had to be stored during periods of drought and the landscape protected from its destructive potential in times of flood. The design process was never one of applying a perfected blueprint but one of constant adjustment, both for aesthetic reasons, as Molesworth acquired new books and visited new gardens, and because the daily observation of the evolving performance of the hydraulic system necessitated it. He revised the design when periods of flood or drought revealed unforeseen weaknesses. Areas of regular and smooth gradient were preferred for orchards, plantations and kitchen gardens. He disapproved of a 'field on ye way to ye hillside over ye

Fig. 8
Second edition Ordnance Survey map of Breckdenston, Co. Dublin, 1874.

A new solution for improving the dwindling water supply was proposed in 1720. Molesworth planned a 'reservoir or large Basin in ye 16 acres', which would be capable of supplying 'constant running water even during ye height of a dry summer'[119] at the western end of the demesne with the 'longest prospect of ye Sea from anyplace about Breckdenston' (Fig. 13). A Mr Costelloe was consulted about the reservoir's design, and he proposed to 'divide' Molesworth's single 'large Basin ... into 2 or 3 lesser Basins'. Molesworth rejected his alteration of 'one of the finest things about Breckdenston'. Costelloe's smaller basins would 'neither contain half so much water, nor ... be pleasant', and far more water would evaporate 'in the smallness of these three or four Basins' than from 'the large Basin ... 5 or 6 foot deep, shelving from ye sides towards ye depth in ye middle'. Costelloe also advised Molesworth to plant acacia trees around the basins 'in order to prevent the operation of the sun and wind' at the exposed western end of the demesne. Molesworth, always dubious about professional advice, chose again to ignore the unfortunate Mr Costelloe. He thought that acacias would 'spoil the beauty' of his new basin, and planted elms '30 or 40 foot asunder, in double rows' instead. A 'fine prospect' would 'appear under their branches and between the intervals of trees' until they grew 'exceedingly old'.[120] Lime trees were also a popular choice for the pond areas, and their habits, like those of the avenues, were strictly pruned into shape. Never lacking in ambition, Molesworth did agree with Costelloe that more basins, if not smaller ones, were required at Breckdenston, and planned 'to have 3 or 4 resevoirs more'.[121]

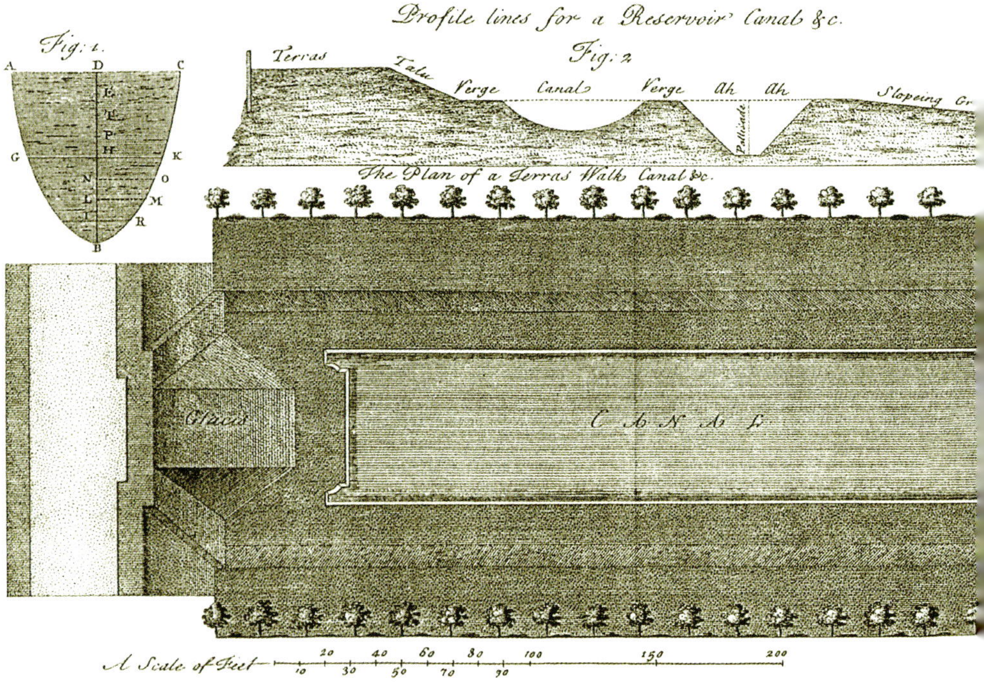


Fig. 12
Stephen Switzer, *An Introduction to a General System of Hydrostaticks & Hydraulics, Philosophical & Practical* (London, 1729): Plate 3, 'Profile Lines for a Reservoir Canal &c.'

In 1721 John Molesworth wrote a long letter to his father with descriptions of gardens reminiscent of the great water and fountain Italian villa gardens. He also sent instructions for their design and construction:

> *Your fountains will be a great beauty to the gardens and to the country: those called basins may be fitted up at small expense; the bottoms and sides are here built with good brick, the margins may be made of a small cornice in freestone, which, if you send the diameters of your basins, may be made cheap at Bristol and transported at an easy rate.*[122]

He particularly advised his father on the other sequence of ponds, fountains and cascades that stepped downhill and eastward through the river valley from Knocksedan. John claimed that 'the fountains on the hillside, and that

Fig. 13
Diagram plan of the passage of water through the demesne, indicating the location of the water features and machines from John Rocque's *Map of the County of Dublin*, 1760, overlaid with the 1874 Ordnance Survey map of Breckdenston, Co. Dublin, 1874.

a Knocksedan Avenue
b Great Avenue
c Avenue to James Hand's
d Avenue to Tom Cullen's
e Lettice's stream
f Dublin Gate & Avenue
g High Walk with Belvedere & South flanker
h Upper Parterre
i Water Cistern House
j New Orchard
k Engine House & Tuckmill
l 18th-century mansion
m 17th-century 'Hall'
n Kitchen Garden & Orchards
o The Great Pond
p The Tuckmill Race
q The Channel around the Pond
r Octagonal Basin & 19th-century mill
s Cascade
t Parterre Fountain
u The Canal
v Ruined sluice building for stream
w Wilderness area
x Sixteen acre field with Reservoir Basin
y Apparatus for moving water from the Tuckmill & Engine House to the Cistern House
z Long pipe connecting the reservoir Basin, the Cistern House and the Parterre Fountain.

at Knocksiddan will yield variety', but that 'their situations' would require 'different ornaments'. One fountain 'lying horizontal, will become a little jet, which, by different tops upon the pipe, will vary itself into stars, sheets or showers of rain, as you please, or spout directly up, as is the common way'.[123] John sent his father 'sketches of fountains' while Molesworth tried to think of 'some cheap yet pretty ornament & line [?] my spring thro' a grotesque or mask face into a shell basin'. John responded:

> *That on the hillside standing in a grove, must be grotesque, and upon the decline of a hill, its source must be pursued till you find that, cutting the hill down perpendicular, the spout would burst out about navel high of a man: that perpendicular must then be faced with a sort of building, which I am about drawing a sketch of.*[124]

The parterre fountain was far more ambitious than those of the Knocksedan hillside, which used the natural water pressure of the hillside springs. Molesworth computed that 'by carrying on ye large pipe to ye Basin' in the 16 acres, the resultant water pressure at the level of the parterre 'would have made ye water spout in ye middle carry up ye water as far as ye spout of ye cistern in ye water house within less than a foot and with a large strong stream' (Fig. 13).[125] This fountain could not have played continuously; at a selected time, probably when guests were gathered in the gallery room, a valve released some of the reservoir's water to create the waterspout. Unlike the construction of the canal, when the 'many outstanding workmen in this country' required no 'expense of bringing anyone out from England',[126] the design and construction of the parterre fountain demanded a degree of expertise not then readily available in Ireland. Molesworth wrote that the parterre fountain could not be finished until 'Bell the plumber goes over again there being nobody in Ireland'[127] who understood it. Other fountain projects demanded further expertise, and George Cartwright wrote that he would get 'a Miller' if Molesworth meant to 'go on with the two fountains this summer in ye high grove & Octagonall basin'.[128] This suggests that, whereas the technology of canal construction, which was similar to that required by such contemporary public projects as land reclamation and inland navigation, was available, expertise in fountain making was not. The lack of indigenous expertise probably encouraged Molesworth to ask his son for information, and may have contributed to the arrival in Ireland of the Italian architect Alessandro Galilei.

By 1721, Molesworth's increasingly turbulent financial position, arising from the South Sea Bubble, had forced him to admit that he was 'not in a condition to go on with the designs of our other fountains'.[129] The same letter stated however that 'ye grove in ye garden ought to have had its fountain finished as soon as we could do it, being ye most pleasant & beautiful place for a fountain imaginable'. This somewhat contradicts Molesworth's attempted financial sobriety. It proved very difficult for him to stop:

> *I am grown a great watermonger & have convey'd a deal of it into Breckdenston gardens and wou'd do more were it not for ye expense wch is great, esp. where Lead is used.*[130]

The last expenditure on fountains followed that of the canal, the great pond and the many other basins, cascades, channels, trees, shrubs and flowers that Molesworth had lavished on his corner of north Dublin. It left the Molesworth family in a precarious financial position and inspired the poignant phrase in a begging letter to his eldest son that, while it was 'the part of a father to give and not to expect gifts from a son',[131] he could no longer afford to continue his improvement of Breckdenston's landscape.

## 'The Farmlike Way of Gardening'[132]

An archetypal Whig, Robert Molesworth has been described as one of those men who 'served to maintain a revolutionary tradition' in the aftermath of the Glorious Revolution of 1688. These men, 'sometimes calling themselves the "Old Whigs", or the "Real Whigs", may be detected less than four years after the acceptance of the Dutch Deliverer', (William of Orange), and 'agitation for reform ... may be said to have begun with the appearance of Molesworth's Account of Denmark in December 1693'.[133] Whig politics promoted enlightened self-interest, the reduction of monarchical and centralist power, and an early form of capitalist economy. Radical Whig tendencies tended to appear whenever it was felt that the 'commonwealth' of the people was not being adequately served by the combined forces of government and crown. The radical Whigs 'cherished ideas about checks on government from within and without, about individual freedoms and about the ranks of society ... but their inheritance of the revolutionary tradition was still tempered by the admiration for the English constitution'.[134] Breckdenston was a locus of radical Whig thought: 'These reformers were to be found in dissenters' meetings and in certain country houses, for e.g., in Essex and at Swords near Dublin.'[135] As a powerful political theorist, Molesworth counted the third Earl of Shaftesbury, Lord Burlington, Jonathan Swift, John Locke, Francis Hutcheson, John Toland and many other Augustan intellectuals among his friends.

England had emerged, triumphantly optimistic and armed with a new constitution, from the turbulent internal crises of the seventeenth century. The empowered Parliament, influenced by the helpful philosophies of Locke and Hobbes, quickly attained the triumphalist and imperial mentality that turned England into a great world power. In the arts this optimism is particularly visible in the work of the early advocates of the landscape garden. Urban Italianate artefacts were translated to rural settings, and when miniaturized, manipulated the observer's perception of the object in the landscape. An associative, interpretative route was developed where the observer 'read' the owner's meaning through a series of frequently esoteric signs. Parliamentary enclosure also helped to form the great Whig landed estates in eighteenth-century England. The landscape was gradually subsumed into capitalist society by a governmental process, and the traditional interpretation of landscape as a nurturing body for human existence lost its meaning, as abstract economic values assaulted the mythological value of land. The rural poor, dispossessed of their physical and psychological links with the landscape, moved to the cities. The land was left vacant and ready for the application of new economic and agricultural theories, and for the aesthetic processes intended to beautify them. For many contemporary observers, the landscape became an indicator and a metaphor for the political machinations that altered it.[136] Conceived at a time when capitalism was emerging as a worldwide system, the landscape garden came to represent capitalism's various patterns of control in landscape form.

The Whig oligarchy of Great Britain has been compared with the oligarchy of the Venetian republic.[137] This was represented architecturally by the Palladian villa, which had been developed by the Venetians for their holdings in the *terra firma* mainland territory, which they had conquered in the sixteenth century. Palladio and his colleagues formulated an architecture and a landscape to establish the ideology of a conquering people, creating houses with 'an imaginative world occupied by a section of the Venetian ruling class and promoted by them as a more refined and morally superior lifestyle than merchant commerce'.[138] This was particularly discernible in 'the programmatic themes of the paintings', which, 'by idealizing the actual rural relationships, were meant to eliminate the contradiction between the beautiful villa and the economic villa'.[139] The Whig doctrine of enlightened self-interest engaged strongly with modern economic theory to demonstrate that clear, rational modes of thinking could forge a new environment with equal opportunities for all propertied gentlemen. The Whig landowner frequently drew his wealth from the city, and the Palladian model harmonized sweetly with his interests. Tory opposition posed the moral and ethical questions of traditional benevolence, which modern 'improvement' and individualism subsequently demolished.

The Tudor plantations, the Cromwellian and Restoration land confiscations, and the subsequent land surveys and settlements had completely transformed Irish land-ownership by the eighteenth century. Many people had been employed to supervise the survey and the redistribution, 'attracted by the idea of Ireland as a tabula rasa for new ideas as well as the chance of personal profit'.[140] Whig ideals of improvement were completely in tune with imperialist and expansionist thought. The elimination of traditional boundaries and earlier palimpsests, the purely economic value of cultivated land, and the advancement of personal power and fortune – matters which were debated within the ruling class in England – were adopted generally in Ireland. Many Whig gardening theoreticians tended to connect taste with conspicuous possession, which was helpful when the ruling ideology was founded on the precept that the relationship between land-ownership and political power was clearly understood. If 'the relationship between Venice and its dominions' was one of 'conquering city state and a conquered, exploited empire, not one of capital and its provinces',[141] Palladian architecture would appear to be more directly translational into the Irish situation. Gardening became a method of differentiation in a colonized landscape.[141] Ruling élites traditionally base the ideology to justify their power and property in the distant past, when the founding stone of aristocratic hereditary power was the provision of defence. The new Irish Ascendancy, however, could generally only use the close temporal proximity of recent events to formulate a new mythology. A mythology tied too accurately to recent events does not easily develop a successful iconography. The eighteenth-century landscape garden, supported by both allusion and illusion, could be misinterpreted in the fluctuating cultural and political Irish environment. The precise ideology and education that its interpretation demanded from the observer required a stable cultural environment, and this was not easily achieved in the colonial situation.

Irish Protestants also had a 'larger mission–to improve the land and its inhabitants, and thereby themselves as well'.[143] Robert Molesworth, in his capacity as an agricultural theorist, published a pamphlet in 1723 entitled

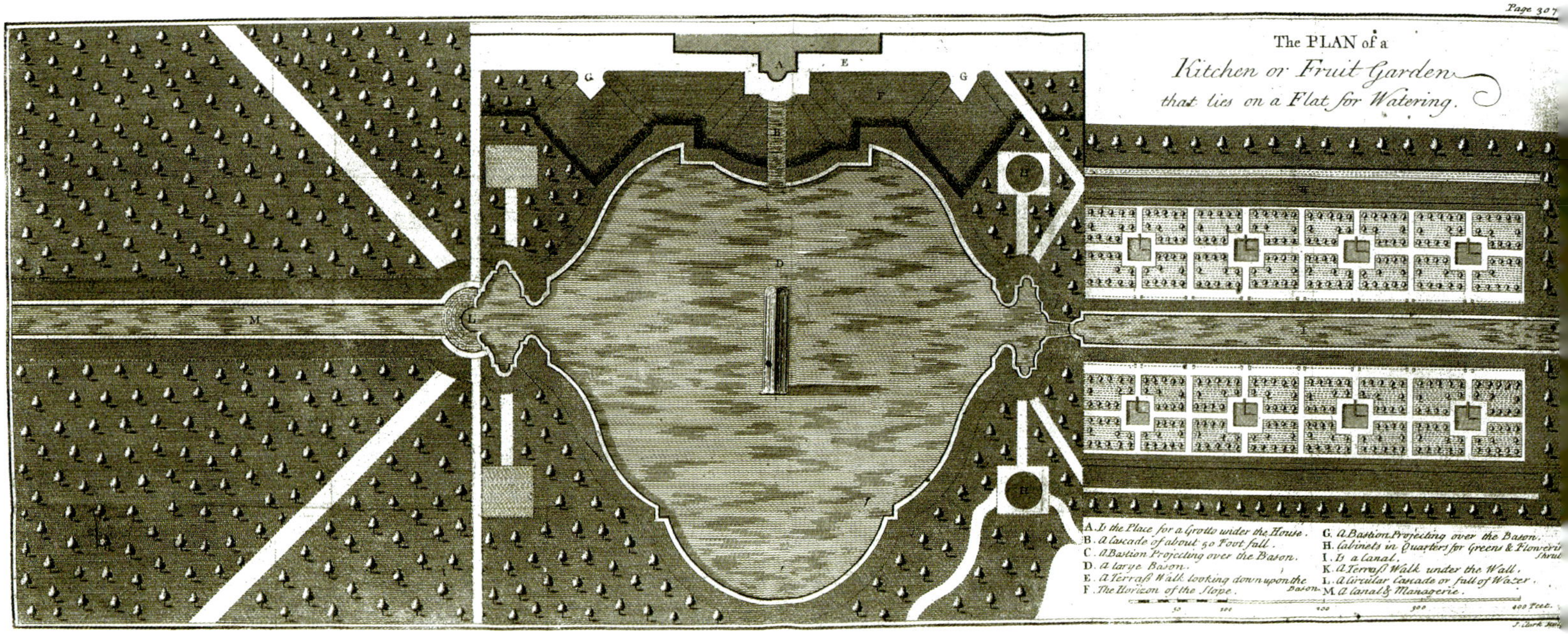


Fig. 14

Plate: 'The Plan of a Kitchen or Fruit Garden that lies on a Flat for Watering', from Stephen Switzer, *The Practical Fruit-Gardener*, London, 1724, p. 307.

*Some Considerations for the Promoting of Agriculture and Employing the Poor*,[144] where he emphasized the obligation of the landed gentleman to improve the countryside in the interest of the public good. Its author showed no false modesty by recommending to his readers that 'the late improvements of the Lord Molesworth . . . would make a noble and useful history'.[145] He wrote that land could be improved by adding 'Marls, Lime, Bog-earth, Shells, Ashes' to the soil, or by 'Burning, Overflowing, & c., & then finding out proper Grains of Hay and Grass'. 'Such Experiments' he considered 'very Pleasant and usually Profitable', and their inspiration came from the 'Experience of Gentlemen and wealthy Farmers'.[146] General employment 'must arise from the Improvement of our Grounds, Fishing & Navigating the Sea, and from our Manufactures'. Molesworth also insisted that the 'Improving of Ground must be carried on by private Industry, and Experiments of ingenious Man, more than by publick Laws'.[147] The economic advantages of the Protestant religion were such that it was 'much better suited to a trading Nation than the Popish'. Catholic workers had 'too many holy-days, & Monks & Nuns, & expensive Vanities & idle errands to take them off their Business'.[148] Hydraulic and drainage projects also improved the gentleman's landscape. Dutch practice was obliquely admired when Molesworth commended the manner in which 'the richest part of Lincolnshire called Holland, hath been recovered' by 'draining their Fens'.[149]

'The first and most striking feature' of Irish eighteenth-century architectural literature 'is its overwhelmingly utilitarian and technical bent',[150] with 'methods of raising water by hydraulic engines, a subject which by the early eighteenth century had assumed a central significance in Ireland'.[151] Molesworth's evident interest in those aspects of garden design and construction with a strong engineering and mechanical emphasis (water drainage, fountains, cascades, canals, mills) may express a general tendency among the Anglo-Irish Ascendancy. Garden theorists took care to set out the extent of their expertise in this area. Stephen Switzer, in his introduction to *An Introduction to a General System of Hydrostaticks & Hydraulics,* traced his descent from the ancient and best contemporary hydraulic theorists. He claimed that his book had been:

> *... deduced from the theory of Archimides, Galileo, Torricelli, Boyle, Wallis, Plot, Hook, Marriotte, Desaguliers, Derham, Hawksbee & others, reduced to practice by Vitruvius, Bockler, de Caus, & other Architects amongst the ancient Romans, Italians, French, Flemmings and Dutch, & much improved by later practice and experience.*[152]

Such cosmopolitan credentials would have increased his stature in Molesworth's eyes, whose interest in all cultural traditions of gardening is noteworthy. He found that 'ye Persians are and allways were ye best contrivers and drawers of Aquaducts under ground by reason of ye dryness of their country'.[153] This cosmopolitan outlook in technical matters, and the picture of Ascendancy Ireland it creates, is borne out by Christine Casey's analysis of the difference between American and Irish 'colonial' libraries of this time: 'The almost exclusively English and Palladian character of the architectural books [in American eighteenth-century book catalogues] ... serves to emphasise the catholic and European tastes of Irish collectors.'[154]

Molesworth improved his distant estate town of Phillipstown, King's County.[155] He decided that 'Phillipstown street should be planted before the doors with a row on each side like a Dutch town' because it had 'a Dutch situation already by reason of the bogs and rivers'. 'Elms or oaks, or ... strong ash or *Abeles* ... paled in like those in St. James's park' lined the streets, and 'every tenant possessor of the plots' was 'bound to preserve' them. Once 'full of trees on ye back sides of their gardens', the town would be 'renewed'.[156] Molesworth's comparison of Holland with Ireland was a popular one at this time, particularly among men with an interest in land reclamation and water drainage. Holland also helped by association to justify Molesworth's statement that 'if the country of Ireland was a Protestant nation ... it would help forward all endeavours for these improvements'.[157] Molesworth's interest in Phillipstown contrasts with his indifference to Swords. It seems unlikely that, with his wide influence and power, he would not have been able to create a more formal architectural or axial link with the nearby town, had he so desired. Alternatively, either the demesne's topography or the intervening landowners prevented a closer relationship, making it easier and perhaps more meaningful to appropriate the town visually from a distance. Molesworth's letters make it quite clear that, where a forceful position was required to control the surrounding countryside, he had no qualms in adopting one. In 1704 he urged his wife to remember that 'the law of England' allowed every freeholder to 'enclose so much of his common as lies upon him . . . provided that he leaves out as much common as is sufficient for those that have a right & disclaims any further title to put beasts on the rest of the common which he leaves out'.[158] This letter suggests that he was enclosing Swords common, a typical stage of Whig land 'improvement' and the focus of much contemporary criticism. By constructing 'a Wall to divide all our Grounds', Molesworth and his cousin Forster (of neighbouring Forsterstown) altered the traditional routes of the countryside so that it became 'almost impossible for the Irish vagabonds to make a highway of our grounds'.[159] The traditional patterning of the countryside was again disturbed by Molesworth's plan to 'divert the footway to Swords (for common passengers) either to the side of the hill or by James Hands and ye lower end of ye Decoy'. As the existing route was not a right of way and only 'permitted' by Molesworth himself, he knew that it was within his power 'to stop up or turn according as we please'.[160] Whig improvers were later heavily chastised for such behaviour, as it was an obvious example of countryside traditions being removed for economic and individualistic motives.[161] By promoting such changes, Robert Molesworth indicated that he saw no economic or symbolic advantage in maintaining the countryside's traditional links with its local town of Swords. He disposed of these links in favour of aggressive land development. Walls were constructed to announce the presence of the demesne to travellers and visitors alike, and 'to preserve any fruit from theives'.[162] He also enclosed 'all ye course rough unimproved land' at his English estate of Edlington by putting it 'under fine grass or tillage' with 'a deal of new closes in hedging & building & repairs & planting'. Edlington town street was 'full of new industrious tenants, the commons taken in and turn'd to ye best profitable land . . . ye Hopps grounds enlarged & thriving, the wood and underwood putting to right order & increasing in value to as now to be worth £10,000'. Molesworth believed that his activities at Edlington had encouraged the local parson to become 'highly content & grown a stiff Whigg',[163] which suggests that aggressive land development was then associated with Whig politics. He kept his Swords tenants as 'tenants at will', betraying a distinct lack of benevolent feeling; his somewhat reprehensible desire 'to keep them in awe' in order to 'hinder them from destroying our estate'[164] demonstrates a manipulative intelligence.

Gardening frequently linked architecture and engineering in the early eighteenth century. The hydraulic and technical projects of the great landowners' gardens acted as test sites for the great tracts of farming land they owned beyond their demesne walls, and for the public projects they instigated and supervised. Such a comparatively small hydraulic exercise as that of Breckdenston could then be put into practice on a much larger scale. Molesworth employed models to create an ideal improved landscape of town and countryside. Phillipstown was redesigned with reference to a London park (St James's); the middle walk of Breckdenston's cherry orchard was also once 'as long as that in St. James' park and as broad'.[165] The interchangeable use of a London park for rural and urban situations expressed the flexibility and ambiguity of Whig design philosophy. By insisting that the economic language of town and country was one and the same, Whig theorists attempted to break down traditional definitions of country and city, and, by extension, their patterns of expression. By using the same vocabulary to design Phillipstown and Breckdenston, Molesworth makes no distinction between the urban and rural environment, and the long arm of improvement stretches to encompass both. Molesworth's assertion in a letter dated 3 May 1724 that Phillipstown was 'really a very improveable, healthy, and even a pleasant, plentiful place to dwell in',[166] indicates that he believed he had achieved some success in urban design.

'The farmlike way of gardening' attracted many eighteenth-century landowners. It sought to attain an elusive balance between nature and art, simplicity and contrivance. The productive, useful and moral 'farm' element was made 'ornamental' by the subtle and careful application of artistic and aesthetic judgement. Ideally, neither identity was lost as the garden developed, but in reality the balance sought was rarely attained, as the more 'farmlike' the garden, the less evident the art, and the more ornamental the garden, the greater the degree of artifice, luxury and conspicuous consumption. The philosophical questions which this paradox exposed were explored by Robert Molesworth's great friend the third Earl of Shaftesbury. Stephen Switzer, the garden theorist invited by Molesworth to Ireland in 1719, proposed a formal design method for the 'farmlike way of gardening'. He had a great theoretical influence on the design of gardens, and he was an instigator and forerunner of the English landscape gardening style. The 'farmlike way of gardening' gradually became entwined with the French *ferme ornée* as the century progressed, but its initial pattern was set by the early eighteenth-century landscape garden and defined by Shaftesbury and Switzer.

The *ferme ornée* in Ireland may at first glance be felt to be a callous and ironic typology to introduce into a country which has had considerable difficulty in adequately providing for its population at certain times during its history. In the eighteenth century however, the concept of the *ferme ornée* was believed by many, Jonathan Swift amongst them, to be a sensible, honest, natural and classical way of combining utility with beauty. The artifice and contrivance which Addison, Pope and Switzer associated with the great Dutch or French formal gardens were felt to be wasteful and profligate. Their high expenditure of money and labour was thought to contradict the garden's ability to create, rather than merely to expend, resources. This criticism reflected a growing British nationalism, as a truly free and advanced society would not squander its assets on the despotic requirements of mere grandeur. Molesworth was always concerned that Breckdenston should function independently and profitably. When he considered renting his property during his long absences at Parliament in England, he predicted that the rate of return on his improvements would allow the gardens to 'surely pay for their keeping & ye repairs of the house & tax'. He also believed that 'whoever is there (if carefull) may easily look after the trees & grounds & increase our nurserys'.[167] Shaftesbury's philosophy, with its moral and stoic overtones and its emphasis on rural solitude and personal self-sufficiency, encouraged the development of this ambiguous design methodology, where a conscious blurring of the boundaries between art and nature, and the useful and the beautiful was explored. Jonathan Swift

> *Workmen . . . so polish'd their piece, and render'd it so natural and easy, that it seem'd only a lucky flight, a hit of thought, or flowing vein of humour; they were then chiefly concern'd lest it should in reality pass for such, and their artifice remain undiscover'd.*[179]

Shaftesbury and Molesworth followed the same design principles. Their gardens were ordered into compartments, which were delineated by orders of trees, perfected by topiary, and directed by perspectival lines of control. Shaftesbury's garden at Wimborne St Giles, Dorset, was similar to Breckdenston, and in 1707 Shaftesbury produced a 'Paper full of Corrections and additions by Lord Shaftesbury on Plantations to be altered and renewed in his estate, under five headings' for his gardener.[180] The headings covered 'the plantation in front of the parlour garden; the second, that near the lower canal; the third part pertains to the old wilderness; the fourth, to the old river walk; and the fifth part considers the plantations by the strawberry garden'. Molesworth's gardens at Breckdenston included exactly such areas, and the planting Shaftesbury prescribed is very reminiscent of Molesworth's instructions for the plantations at Breckdenston. Shaftesbury's 'plantations by the lower canal on the south side', like the canal at Breckdenston, were planted with elm, with 'every other elm . . . taken away and in their place the remaining elms . . . cut into globes in imitation of the globe yews on the same line as the upper canal'. The maples in Shaftesbury's 'plantation in front of the parlour garden' were 'set to answer again to the intervals of the hollys: having over against every holly a good straight yew-plant to run up to a pyramid'. The 'same order' was 'to be continued from the grotto upward from behind the bowling green, where the yew hedge in the same manner is to be removed backwards, but the Scotch firs to stand as they do, there being no prospect for them to hinder'.[181]

Shaftesbury contributed plants to the Breckdenston gardens. Molesworth sent 'two bundles of vines, the larger bundle of which he had from Lord Shaftesbury', to Breckdenston in 1710.[182] Lettice was advised to consult 'Bradley & Lawrence' for their 'right dressing and pruning' and to ensure that they were planted in the 'right places'.[183] Molesworth also pressed his son 'to secure' for him 'a small sack of acorns of the ilex, or evergreen kind, whereof there is a great wood near Pisa', and 'some seed of the white mulberry tree so common in all the hedges in Piedmont for their silkworms'.[184] These apparently did not arrive, as on 5 March 1723 Molesworth had 'not heard one word about the mulberry trees and black oak acorns'.[185] If they had arrived, they would have supplied the garden with some native Italian plant material, which would have enhanced and proclaimed its Italianate and classical character. Italian plants would also have strengthened the iconographic programme, which undoubtedly contained much classical allusion. During Shaftesbury's final years, which he spent in Italy, 'he became just as friendly and as frank about public affairs with John, Robert Molesworth's eldest son',[186] who advised his father on all designs with an Italianate and classical emphasis. The influence of Lord Shaftesbury may be detected in many of John's recommendations. On the choice and siting of statuary, which played a prominent part in the garden, he wrote that he 'supposed' that the statues in the 'niches in the corner of the parterre . . . would be fauns and dryads'. John Molesworth also corrected current English practice with his authoritative knowledge of the Italian originals, from which much of the decoration at this time was derived, writing that, 'whereas it is common in England to plaster and whitewash those niches, it ought not to be so'. The choice of appropriate classical inscriptions for the numerous fountains, grottoes and buildings dotted throughout the grounds was also a matter for John's judgement. He decreed that the Knocksedan fountain was to be supplied with a 'Greek motto', which was designed to 'agree with' the 'fountain under the house, upon the side of the hill, its situation in a gloomy grove, authorising an air of mystery'.[187] The sequence of fountains leading down the hill from Knocksedan thus appears to have terminated under the house, and the beginning and end of the sequence seem to have been punctuated with answering mottoes. This was a sophisticated and Italianate design device and suggests a complex iconographic programme. The programme's interpretation or possible misinterpretation was also a matter of some concern:

> *Men of sense will not think your inscription to Sanctus Columba either superstitious or Popish: you may be accused indeed of a design to reconcile yourself to High Church: the first motto Fies nobilium & c. is very proper: the other infermo capiti & c. is liable to a joke besides an ugly idea at the latter end of it; in its stead I would offer Splendidior vitro.*[188]

The detailed analysis of whether the inscription could be construed as Popish or High Church reveals both the political character and intent of including such elements in a garden design, and the inflammatory effect an ill-considered quotation could achieve in the politically confessional Irish environment.

Jonathan Swift dedicated letter V of *The Drapier's Letters*, which described a visit to Breckdenston, to Viscount Molesworth:

> *Since your last residence in Ireland, I frequently have taken my nag to ride about your grounds; where I fancies myself to feel an air of freedom breathing round me. But I have lately sold my nag, & honestly told his greatest fault, which was that of snuffing up the air about Brackdenstown; whereby he became such a lover of liberty, that I could scarce hold him in.*[189]

'As Politicks run', Swift did 'not know a person of more exceptionable principles'[190] than Robert Molesworth. Swift was a staunch Tory, yet found Breckdenston 'as in traditional country-house literature, . . . the concrete embodiment of the values of its owner', and those values of 'Liberty' were 'hardly the orthodox ruling-class values typical of the conservative aristocrat'.[191] His effusive regard for Breckdenston stemmed from his belief that Molesworth, both in his pamphlet *Some Considerations for the Promoting of Irish Agriculture* ('an excellent Discourse

. . . full of most useful hints'[192]) and in the actual management of Breckdenston, was achieving a truthful and moral version of the country-house ideal, and that this in turn was concerned with the greater public good. The wilful romanticism and illusion he associated with the arcadian myth of the country house, particularly in the poverty-stricken reality of late seventeenth-century Ireland, were apparently absent from this corner of Co. Dublin. By contrast, the character of Speaker Conolly, the owner of Castletown House, was derided by Swift with such vitriolic statements as: 'There was a fellow in Ireland called Conolly, who from a shoeboy grew to be several times one of the chief Governors, wholly illiterate & with hardly common sence.'[193]

Jonathan Swift could not forget that 'all power structures as well as property rights are determined by brute force and greed, not by providential plan or benevolent human design'.[194] He possessed a lucid understanding of the 'paradox that is at the heart of the eighteenth-century attitude towards nature: the simultaneous embrace of the pastoral mode and the rejection of rural realities'.[195] In practice Molesworth and his landscape did not live up to Swift's ideal. Breckdenston contains many examples of purely aesthetic interventions, and the wanton expenditure of funds on landscaping features caused the financial difficulties that Swift considered both irresponsible and immoral. Yet Swift was convinced that Breckdenston embodied more of his ideal landscape than either Dr and Mary Delany's adjacent Glasnevin demesne of Delville or Alexander Pope's garden at Twickenham, both of which he disparaged.[196] At Breckdenston 'as presented by Swift, temperament and politics, ideology and landscape come together'.[197] While Molesworth did not completely share 'Swift's highly idiosyncratic, predictably parodic, and almost literally subversive version of the detached aesthetic contemplation of nature'[198] – his appreciation of the view of Dublin Bay from his bed could not accord with this – the manner in which he wrote and thought about his landscape is consistently earthy, rational and practical. His landscape remained useful as well as beautiful and none of the letters suggest that his intention was to practise the detached appreciation of 'arcadian scenes set in contemporary topography'[199] that Swift attempted to deconstruct.

Jonathan Swift considered the Tory ideal of benevolent tradition fostering an ordered and natural system of power in the countryside unrealistic in the Irish environment. Any exact match between political alignment and Irish landscape design was also confused by the grim reality of that environment. Despite the fact that the Delaneys were much closer to him in political outlook than Molesworth, Swift found that Delville's 'structural features . . . do not alter themselves naturally and freely, of their own accord and by an inner mystical movement, in order to accommodate themselves to their master's measurements, but instead are continually being destroyed and rebuilt by him, victimised by his ever-changing whims'.[200] Breckdenston never became part of 'a fantasy world in which Delany, as a result of his building endeavors, becomes enmeshed in comic delusion'.[201] The letters, and the site itself, reveal that its landscape developed in an additive and logical manner, and that the expensive waterworks formed part of an essential watering system. The scraps of evidence which suggest that Breckdenston's iconography may have been politically subversive – John Molesworth's concern that the fountains' inscriptions should not be misconstrued – also suggest that Molesworth may have employed the muses' statues in his gardens to communicate a personal and political philosophy. This may explain why Breckdenston escaped the derision that Swift heaped upon the nearby Delville, whose design vocabulary, although outwardly the same, was evidently thought by him to communicate a vastly different agenda:

*To Fame a Temple you erect,*
*A Flora does your Dome protect;*
*Mounts, Walks, on high; and in a Hollow*
*You place the Muses and Apollo;*
*There shining 'midst his Train, to Grace*
*Your whimsical, Poetick Place*
*These stories were of old design'd*
*As Fables: But you have refin'd*
*The Poets Mythologick Dreams,*
*To real Muses, Gods and Streams.*
*Who wou'd not swear, when you contrive thus,*
*That you're Don Quixote Redivius?* [202]

Like the third Earl of Shaftesbury, Swift concerned himself with cultural meaning. The artifice of Delville was far too overworked to attain the nonchalance of Breckdenston.

## The Necessity of Luxury

*Breckdenston, a plain rural seat without artificial ornaments (and so likely to continue), but highly beholding to nature.*[203]

Molesworth believed that people should dispose of the financial rewards of agricultural improvement by spending 'their spare money in politeness and building, and neat furniture of their houses'. 'Much eating . . . feeds diseases, wastes time and perishes in the using', and construction projects were 'more ornamental to a nation & more lasting'.[204] This approaches the paradox of the *in utile dolce* landscape by avoiding the point at which improvement became a luxury, or an act of conspicuous consumption, with no moral value attached to it but that of being 'ornamental' to a nation. The illusion that the moral Whig landscape wished to uphold, that aesthetic and economic decisions were one and the same, was always difficult to establish, as the fact that a luxury is 'more lasting' holds little moral weight:

> *Vast and expensive Gardens, that the Folly of this and past Ages is run into, become a Burthen too great for the biggest Estate, and the Gardens themselves not at all answerable to the needless Expense that is laid out upon them.*[205]

Molesworth perceived the landed estate to be an abstract place of escape, productivity and pleasure with no obligation to the culture and countryside it supported. This belief expressed the essentially unrooted and urban character of the Whig villa landscape. Breckdenston's connection with Dublin was emphasized by the construction of the Dublin gate approach route and the manner in which raw material from the city and its outskirts (pipes, etc.) was sourced for the garden's construction. This underlined the landscape's suburban, abstract and cosmopolitan qualities and freed Molesworth from any benevolent conscience he might have developed in a more rural environment. In 1723 he warned his son and heir (who inherited the estate upon his father's death in 1725) that he 'must try to bring down yr sentiments to yr fortune & to value an Irish seat & estate'. Molesworth thought that although Ireland could not 'approach to ye finery & expense of a more happy climate & greater riches [yet] there is luxury even in commendable improvements such as Building, gardening'.[206] This statement, in view of the fact that the family was under severe financial pressure at the time, may indicate that Molesworth was warning his son against the danger of investing too much money in the 'luxury' then visible at Breckdenston. Alternatively, he may simply have been promoting the lush productivity of Breckdenston's groves, gardens and ponds. The extract also suggests that the moral qualities of the economic landscape had been rendered truly ambiguous. Molesworth seems to suggest that, where the landscape had been rendered as productive and economic as possible, there was indeed only one other course open for the successful Whig landlord: to do it again elsewhere or to justify 'luxury' as an eventual end. The design of Breckdenston eventually departed from its 'real Whig' economic and design principles of sobriety, rationality and strict Protestant morality. Molesworth still hoped that his son John would 'improve it [Breckdenston] by those acquisitions of knowledge'[207] he had assimilated in Turin, but he was concerned that wanton expenditure on such activities would contradict some of the meaning he had tried to instil into his landscape. The grandiose gestures he made at the end of his life were to be avoided by his son, for economic, political and aesthetic reasons.

The philosopher Francis Hutcheson wrote his influential aesthetic treatise *An Inquiry into the Original of Our Ideas of Beauty and Virtue* while a member of Molesworth's intellectual circle, which gathered at Breckdenston. 'For Hutcheson, the importance of Molesworth's interest in empiricism and improvement was in the support it offered to his more philosophical interests. Both men linked the project of aesthetic improvement to that of moral development.'[208] The 'Inquiry Concerning Beauty' developed a 'theory of beauty that depended upon the comparison of ideas of uniformity and variety, which was perceived by an internal sense of beauty, or a capacity for aesthetic judgement'.

> *Hutcheson's empirical method corresponded to the practical work of Molesworth on his estate, and his theoretical definition of beauty to Molesworth's vision of a mixed or Dutch style of garden that depended upon its imitation of nature for its aesthetic effect. It also coincided with Molesworth's ethical imperative to improve the environment in a context where most of the country was ruinous. Like Swift, Hutcheson found Breckdenston's landscape inspirational. Molesworth used his garden to express his moral, aesthetic and political philosophy and this ambition gave it an influence beyond the parameters of garden design.*[209]

Molesworth was patriotically compelled to produce innovative improvements at Breckdenston as a visible display of wealth, sophistication and independence. He exemplified 'the tendency of successful Dubliners to fashion material and mental cultures from assorted elements: some local, others imported, and it was in these quarters, where occasions for public display of resources abounded, that innovations were most likely to begin'.[210] Some degree of luxury was excusable for patriotic and moral reasons. Toby Barnard has written about the occasional 'Irish fury at what was imposed – in government or in taste by London' and that 'such anger nourished a fitful Irish patriotism . . . In this mood, the smart decreed that the modish should henceforth be Irish. Thus the public displays of wealth could be read as all too legible indices of patriotism'.[211] The cultivation of vines was a cause for patriotic concern in the early years of the seventeenth century 'when all the world sees the Scotch wine is admitted', and Molesworth was keen to prove that it was not impossible 'to get some from Ireland'[212] as well. Melons were a great source of pride and regarded as 'the principal fruit of all kinds . . . the richest flower and taste of any of them . . . as Palladius and from his, Bauhinus testifies'.[213] Molesworth's glee 'that about Dublin they should not as yet have attained among all the gardeners to the art of raising melons', which 'we did at Breckdenston with great success years ago',[214] had no such classically objective sentiment as its source.

Lettice Molesworth, as the chief overseer of all the alterations to the Breckdenston landscape during Robert's long absences in England, must have had considerable influence over the design of the estate, as she made all the day-to-day and detailed decisions. The few letters from wife to husband in the Breckdenston correspondence testify that she was generally preoccupied with carrying out his wishes and with the practical management of an estate. She knew the gardeners and workmen personally and her letters remind us of the countless small transactions and decisions that affected the overall design. As the years passed, Lettice, the practitioner on the ground, became more and more critical of her husband, the distant specialist. Her confidence increased with practical experience and in 1722 a dénouement over the family fortunes and estates took place. In its aftermath Robert Molesworth was 'sorry to acknowledge' that Lettice had 'bin long uneasy that she had not the entire management' of the family's 'fortune' and gave three reasons in a letter to his son John for Lettice's unrest. First, she thought that his 'necessary attendance in Parliament at London' had kept him 'from such a thorough acquaintance of it [the management] as was fitting'. Secondly, she had not allowed 'herself and her own Designs a greater proportion' of resources because she thought that Robert would not be 'willing' to give them to her. Lastly, she considered Robert 'too wastefull' having 'laid out ye income some other way than was needful or agreeable'. Lettice's criticisms evidently hit home. 'Whether upon all or any of these considerations', Molesworth 'thought it proper to ease her mind as well as to relieve my self from Solicitude & to give scope to all her projects & good husbandry by giveing her an entire power over my whole Estate'. This included the power 'to lett leases, to manage ye demesnes, to receive and pay all Rents, debts, and interest of monyes, to buy and sell, take and remove servants, in short of everything relating to my [Molesworth's] poor fortune'. Having handed over his estate to Lettice, Molesworth had to 'content' himself 'with ye poor shory allowance of 25 sterling a month'.[215] It seems clear from this letter that Lettice did indeed have 'her own designs' for the gardens' development and that some 'proportion' of them had been put into practice. She wrote that her 'endeavours to draw water to it [the Decoy] goes on well',[216] indicating that the stream which appears at the southern end of the garden in John Rocque's map of 1760 (Fig. 3) but in no subsequent one was probably one of her interventions. The fact that Robert considered the possibility of transferring his entire estate to his wife before his death reveals both Lettice's formidable managerial abilities and the financial power eighteenth-century wives sometimes managed to wrest from their husbands. It also reveals either Robert's exceptional enlightenment or the exceptional condition in which he had left the family finances. Whatever the reasons for his decision (which he had no desire to clarify completely to his son), such scenarios enabled women to play a part in the design process, as clients, clerks of works and designers in their own right.

The advice contained in *Some Considerations for the Promoting of Agriculture* presented the author as a more sober, rational and economic man than the last developments at Breckdenston suggest. Molesworth's financial decline from over-expenditure on waterworks indicates how far the landscape of Breckdenston had departed from the ideal utilitarian working landscape of Swift's *Drapier's Letters.* His final letters to his son seem to suggest that the ambiguous definition of luxury in the *ferme ornée* landscape was more lucidly evident to him in retrospect. Yet Breckdenston's landscape embodies more of Swift's, Shaftesbury's and the New Junta's radical Whig thought on landscape design than any other garden in Ireland as yet documented. Molesworth's concern for all aspects of his garden's design, his obsessive regard for its agricultural variety and productivity, and his patriotic concern that it would serve as a scientific and technological model for the Irish landed gentleman, indicates that his ambition to advertise the Whig philosophy in landscape was convincingly achieved. His letters reveal the moral questions that sometimes plagued him after a particularly extravagant piece of expenditure, and the Whiggish logic he employed to relieve himself of such conscientious qualms. The landscape of Breckdenston contains in its design traces of these qualms, and its philosophy reflects some of the grim honesty Swift brought to his analysis of contemporary landscape design. The latent ability of Whig economic theory and landscape design graphically to reveal the power structure of society, while not containing many seductive panaceas, may (as Swift and Molesworth sensed) have proved a better model for the Irish landscape than those which the following chapters will explore.

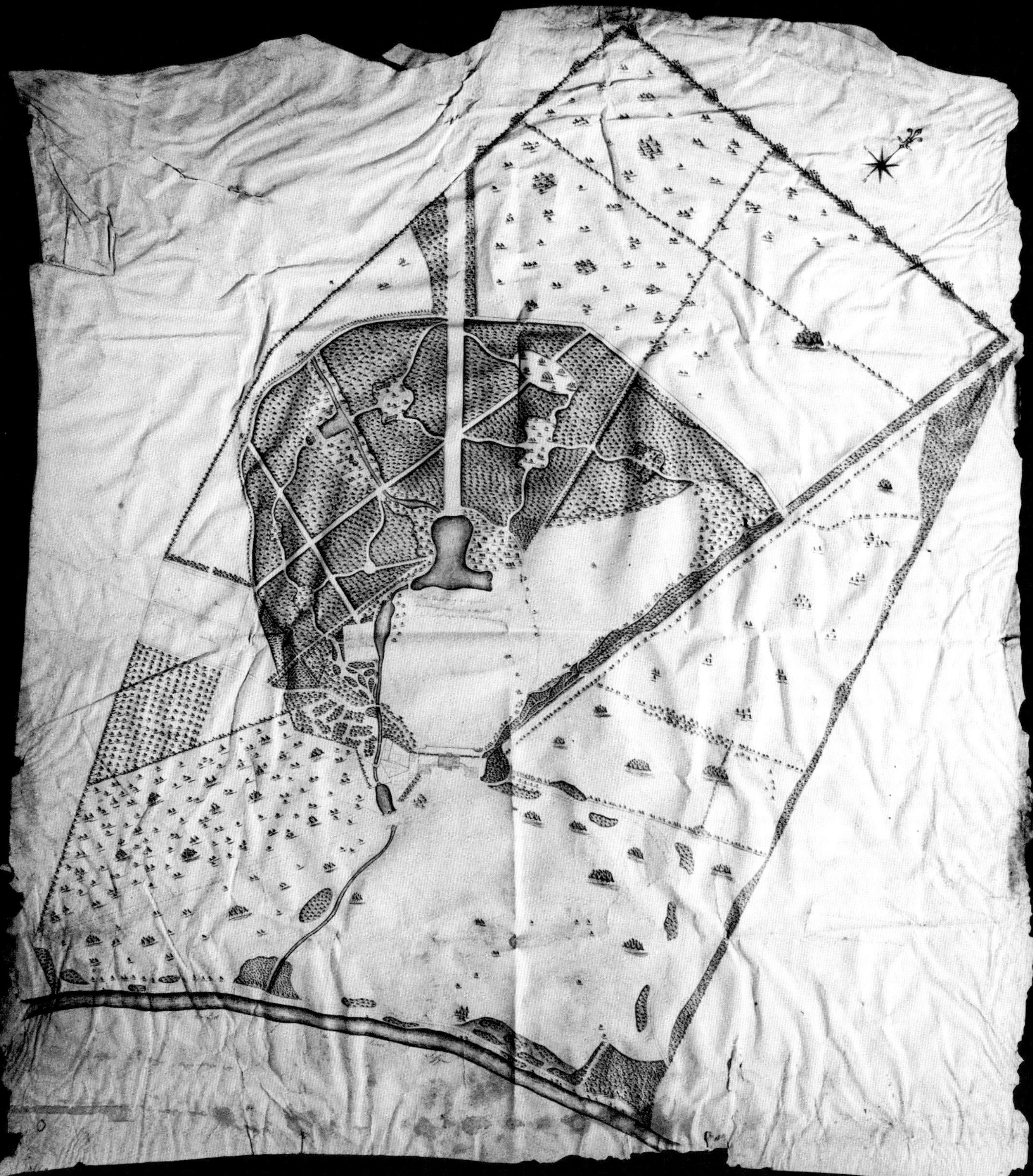

Chapter 2

# The Landscape of Castletown House

Fig. 16

Demesne plan of Castletown, *c.* 1739.

Fig. 17
South façade of Castletown House.

Alessandro Galilei's contribution to the history of Irish architecture was his design for Castletown House. His client, Speaker William Conolly (1662 –1729), patriarch of the untitled Conolly family, had amassed great wealth in the late seventeenth and early eighteenth century, and required a new seat to express the political and financial power he had attained. He married Katherine Coynyngham, the daughter of Sir Alfred Coynyngham, a Williamite general of Ordnance, in 1694, and their first home was at Rodanstown, Kilcock.[217] Speaker Conolly acquired the Castletown estate of '502 acres, very good land, a very good dwelling house, with garden of pleasure, a good kitchen garden and good orchard, a fine wood also and hop yard',[218] for £15,000 in 1709 from the Dongan family, who had lived at Castletown since 1588. The Dongan's 'manor of Castletown of Kildraught, with the town and lands of Kilmacredock', was described by a government Inquisition of 1688 as a 'castle with a stone hall, 40 messuages'[219] and 'a watermill with a mill-race'. It also contained 'the mill park' and 'a weir on the river Annliffey'. The land included '500 acres arable, 20 acres meadow, 120 acres pasture, 800 acres wood' and '40 acres moor'.[220] Castletown House, the central focus of a demesne of 666 acres, which the landowner farmed and managed himself, is connected to its estate town of Celbridge by an avenue of lime trees at its southwestern edge.[221] The river Liffey forms the southern boundary of the demesne. A further two entrance routes lead to the house, one from the southeastern Dublin gate and another from the north.

Construction of the new house, a paradigm of Irish Palladian architecture, began in 1722. Although Alessandro Galilei designed the house itself, it was constructed without his direct supervision, as he returned to Rome in 1719. Thus it was Sir Edward Lovett Pearce, who had returned to Ireland from Italy in 1724, who supervised the construction of the most ambitious Palladian house ever constructed in Ireland. It 'may have been Molesworth who urged (Speaker) Conolly to commission designs for Castletown from Galilei', and John Molesworth had also written 'to Galilei in Florence saying that now that Mr. Conolly was building he would welcome Galilei's advice now and then if Galilei were back in Ireland'.[222] The letter Molesworth wrote to Lettice on 18 May 1717 proves that he had played some part in making the introduction and that he had encouraged Speaker Conolly's patronage of the Italian architect. In this letter, which is unfortunately damaged, Molesworth asked Lettice to 'thank our Lord Justice Conolly for his – to Mrs. Ekensall [?] at my request and in re – [torn] his architect both for ye disposition of his – [torn] at least. I am sure I will carry over with me the best Architect in Europe'.[223] This suggests that Galilei was Speaker Conolly's architect by this time and that, by bringing Galilei over from Europe, Molesworth had played the primary role in securing his services for the Speaker. In 1721 Galilei wrote to John Molesworth to reassure him that he was following his 'advice especially as to studying architecture and the making of aqueducts and fountains'.[224] Galilei was employed by Molesworth, and by extension Speaker Conolly, for his

Fig. 18
Drawing from the 1729 Castletown demesne plan (Fig. 16).

a Castletown House
b The River Liffey
c Celbridge Avenue
d Kitchen Garden
e Forêt Ornée
f The Lake on the back lawn
g 'A Proper Place for an Houre Garden'
h Shrubbery
i Flower Garden
j The Crodaun Stream

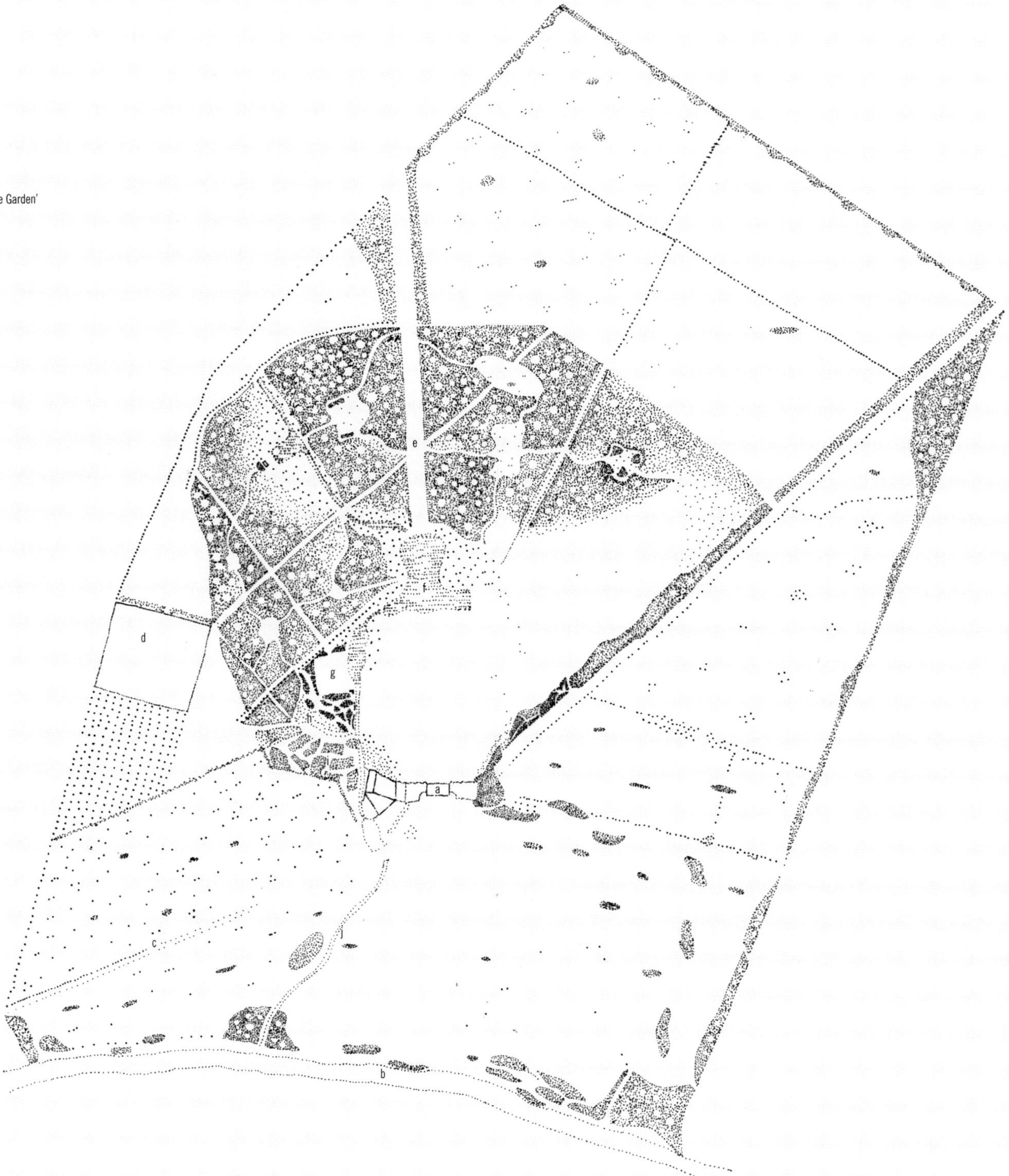

The accounts also prove that Rocque's small map is an accurate depiction of what actually existed at Castletown:

| | | | |
|---|---|---|---|
| *1778* | *Apr. 30th* | *To removing 674 yards of Earth on the terrace* | *£10,6,1* |
| | *May 30th* | *To removing 254 yds of Ground on the Terrace at the Old Garden* | *£2,15,2* |
| | *July 4th* | *To removing 2003 yards of Ground on the Terrace at the Old Garden* | |
| | | *To stub 93 trees on do.* | |
| | | *To making a shore on do.* | |
| | | *To 32 men sanding the edge of the pond* | *£23,5,11* |
| | *Nov. 20th* | *To 4 weeks filling the Haha by the River side by the new Bridge* | *£7,3,6* |
| *1779* | *Nov. 27th* | *To levelling the Old Garden making a Drain at the Lime Kiln and a Shore from the haha* | *£3,15,10* |
| | | *To trenching the Bank in do. for Planting by Agreement* | *£5,2,4.5* |
| | *Dec. 24th* | *To digging out the Road by the Beech Trees in the Old Garden and trenching by do.* | *£7,4,8 232* [229] |

It is also possible to distinguish elements of the seventeenth-century Dongan landscape from those that date from the construction of Castletown House (Fig. 21). It is probable that the straight avenues, which led to the Liffey west of the terraced gardens and to Celbridge, were geometrically linked to the Dongan house. This would also explain their lack of axial connection to Speaker Conolly's mansion. The old Dongan kitchen garden, like that at Breckdenston, was probably also positioned axially and adjacent to the mansion it served. The post-1768 demesne map carefully named the various avenues that cut through the northern woodland. One of these avenues, Dangan's Walk, must date from the Dongan period. Figure 21 attempts to locate the position of the Dongan mansion by connecting the axes of Gay's Avenue, Dangan's Walk, the Celbridge Avenue and the Avenue from the *rond-point*, as depicted by Rocque. The focus at which they meet probably pinpoints the location of the Dongan mansion. Speaker and/or Katherine Conolly must have laid out the avenues, which do not relate to this older geometry, when the landscape was redesigned to enhance the new mansion. Naturally enough, they were focused upon the new mansion, and include the Broad Walk and the Avenue leading to the Dublin gate. Speaker Conolly and/or his wife (Fig. 21) must also have laid out the canal, which Rocque places on axis with the house and the Broad Walk.

Castletown's woods were regarded by many as the defining beauty of the Castletown landscape, which was sometimes considered by contemporary observers to be 'too flat to make a pretty picture'.[230] The *c.*1739 map of Castletown describes a large park in the French *forêt ornée* garden style situated north of the house, with long axial avenues cut through its woodland and a boundary walk separating the designed landscape from the surrounding countryside (Fig. 16). Ornamental forest brought woodland into the garden by cutting avenues or

Fig. 21
Analytical drawing of the vegetation and landscape of Castletown depicted by *Rocque's 1760 map of Dublin* (Fig. 19).

a Dongan kitchen garden
b Dongan terraced gardens
c Dangan's [Dongan's] Walk
d Gay's Avenue
e Celbridge Avenue
f Avenue from the Rond-Point
g Avenue to the Liffey
h Broad Walk
i Dublin Gate Avenue
j canal
k Pond
l Rond-Point
m The Ring in the Wood
n Outline Position of the Dongan House
o Castletown House

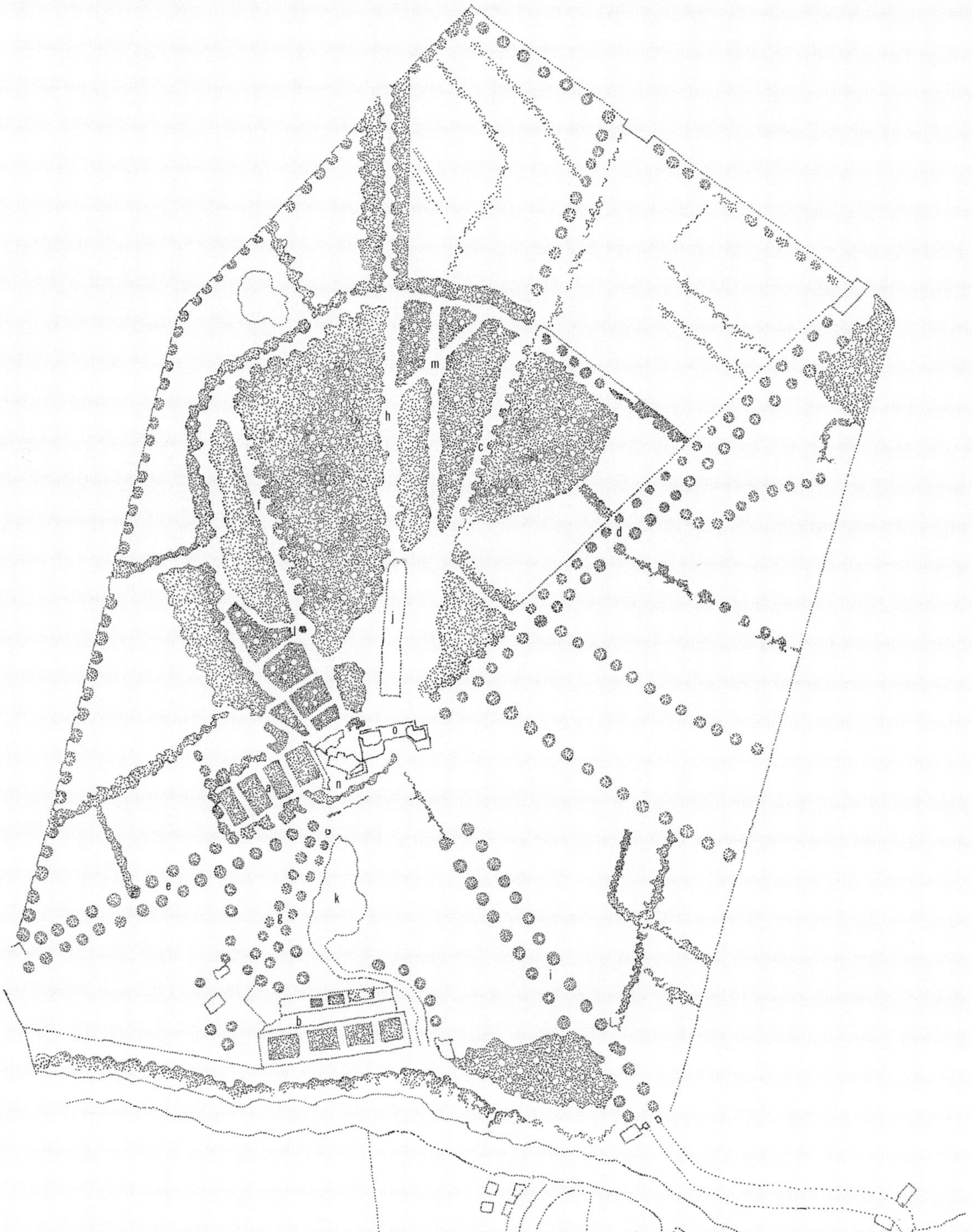

allées through acres of mature woodland. The avenues enabled the visitor to perambulate pleasantly through the woods, admiring the quality and variety of the timber, without having to stumble through the undergrowth. They were orientated towards specific topographical features in the surrounding countryside. The various powerful families who lived along the Liffey valley created a great designed landscape together by uniting their landscaping efforts so that a greater whole might be formed from the sum of the parts. Speaker and Katherine Conolly planted formal axial avenues to co-ordinate their landscape's design with the surrounding countryside and to respond to its topographical position as one of the principal gentlemen's seats along the route of the river. The geometric origin of the Broad Walk (Fig. 22 & 24) is clearly that of a perpendicular axis from the north front of Castletown House, and its focus at the Conolly obelisk was constructed by Katherine Conolly in 1740. An account for 'planting Poplars and Beech in the Broad Walk'[231] suggests that it was a linear clearing of mixed planting. An avenue once extended the axis of the Broad Walk to the obelisk on a hill, and this hill and the river Liffey probably fixed the orientation of the house. The '93 lime trees in Coffy's Walk'[232] led towards Griffin Rath, and Guy's Avenue led the eye to the small hill northeast of Ravensdale House (Fig. 22). Some of the avenues were not made from carefully spaced trees but from hedges. Other great houses in the vicinity responded to the Castletown interventions by orienting features in their landscapes towards Castletown's. The approach avenue to the house of Back Westown (southeast of Castletown) was oriented on the Wonderful Barn (Fig. 22). By ambiguously blurring the perceived boundaries of their estate, the family's influence over the surrounding landscape was magnified. The Fitzgerald family, Earls of Kildare, probably colluded in the obelisk's successful design, as it is visible from within Carton demesne and built on their land.

Fig. 22

James Taylor, *Map of the County of Dublin*, 1783. Detail.

The Castletown accounts record the estate's good woodmanship and management, which maintained the woodland's renown. The wood's sub-sections generally shared the name of an adjacent avenue – Coffy's Wood was named after Coffy's Walk – and fortunately these were included on the post-1768 map of the demesne (Fig. 24). The avenue and shrubbery walks were laid with gravel and, as the drainage channels and ha-has generally followed the lines of the walks, their outlines have been conserved. The demesne map of about 1739 described how the woodland portions were divided by the grand axes and then sub-divided by twisting paths leading to small groves and clearings (Fig. 16). The filigree detailing of the area immediately west of the house suggests that this was where the flower-gardens and shrubberies were situated. Stephen Switzer's style is visible in the map's integration of a formal axial plan with minor curvilinear walks and garden rooms. The desire (as at Breckdenston) to create a variety of atmospheric spaces by manipulating scale, dimension and the patterns, tones and hues of the plant material is also evident. The wood today is still semicircular in outline and the avenues, walks and walls, which separated the wood from the farming and deer-park land to the north, can still be discerned. The Celbridge linear approach avenue was planted with limes, flanked by a hedge and a nursery screen of fir trees, with 'shores' or edges which were banked and sodded.[233] Molesworth's shelter avenues at Breckdenston were also of fir, and Bryan Kavanagh's 1769 account for digging up '112 firs in the Avenue leading to Celbridge'[234] reveals that the limes were then mature enough to allow their nursery trees to be removed. This suggests that the Celbridge Avenue was replanted by Speaker William and Katherine Conolly.

The Speaker died in 1729 with the house still unfinished. He left 'the estates in Wales, his mansion house in Dublin, Castletown, and all his estates in Kildare, Meath, Westmeath and Roscommon ... to his wife for her lifetime, and thereafter to his nephew William'.[235] This bequeathed Katherine Conolly considerable financial independence and power, and many of the subsequent landscaping interventions, which followed the construction of the house, may have been hers alone. The next hundred years of Castletown's history revolves around the aesthetic tastes and ambitions of two women. Speaker Conolly's grand-nephew, Thomas Conolly, married Lady Louisa Lennox in 1758. Katherine Conolly and Lady Louisa Conolly turned Castletown demesne into one of the great designed landscapes of Ireland, visited and admired by both foreign and native visitors until its period of decline in the nineteenth century. They controlled, designed and commissioned the creation of the Castletown demesne between 1729, when the Speaker died, and 1821, when Lady Louisa Conolly died, with a gap of only six years between Katherine Conolly's death in 1752 and Thomas Conolly's marriage in 1758. Katherine Conolly began her life at Castletown following a period of immense unrest in Ireland, at a time when the Anglo-Irish Ascendancy consolidated its position as owners and rulers of the land. Louisa Conolly began her life at Castletown in the heyday of that Ascendancy and died after witnessing the impact of the French Revolution, the United Irishmen's 1798 rising, the Act of Union and the inevitability of Catholic Emancipation on her family, friends and class.

Katherine Conolly directed her attention towards the surrounding landscape during the twenty-three years of her sole occupancy of the Castletown demesne between 1729 and 1752. The planting of trees, the interventions described by the *c.*1739 map and corroborated by the accounts, and the construction of the Conolly obelisk and other outbuildings were Lady Katherine's major contributions to the Castletown landscape. She also rebuilt the Protestant church at Celbridge, with a monument therein to her late husband's memory, having found the church 'much too little for the People'. Although many people had promised to 'contribute towards rebuilding the old church', she eventually had to do 'it all at my own expences'. When complete it was 'larger and ten times handsomer than the old church'[236] and had cost her '2000 pds at least'.[237] Despite the many building projects completed at Castletown during her occupancy, she rarely wrote about her activities, and no accounts for those years are known to have survived.

Fig. 23
M. Dahl, *Katherine Conolly & Niece.*

Lady Anne Wentworth married Speaker William Conolly's nephew and heir, William James Conolly, in 1733. Katherine Conolly did not always see eye-to-eye with her nephew's new wife, and found her 'fond of diversions ... always the feat of young women kept in a nursery and never let go abroad to see anything till they are married'.[238] She also objected to the young couple's frequent sojourns in England. They once departed with 'all spent and little or no debts payd', which 'grieves me much' as she recalled 'an old and true saying a rolling stone never gathers moss'. Lady Anne Conolly's spendthrift ways led Katherine to remark that 'English wives ought to bring large portions' with them to Ireland, which she had 'never heard' was the Irish case. The English wife's extravagance was 'all to come'.[239] Lady Anne was not impressed by the Castletown landscape. Her father, the Earl of Strafford, had educated her to appreciate his improving tendencies at Wentworth Castle in Yorkshire. This great estate was situated in the same county as Bramham Park, Castle Howard and Studley Royal, the most ambitious and successful contemporary examples of the garden style Castletown also sought to create. In a letter to her father in 1733, Lady Anne complained that Castletown's wood was 'a good distance from the house' and had 'no shelter', since there was 'very little timber in it'.[240] She found that Ireland in general had 'but few places that are anyway like a seat' and that they appeared to her to 'have all one fault and that is the want of trees, by which reason every place looks terrible raw and cold'. In 1733 she considered Leixlip Castle, where she and her husband lived until the death of Katherine Conolly in 1752, to be much more agreeable, Castletown being 'so very unfinished without doors' and not 'very pleasant'.[241]

The great aristocratic gardens of England depended for their effect on enormous areas of mature woodland. Plantations of trees also symbolized the power and sound business sense of the great lord. As an indispensable national resource responsible for the construction of her warships, the woods symbolized the country's power and freedom for all patriots.[242] England's national identity in the eighteenth century was intimately linked with the mythology surrounding her verdant 'heart of oak', which became 'the bulwark of liberty, all that stood between freeborn Englishmen and Catholic slavery and idolatry'.[243] What remained of the Dongans' 'fine wood' was inadequate to express the new power and wealth of the Conolly family, and it became imperative to revive the woodland. Great demesnes nearby, such as those of Carton and Lyons, did not have Castletown's woodland heritage and never developed extensive forest gardens. They had not the incentive of an existing stock of mature trees to encourage an ornamental woodland design. The extent of the tree-planting carried out at Castletown in the first half of the eighteenth century may be judged from a 1762 letter of Emily, Duchess of Leinster. Castletown's woodland was then 'worth a million to people who live here in winter, besides the beauty of it in summer, for to have so charming a walk or ride where no wind comes nor wet underfoot is delightful'. This suggests that the tree canopy was then dense and old enough to protect people from the elements, and that the Dongan remnant was more substantial than Lady Anne would admit. Referring to Carton's lack of such an amenity, Emily Kildare wrote: 'It's a pity us poor invalids have not such a one; I hope that is not coveting one's neighbour's goods.'[244] Sixty-one acres of woodland remained within the demesne wall by the late eighteenth century.[245] These were probably harvested, and an old pollarded oak, which still exists in the woodland immediately east of the house, reveals that some of the trees remain. Arthur Young, who visited Castletown in 1776, found it 'the finest house in Ireland . . . quite surrounded with fine plantations disposed to the best advantage to the north, these unite into very large woods, through which many winding walks lead, with the convenience of several ornamented seats, rooms &c'.[246] Lady Katherine's landscape developed into a critical success.

William James Conolly and Lady Anne Wentworth spent a mere two years in residence at Castletown before William James's death in 1754, but Lady Anne probably influenced her mother-in-law during their long period of residence at Leixlip Castle. Her letters reveal that she was a woman both knowledgeable and critical of gardening taste. Lady Anne and her father were very close, and she advised him on garden developments at Wentworth Castle. In 1734 she found the obelisk he had built there 'one of the finest' of his 'improvements', but that the 'Lew Lake' had been 'wholly neglected' when he 'quite left aside the thoughts of a temple there'.[247] She visited many Irish gardens and found Rathfarnham Castle to be 'the best' of any she had 'seen in this Country'. 'An old castle with square towers at each corner', it had 'the Air of an English Nobleman's seat', with a 'pritty' garden and a 'vastly well wooded' park with 'a racing water going thro it, besides a great many fine fishponds' with 'the largest Carp' she had ever seen. It was 'not near so grand' but 'more agreeable than Castletown'.[248] Such frank and critical remarks from a daughter-in-law with an 'unhappy way of speaking harshly with out thinking'[249] appear to have goaded her mother-in-law into action. The obelisk at Wentworth Castle was constructed in 1734 and, as the construction of Castletown's obelisk began in 1740, a resonance between both landscapes is suggested.[250] Katherine Conolly had a life interest in much of the Conolly estates, including Castletown, and Lady Anne's husband 'did not come into possession of them until her death'.[251] Katherine Conolly died in September 1752 and William James Conolly in January 1754, which gave him little time to spend any of his uncle's money or to alter Castletown. Although Anne

W E S
Night Park A R P 9 = 3 = 33
No 1 Deer Park A R P 16 = 2 = 10
A R P 3.3.27
No 2 Deer Park A R P 26 = 2 = 30
No 4 Deer Park A R P 23 = 1 = 20
Abbey Field A R P 10 = 1 = 37
Pond field A R P 9 = 1 = 3
Ditto
A R P 6 = 2 = 15
No 3 Deer Park A R P 20 = 0 = 20
Road round the Wood
Ring
Broad Walk
Paddock A R P 5 = 0 = 31
Coffy Walk
Walk
No 1 A R P 34 = 0 = 10
Back Lawn A R P 36 = 3 = 35
Kitchen Garden
Gaw Avenue
A R P 17 = 3 = 18
Sunk Fence
Road from Kitchen Garden
A R P 3 = 1 = 21
No 2 A R P 18 = 3 = 30
Bryan Cavenagh
Barnfield A R P 8 = 3 = 18
Paddock A R P 4 = 2 = 10
A R P 8 = 3 = 18
7 = 3 = 15
No 3 A R P 38 = 3 = 30
A = R = P 28 = 2 = 2
Kennel Field A R P 21 = 1 = 10
A R P 15.3.00
River Liffy
Denominations A R P
Barnfield 17 3 18
Ditto Do 8 3 18
Ditto Do 3 1 21
Foal Paddock 4 2 10
Field next Celbridge Lodge 8 3 18
Kennel Lawn 21 1 10
A R P 64 = 3 = 15
Front Lawn 38 3 30
2d Division of Ditto 18 3 30
3d Division of Ditto 34 18 0
Back Lawn 36 3 35
Wood Paddock 5 - 31
Wood About 61 - 6
A R P 139 = 2 = 6
deduct for Kitchen garden & Strip Garden &c
besides by the River side, Ring in the Wood, Broad Walk in Do, Little Field between Wood & Sunk Fence, & Broad Plantation Walk
Pond Field 9 1 3
Ditto Do 6 2 15
Abbey Field 10 1 37
Night Park 9 3 33
36 = 1 = 8
No 1 Deer Park 16 2 10
2 Ditto Do 26 2 30
3 Ditto Do 20 - 20
4 Ditto Do 25 1 20
88 = 3 = 0
Total 389 1 35
Road to Dublin
River Liffy
Cottage Ground

Conolly's involvement is not confirmed, it appears more than coincidental that many of Katherine Conolly's improvements to the Castletown landscape took place after her daughter-in-law's arrival in Ireland.

When William James Conolly died in 1754, his son Thomas Conolly (1734–1803) inherited his father's estate before coming of age. The next phase of Castletown's development began with his marriage to Lady Louisa Lennox (1743–1821) on 30 December 1758. Louisa had lived with her sister Emily, Duchess of Leinster, at the neighbouring estate of Carton from the age of eight, following the death of her parents, the Duke and Duchess of Richmond, in 1750 and 1751 respectively. Thomas and Louisa's marriage united the Conolly family with the great aristocratic families of Lennox (Richmond) and Fitzgerald (Kildare) and it also united the development of both estates, as ideas, books and plants travelled between them. The young couple inherited a maturing landscape with a developed structure of woodland, water features, follies, statuary and service buildings. Lady Louisa Conolly took this blueprint and developed it to fit her own personal taste and inclination, while retaining its basic guidelines. She brought many of the ideas formulated by Speaker and Katherine Conolly in the early eighteenth century to fruition when she removed the terrace gardens, avenues and other selected elements of the Dongan landscape and constructed the new kitchen garden. She also implemented the landscaping of the Crodaun stream and reinforced the estate's Liffey aspect by creating a great riverside walk of her own design. The demesne developed progressively southwards, and design interest in the *forêt ornée* was gradually replaced by the Brownian parkland vocabulary. Her new riverside walk eventually stretched as far as the demesne's interface with Celbridge, where she constructed her church and co-denominational school. When Thomas Conolly died in 1803, his estate was far less lucrative than the one he had inherited. The financial stability required for large landscaping ambitions was never achieved again.

Fig. 25
Thomas Ryder,
Decoration between the windows on the north wall of the Long Gallery of Castletown House of Thalia, Muse of Comedy in an antique landscape setting, *c.*1761–63.

Fig. 24
Demesne plan of Castletown House, *c.*1768.

Thomas and Louisa Conolly completed the construction of Castletown House and, in particular, its interior. Castletown's great Long Gallery is situated on the first floor of the garden front. Louisa found it a 'charming room' with 'such a variety of occupations in it, that people cannot be formal in it'.[252] The interior façade of its external north wall frames views of the northern parkland for those seated within the room. The 'underlying theme' of this

## Adorning the Country with Ruins:[275] Louisa Conolly's Gothic Walk

*St. Wolstans is a very beautifull place the house commodious in all respects – the grounds well laid out a river runs within a hundred yards of the windows which are cut down to it, with a fine bank of wood & Mr. Connolly's seat on the other side . . . I have the bank the river the cascades the summerhouses all before me as I sit at my work, not the sleepy, dull, old, river called Father Thames, not the Drunken, boisterous, galloping, rivers of our Scottish mountains but a pretty sort of cantering river . . . this place originaly was a monastry & was inhabited by some hundred monks, the ruins of the Abbey remain in detached pieces & form fine objects.*[276]

In 1767 the Conollys began 'a new piece of work which will make Castletown beautifull'. They started to 'dress' the banks of the river by 'scooping some parts of the ground and adding it to the other to make a little rising ground for alas! that is what this pretty dear place wants'.[277] Their plan to develop the riverside gathered momentum when they managed to acquire a 'little addition of ground by the river side . . . a very little bit, but very pretty' in 1768.[278] The 'little bit' was an addition of '3 acres, 1 rod and 17 perches', surveyed by John Simmonds for a 1768 indenture between Dean Bernard, owner of the estate of St Wolstan's, and Thomas Conolly.[279] The 'piece or parcel of land . . . commonly called the wood and hopyard of St. Wolstan's situated on the north side of the River Liffey' was eventually acquired outright by Thomas Conolly in 1796.[280] 'The Cottage Ground' was carefully included on the demesne map of about 1768, and Louisa's plan to enclose the old public right of way by the riverside, where the walled terraced gardens of Rocque's map still stood, began to take shape (Fig. 30).[281] She designed a route from Celbridge to the Dublin gate with a topographic section carefully moulded to expose riverside vistas of new and existing buildings (Fig. 31). The use of small buildings to define the mood and atmosphere of particular locations within the garden, and to orientate the visitor along certain preordained routes, was well established by this time. The garden theorist Thomas Whately, whose book *Observations on Gardening* was in the Castletown library, believed that the building of follies dramatized the landscape. While 'the interior of buildings should not be disregarded, it is by their exterior that they become objects; and sometimes by the one, and sometimes by the other and sometimes by both, they are entitled to be considered as characters'.[282] Whately maintained that 'in a garden every species of architecture may be admitted from the Grecian down to the Chinese',[283] and it appears that Louisa took such eclectic advice to heart. Classical, Gothick and gothic buildings were gradually accommodated into Castletown's design.[284]

In 1769 Bryan Kavanagh reinforced, levelled and re-sodded the ground by the riverside, while removing 2,128 'yards' of earth.[285] The terraces of the old garden were finally removed in 1778–9 and the varied views of the river provided by their three platforms probably suggested to Louisa that her riverside walk would be enhanced by the use of different levels. An exhaustive amount of earth-moving, concentrated in the area between the lime kiln

Fig. 30
George Barret, Castletown, *c.*1764.

and the ice house, then took place and a cursus or running-track for Thomas Conolly's horses and dogs was laid out at the western end.[286] Louisa developed a sequence of views leading from the pond eastwards, past the bathing house, the ice house, the tower, abbey and gate of St Wolstan's and terminating at the Batty Langley lodge, whence one could return to the house or continue to a final vista of St Wolstan's House. This walk is substantially intact today. Its upper level still commands long-distance views back to the house, towards the follies and out to the neighbouring country houses of St Wolstan's and Donaghcumper. The lower level engages closely with the sound and form of the river itself, and the high bank of the upper walk protects the stroller from the gaze of the enormous façade of Castletown House. At the river's eastern end the two levels merge, and views of the old abbey, the tower and the gate in the park of St Wolstan's become visible across the river. The orientation of both the

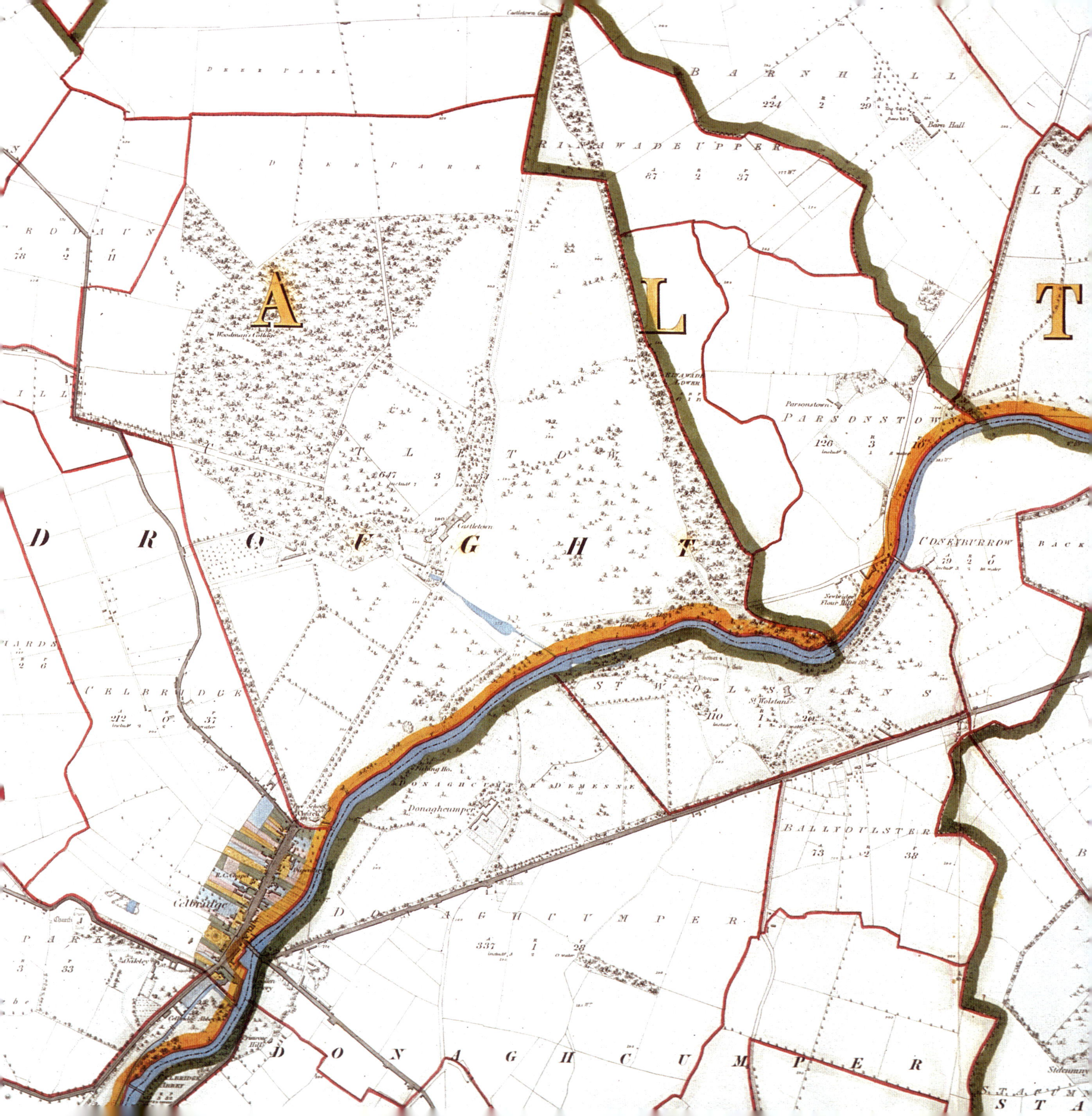

Castletown Gate
DEER PARK
BARNHALL
Barn Hall
RINAWADE UPPER
A
L
T
Woodman's Cottage
Castletown
PARSONSTOWN
Parsonstown
CONEYBURROW
Newbridge Flour Mill
ST WOLSTANS
St Wolstans
CELBRIDGE
Celbridge
Fishing Ho.
DONAGHCUMPER DEMESNE
Donaghcumper
BALLYOULSTER
DONAGHCUMPER
Oakley
Stacumny

Fig. 32
View of the bathing house to the right-hand side and Mrs Siddons' Temple on the left-hand side on the upper level of the riverside walk.

bathing house and the ice house suggest that the preferred route was from west to east but this could be reversed to follow Barret's distant vista of the bridge over the Liffey at Celbridge or, latterly, the church Louisa built in 1806. The greatest height differential between the two levels occurs in the region of the old quarry and lime kiln. This was manipulated for effect in the nineteenth century when the planting of exotic conifers emphasized the romantic and sublime possibilities of the steep gradient. Louisa constructed cascades in the river for visual and aural effect and the planting at the lower level was more intricately laid out. Precedents for the design of riverside walks are to be found in many other eighteenth-century landscape gardens. Rievaulx Abbey, Stourhead and Painshill Park in England (the latter being one of Emily Leinster's models for Carton) all manipulate the natural topography in order to allow the landscape to be viewed from different levels. In her travels in England and Ireland Louisa evidently acquired an appreciation of the careful control of the landscape section.

After a left turn at the mature beeches which mark the confluence of the pond and riverside walks to cross the rustic bridge over the Crodaun stream, a right turn leads down a grassy slope towards the broad lower plateau of the riverside walk. Towards the east, the ruin of the bathing house, a popular folly type along the river Liffey, comes into view (Fig. 32). Luttrellstown and Lucan House each possessed an eighteenth-century classical bathing house with the required stream, cascade and plunge-pools, although that at Lucan had a Gothick interior. Typically the bathing house took the form of a small Doric temple, inspired by the many eighteenth-century paintings of figures from classical mythology bathing in secluded groves (Fig. 33). The social function of the bathing house was a private one, in that 'no invitations to bathe' were given in the manner of 'invitations to take tea'.[287] The new Castletown bathing house was constructed in the years 1778–9, and designed by Louisa Conolly herself. In 1778 she had been 'drawing a Plan' for 'a little room of 19 feet square for a bathing dressing room'.[288] She wanted its garden to be 'planted this Season', which meant that she had had 'no time to lose, for fixing the foundation'.[289] As it was located 'in a conspicuous place', by the riverside, Louisa found it 'necessary to ornament it a little'. Her 'contrivance' had been 'great, in making the Pillars of some Doorcases taken out of the Gallery do' for the portico. These were probably wooden and the '3.5 Plinths to Columns of do., Portland Stone 2.5 ins. thick'[290] prevented them from rotting. The exterior was finished in 'French rusticating work', the roof slated and the windows glazed. The interior had a coved stucco ceiling with applied mouldings and plastered walls, a Scotch stone hearthstone, a coalhole and a chimneypiece. By May Day 1779, the building was complete.[291] The planting complemented the 'Bath Stone Urn and Pedestal', which was probably placed in front of the portico.[292] The absence of a plunge pool or cold bath in the existing ruin suggests that, if any bathing did take place, it took place in the river.

Fig. 31
First edition Ordnance Survey map of Castletown, Co. Kildare, 1839.

Fig. 34
Photograph of a view through the Gothic temple to the Moorish tent across the valley, Painshill Garden, Surrey.

Placed in counterpoint to the bathing house, Mrs Siddons' Temple on the upper walk level was built during the years 1780–1 (Fig. 32). Designed as a focus for both levels of the riverside walk and also for Castletown House and the Dublin approach route, its circular form is effective precisely because it has no hierarchy of orientation. Four freestanding columns (which cannot be appreciated from the long-distance views) open the building to the riverside route and allowed the occupants, who drank tea there, to view the riverside. The absence of any construction elements (doors, windows and chimneys) that might accurately reveal the temple's scale was a common technique used in the construction of many eighteenth-century garden buildings. By removing such details, the scale of the landscape was manipulated. The Turkish tent at Painshill, Surrey, when viewed from the Gothick temple across the valley, lacks any detail that might indicate the real physical scale of the building. It thus succeeds in rendering ambiguous the scale of the landscape in which it is set (Fig. 34). Such a manipulation of scale is also achieved by Mrs Siddons' Temple when viewed across the front park of Castletown (Fig. 27). These techniques must have been more effective when the trees were not all mature (as they are today), and when the eventual scale of the exotics introduced at this time was unimaginable. Pruning techniques were probably also used to manipulate scale and confuse the viewer, as a young tree could be pruned to look as though it had a much older habit. The landscape was also designed for the speed of a carriage; the contrived views and vistas followed each other in such swift succession that small design discrepancies were easily overlooked (Fig. 35). Disbelief cannot be as easily suspended at pedestrian speed and height.

Fig. 35
Design for a Carton carriage.

If one moves below Mrs Siddons' Temple to cross a small ornamental stream, which drains the ha-ha in the front lawn, Castletown's ice house comes into view (Fig. 36). Constructed of brick with a small pitched entrance façade of cut stone, a tunnel descends to the circular brick chamber below ground level. The ice house was a utility building common to all country houses which provided ice for preserving foodstuffs and preparing iced foods. In 1853 Charles Mc Intosh described 'the principle on which ice-houses have previously been built' as constructing 'three-fourths of the building ... under the ground-level, the remainder being covered with soil, and rendered perfectly impermeable over the top'. The 'best of all places for an ice-house' was the 'side of a hill covered with large trees ... the top being covered over with earth and ivy ... on the side of a hill or sloping ground, perfectly dry, and if possible facing the north'.[293]

Fig. 33
Francis Wheatley,
*Nymphs Bathing at the Salmon Leap, Leixlip,*
*c.*1782. Detail.

The Castletown ice house follows the Mc Intosh prescription, except for the recommended northern orientation. Its southern aspect was determined both by the necessity and convenience of having the ice house beside the source of water from which it was filled, and by its secondary role as a focal point for the riverside walk. It was constructed in the last few months of 1775 to coincide with the initial development of the riverside and the alteration of the pond, when an older ice house sited in that area was probably demolished. The environment required for storing ice was improved by the tree planting, which also screened its ungainly form.

Fig. 36
View of the ruined Castletown bathing house with the ice house in the distance.

On leaving the ice house, the medieval ruins of the abbey, tower and gate of St Wolstan's come into view across the Liffey. Louisa included these picturesque and fashionable gothic ruins in her new riverside landscape as borrowed additions suggesting the name 'Gothic walk' (Fig. 37). Their existence may have inspired the river walk's development, as these ruins and St Wolstan's House appear to have been the only riverside buildings in existence when the Conollys acquired the cottage ground in 1768. The abbey (or Grey Abbey) is a mysterious building, which appears in the accounts quite frequently between the years 1775 to 1787. An account was submitted in 1770 for '1 man 2 Days at the Abby repairing the dashing and plaistering the false Windows',[294] and in 1779 a shed attached to the Grey Abbey was completely renovated and re-glazed.[295] A field titled 'Abbey Field' appears on the post-1768 map at the other end of the demesne (Fig. 24). The accounts most probably refer to the Abbey of St Wolstan's, and the word 'abbey' never appears again on a Castletown demesne map. John Coates's 1786 account for taking stone 'to a large gate at the back of the Abbey'[296] may refer to the medieval tower and gate of St Wolstan's, and reveals that the Conollys were involved in their maintenance. John Hobart, Lord Buckinghamshire and brother-in-law of Thomas Conolly, was Lord Lieutenant of Ireland from 1777 to 1780 and rented St Wolstan's from Dean Bernard as a country retreat.[297] The Conollys may have maintained St Wolstan's gothic antiquities both to convenience their important relative and to allow Louisa to influence the design of the neighbouring estate that had such an impact on their own. Accounts for the abbey's maintenance also exist for both before and after the Lord Lieutenant's occupancy. As Dean Bernard was a friend of the Conollys, he may have permitted Louisa to become involved in the design and organization of his own demesne. Her husband, sisters and friends were all accustomed to turn to her for advice on building and planting, and her good friend Dean Bernard could easily have consulted her about the design of a landscape that concerned them both. Alternatively, the Conollys may have simply imposed their superior wealth and power on a weaker neighbour.

In the mid-eighteenth century a taste for the gothic was associated with English patriotism and anti-Catholicism. 'Nationalistic pride and Enlightenment confidence helped to create the Gothic Revival, but

Fig. 38
Robert Healy,
*Unidentified Gothic Landscape*, c.1768.

ironically the movement often put great distance between itself and England's feudal and Catholic past.'[298] Horace Walpole, acknowledged leader of the Gothic Revival, believed with patriotic fervour that the English had 'discovered the point of perfection' in the English landscape garden, and had 'given the true model for gardening to the world'.[299] He found that 'old castles, old pictures, old histories and the babble of old people . . . cannot disappoint' when used as focal points in a garden, because 'the dead have exhausted their power of deceiving'.[300] The anti-historicism of ruins may have proved popular among the Anglo-Irish, whose power and position rested on a strong rebuttal of the larger Catholic cultural environment. Louisa believed (unlike Robert Molesworth) that 'universal representation' was 'absolutely impossible in Ireland, without submitting to become a Catholick country, the consequences of which are obvious, to make a doubt about the imprudence about wishing such a change'.[301] Louisa Conolly and her extended family were closely aquainted with Horace Walpole and his 'Strawberry Hill' Gothick style. She and Emily carried books and letters to him from France,[302] and Emily was one of 'his favourites'.[303] Walpole had worked for Thomas Conolly's uncle, William, second Earl of Strafford, at Wentworth Castle, where he constructed 'the Gothick market cross in Menagerie Wood', which provided 'a very pretty summerhouse' in the 'very early experimental days for Strawberry Hill Gothick'[304] around 1759–62. Louisa and Thomas visited Wentworth Castle in 1759 and again in 1783:

> *It is really the prettiest place that ever was . . . The Grounds are Charming. He has an immense [Ld Strafford] quantity of Wood and vast command of Water with the prettiest rising grounds that can possibly be. There are many pretty Temples in the Park, there is a vast deal lay'd out upon it and really I do believe with the prettiest taste in the world.*[302]

Louisa through her Lennox and Conolly connections may be presumed to have fully understood the patriotic and anti-Catholic ideology of the Gothick style. 'The idea of a monastery had been constructed by the eighteenth-century Whigs as a threatening and alien other to Hanoverian supremacy.'[306] Both 'low and elevated views of abbeys were available to visitors throughout the second half of the eighteenth century' and 'their responses would have been at least heavily influenced by specific cultural factors'.[307] These 'cultural factors ensured that abbey ruins were typically the focus of Protestant Whig hatred of Roman Catholicism'.[308] The Conollys commissioned a view of an unidentified landscape with gothic ruins from Robert Healy in the 1760s, indicating their awareness of the contemporary movement in taste (Fig. 38).[309] By including gothic ruins in their garden they may have intended to

Fig. 37
Reconstruction drawing of the Gothic landscape of the Castletown river walk.

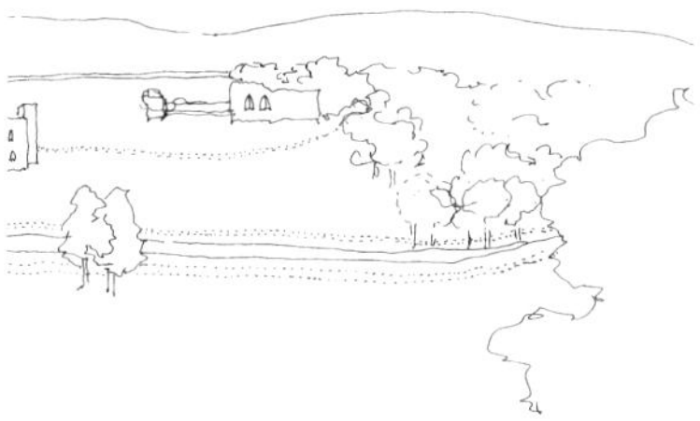

R. Healy Delin 1768

## Designing Women

*... but young men and old women seldom thinks the same way.*[378]

Katherine Conolly, 1730

Louisa Conolly's direct involvement with her workmen and the dynamic of the construction process led her to observe contemporary labour relations and to acknowledge the eighteenth-century landowner's obligation to provide work. In this she continued the path worn before her by Katherine Conolly; both women, being free from childbearing and child-rearing duties, appear to have acquired rewarding occupations. Katherine Conolly, in the manner of a great political hostess, continued to entertain 'the government and a 100 more all the holly days'[379] of Christmas 1739, some ten years after the Speaker's death. She managed the extensive Conolly estates, lamenting in 1742 that she had to buy her hay, 'which is very hard on me that has so such land in my own hand'.[380] She made many observations about the 'miserable condition' of the poor, writing in 1740 (around the time of the obelisk's construction) that they had had no rain, 'which is to be feared will ruin the farmers in many parts'. She believed that 'if the tennants be in such a way the landlords must be the sufferers also'.[381] Louisa Conolly did not consider herself 'a great politician with regard to Ireland'[382] and yet she was consulted by powerful men about Irish politics. She was certainly sometimes prejudiced against the native Irish workmen, and found it 'extraordinary to say of Paddy workmen in general ... that the Stone Cutters work and Iron work are so well finished for the sort of materials that they are done in, that it is quite pleasant'.[383] But she did believe that she could 'do no good, but employ the poor people, which as long as one has a shilling to spare ... is the best way of spending it'.[384] In her old age she became even more convinced of the need for benevolence by the rich to the poor:

> *I cannot help hoping that with the help of wise Heads, I may see the principle established, that the Poor, ought to be the first care of the Rich – The Labouring Class are the most Populous in most Countries, it is thro' their bodily Labours that the productions of the Earth are to be had & justice calls for their receiving that share of them, that is necessary for their maintenance and comfort.*[385]

Both Katherine and Louisa Conolly refused to remain enclosed within the demesne and oblivious to its power over the wider countryside and its people. Improvement for these two women did not merely mean a pleasant flower border and a well-mown lawn.

As Louisa grew older she became more involved in the design process itself. In the late 1760s she began to go out on site and her letters describe a day-to-day familiarity with the workmen and the works. In 1768 she went 'out, to give some directions about a sunk fence, a business of the utmost importance'[386] and by 1778 she did 'nothing but wear out my stumps', which were 'hardly able to carry me thro' the work of the day'.[387] Her worried

Fig. 45
Robert Healy,
*Louisa Conolly with her Gamekeeper, c.1768.*

Chapter 3

# ‘To Mix Foreign Trees with the Natives’[405]
# The History of Carton Demesne

Fig. 47
Aerial photograph of Carton demesne.

Carton House and demesne, once principal seat of the Fitzgerald family, earls of Kildare and dukes of Leinster, is a large demesne of about one thousand and seventy acres, situated on the old turnpike road from Dublin to Galway at a distance of approximately eighteen miles from Dublin. Maynooth, the estate town, is connected to the demesne by an avenue of lime trees. The ruins of the Fitzgeralds' old castle and church are situated at the opposite end of the town from the demesne gates. The formal stone façade of Maynooth College, founded in 1795, extends and terminates the main street axis. The noble Norman family of Fitzgerald contributed many colourful and inspiring figures to Irish history, notably the great Elizabethan chieftain Gearóid Mór Mhic Gearailt and Lord Edward Fitzgerald, the United Irishman and francophile. Unlike many of the Ascendancy gentry, the Fitzgeralds could lay long claim to their landed property and the power they derived from it: the manor of Maynooth had been granted to Maurice Fitzgerald, Lord of Maynooth, in 1176.

Gerald, the fourteenth Earl of Kildare, granted the lease of Carton to Sir William Talbot in 1603 'and it was he who built the house at Carton, which is the nucleus of the present mansion'.[406] 'The Civil Survey' of 1654 described the property as 'one Stone House . . . being now ruined and decayed', and the 'lands of Cartowne' also contained 'one chapell of ease, one ruined stone house, with a garden and orchard thereunto belonging; one decayed water-mill and one decayed Dove-house'. Richard Talbot, Earl of Tyrconnell, died in 1691, and was subsequently attainted for his support of James II at the Battle of the Boyne. Carton was then described as 'meadow and pasture' with 'a very fine House' and 'all manner of convenient offices and fine gardens' in the 'Book of Forfeited Estates'.[407] A contemporary plan had recorded the 'fine gardens'[408] that surrounded the duke's residence (Fig. 48). The house separated the northern plateau of walled gardens from the southern entrance courtyard. The plan's legend listed many of the typical features of a late seventeenth-century landscape: a walled court, a walled pleasure-garden, an orchard, a terraced walk, a flower-garden, a canal, plum, cherry and 'sparragrass' gardens, a walled kitchen garden, two turrets, a mound of earth and a variety of related service buildings (Fig. 48). Entrance to the estate was by carriageway from the northeast, where the Dunboyne avenue's strict lines of elm led the visitor into the enclosed railed courtyard in front of the house. This formed the hub of the prospect avenues, which radiated out into the countryside. By penetrating the symmetrical block of the house, one emerged into a stepped series of walled gardens and terraced walks. The gardens took advantage of the falling ground of the Glashrooneen river valley and distant prospect of Maynooth castle to the west. The western wall walk overlooked a canal in the plum garden, which in turn overlooked the cherry garden. A gate led from the cherry garden to the Glashrooneen river, where boating parties could embark downstream. Connecting the garden with a natural water feature was a popular gesture in contemporary Anglo-Dutch gardens. 'Something Dutch can be identified in the sense of enclosure, of intimacy, and of the relationship of buildings especially pavilions to water.'[409] The steep slopes of the Glashrooneen valley were more than adequate for constructing a cascade or an elementary fountain. Carton's flat, elongated water channels are reminiscent of 'most Dutch gardens' where 'the waterworks were of a static character'.[410] This lack of moving water at Carton, when it was common by this time to include such features in a garden, is stylistically Dutch.

Sir Richard Ingoldsby purchased the Carton estate for £1,800 in 1703. When he died in 1712, his son Henry Ingoldsby inherited the estate. He was fond of Carton and intended to 'live and die there'.[411] Henry Ingoldsby directed the design of Carton demesne until his death in 1731.[412] He initially spent many impecunious years in London, where some of his 'Irish rents – calculated at £1200 a year'[413] bought trees, plants and seeds for the Carton gardens. His uncle William Smythe took care of Carton when Henry was in London, and reported regularly on the condition of the estate. Both John Dodson and a Major Sawyer worked as gardeners in the 1716–24 period and William Smythe sent his nephew lists of the plants, trees and seeds that they needed in the gardens. Stocking the estate with trees was evidently a primary concern, and trees were bought in London in 1716, with more trees sent over in 1718 and 1724.[414] In 1723 Dodson put in a request for 'some peaches and Apricott trees'[415] and Henry 'bought four Mulberry Trees, ten Catherine Peaches & ten choice apricocks some choice flower rootes and some garden seeds'[416] for the gardens in 1724. Malts were sent over specifically 'for the preservation'[417] of fruit, and the fruit was also sold for profit. Henry

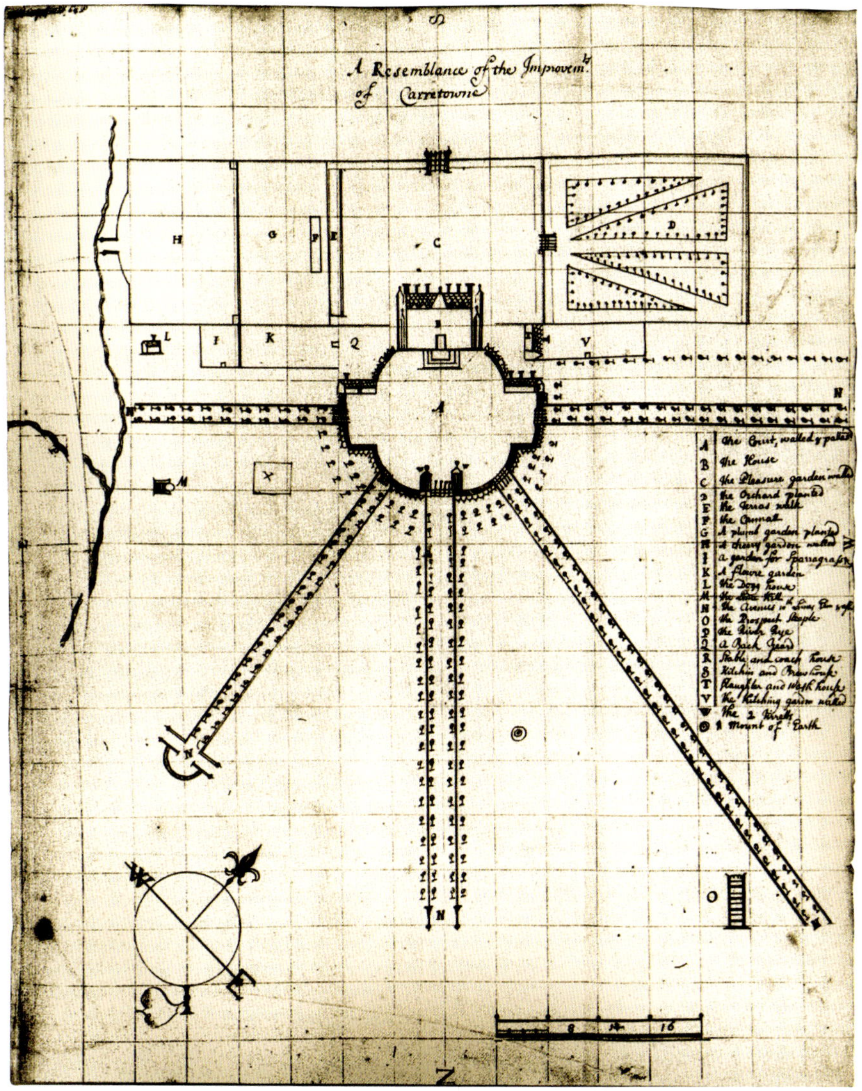


Fig. 48
Anon., *A Draught of Carton,*
*The Duke of Tyrconnell's house;*
*A Resemblance of the Improvements at Carretowne.*
Late seventeenth century.

A the Court, walled
B the House
C the Pleasure Garden, walled
D the Orchard planted
E the Terras walk
F the Cannall
G A plumb garden planted
H A cherry garden walled
I A garden for Sparragrasses
K A Flowre garden
L the Dogg House
M the Little Kill
N the Avenue wth Lime Elm
O The Prospect Steeple
P The River Rye
Q A Back Yeard
R Stable and coach house
S Kitchin and Brew house
T Slaughter and wash house
V the Kitching garden walled
W the 2 turretts
@ A Mount of Earth

Fig. 49
Johann van der Hagen,
*A View of Carton House*, c.1738.

Ingoldsby was a farmer and very concerned with his animal stock. In 1716 Major Sawyer was instructed to 'buy his cattle in Munster this season' and not to let Henry 'be bamboozled' as he had been the previous year. Sawyer was also instructed to 'make up all his fences and lay up all his meadows and turn out all his horses to grass and let them rest' before the cattle were bought. William Smythe advised Henry about the letting of his tenanted land, and in 1724 Henry thought that he would let 'all the Moygaddy lands' except for 'that part which Dick Grehane held behind my Gardens'.[418]

Henry Ingoldsby believed that England 'had arrived to such a perfection in Gardening that a man twenty years ago a Gardner scarcely knows anything of the matter', so far had it advanced. He was 'amazed' by the contemporary gardener's ability to 'raise & doe what they p*lease at any time of the year here'.[419] Henry employed George Lamb, 'a thorough working Gardner'[420] in London in 1724, who came 'well recommended',[421] to rectify the Irish situation. The newcomer had 'the caracter of being a thorough Good Gardner & particularly a good pruner as good [as a ] Nursery man'.[422] He was also able to identify 'Auriculas and ten Carnations . . . from ye rest'[423] when Henry sent some over for a friend. The new English gardener was horrified by the state of the Carton gardens, and immediately wrote to his employer to describe 'all his frights both in respect to ye old wall trees & ye badness of the foil in the Borders'. 'Not being used to such sights here in England', Henry considered that the shock had unfortunately 'discouraged' Lamb in his work. He tried to deceive himself that the bad reports he received from William Smythe merely demonstrated the earlier 'negligence of John Dodson, who was not very apt to dress ye Gardens in their best apparell without a strict eye over him'.[424] But the new gardener never recovered from the 'frights' of Carton's gardens, and did not turn out well.

An undated painting by Johann van der Hagen of *c.*1720–38 depicts Henry Ingoldsby's Carton landscape (Fig. 49). The Baylie and Mooney map of 1744, commissioned presumably by the nineteenth Earl of Kildare following his purchase of Carton in 1739, describes the landscape depicted by van der Hagen in plan (Fig. 50). The painting and the map together suggest that the walled gardens of the Holkham Hall plan (Fig. 48) were still substantially intact in 1744. The straight lines of trees probably included some from the seventeenth-century orchards, and the brick walls were decorated with a productive covering of espaliered fruit trees. The pleasure-garden's four grass *plats* were ornamented with cones and spheres of topiary and some decorative statuary. The terraced walk was still in place, and a curved wall terminated the gardens where they met the river. The canal is not indicated on the Baylie and Mooney map, nor is it visible in the painting, although it may have diminished in scale to become a small channel. All these factors indicate that the garden still retained its predominantly late seventeenth-century and Anglo-Dutch characteristics well into the eighteenth century. Notwithstanding this Dutch inclination, the grass *plats* of the parterre are typical of an English garden of the late seventeenth century when 'the use of grass as the main feature of parterres remained popular in England throughout the seventeenth century and was clearly identified as a national characteristic'.[425] The elaborate parterres and flower borders that William and Mary encouraged on their arrival in England, when they contrived to amalgamate features of both the Dutch and the French styles into their new palace landscapes, do not appear to have been adopted at Carton.[426] The parterre at Breckdenston, which was also composed of grass *plats* dotted with statuary, must have been similar to that depicted by van der Hagen. The visual effect achieved by the belvedere walk at Breckdenston, which allowed the observer to view both the surrounding countryside and the lower parterre, was also achieved at Carton. Its terrace walk afforded an elevated prospect of the distant countryside and views of the nearby canal, plum and cherry gardens. Both the terraced walks and turrets at Carton and the belvedere walk at Breckdenston were derived from earlier defensive practice. Such features distinguished many Dutch gardens from their French counterparts and led to the 'persistent view of Williamite gardens as fortified'.[427]

The van der Hagen painting (Fig. 49) and the Baylie and Mooney map (Fig. 50) also describe the extension of the late seventeenth-century formal gardens to the north. The extension was more geometrically complex than the original, with an octagonal clearing and many more sub-divisions. *Bosquets* of trees, wildernesses and tree-lined *allées* directed the viewer towards chosen features in the northern countryside. A new *patte-d'oie* was laid out to echo that of the entrance court, which (like that at Breckdenston) was focused on the termination of the central parterre walk. The painting indicates that the *bosquets* planted between the avenues of the *patte-d'oie* were of the type of 'middle height with tall hedges'[428] and developed logically from the sequence and geometry of the older walled gardens close to the house. The planting is also reminiscent of Robert Molesworth's hedged walks and groves. The avenues leading from the house to the lower right-hand side of the van der Hagen painting were stilted and cropped by the painter to separate the land of the prospect tower from that of the designed landscape (Fig. 49). Outside the tight geometry of the parterre garden, the baroque instinct to connect objects in the landscape was re-established. Maynooth Castle answers the Prospect Tower diagonally across the picture plane and a mysterious tower in the Moygaddy townland punctuates the central section. The baroque tendency to extend the garden into the wider landscape is strangely curtailed in the painting by a square of trees, which marks out a boundary between Carton and the surrounding countryside. This figure does not appear on the Baylie and Mooney map (Fig. 50) and is reminiscent of van der Hagen's native Holland. A frame of trees was a familiar feature of the polder-landscape of Holland, where 'the basic formality of the surrounding polderland ensured that the axially-developed gardens were integrated smoothly into their settings through avenues linking with estate woodland and canal plantings'.[429] No such smooth integration is evident in the painting, and the lines of trees seem to impose upon the Carton landscape a flatness that the gradient of the Glashrooneen river thwarted in reality. Johann van der Hagen may have been commissioned to paint an Irish interpretation of his own 'native' landscape and he succeeded in doing so. Carton's gardens exhibit here the 'forced awkward adjustments to geometrical planning in the French mode exactly as did sites in the Low Countries'.[430] The painting does not suggest that the aesthetic theories of Joseph Addison or Alexander Pope had any influence at Carton at this time. The rigid lines of the fruit orchards must have been easily visible from the house, and the topiary, so derided by Pope, is proudly in place.

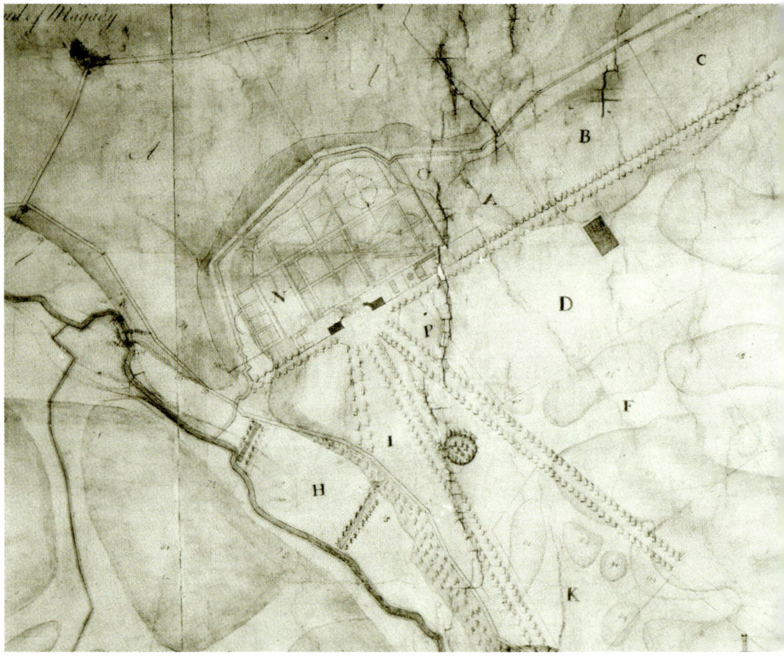


Fig. 50

Charlie Baylie and John Mooney, *A Map of the Demeasne of Carrtown Together with a map of the Adjacent Lands intended for a Deer-park*, February 1744.

A The Elm & Ash Groves
B [?]
C The Clover Field
D The Bullock Field
E The Bullock Field
F The Rock Field
G The Honeysuckle
H [?]
I The Avenue Field
K The Ten Acres
L The Sheep Walk
M The Steeple Field
N The Gardens
O The Intended Water
P The Nursery

The Baylie and Mooney map shows no departure from the baroque style, which might have been expected by 1744. The form of the estate and the positioning of the various elements and functions within it had not changed from those depicted in the Holkham Hall map. The Baylie and Mooney legend does show a marked increase in the demesne's agricultural and aesthetic ambitions, but it still contains few decorative features (Fig. 50). Areas labelled 'The Elm & Ash Groves' and 'The Nursery' suggest that the planting of trees continued to be a primary consideration. The letter O marked out a site north of the house in the valley of the Glashrooneen for 'The Intended Water', but there is no proof that the rigid geometry of canals was abandoned for a more sinuous and 'natural' design. No evidence that the 'intended water' was ever constructed exists and any design for a formal or flooded water feature must have been abandoned. The map also included a table that detailed the bearings of 'several gentleman's seats and eminent places taken from the steeple'.[431] Calculations for possible prospect points were evidently made and considered important for the landscape's successful design. Bearings for 'The Mighty Barn' (The Wonderful Barn) are given as 24 degrees to the southeast.

The scale of the Carton's early eighteenth-century extension was much smaller than those made at Castletown and Breckdenston in the same period. Henry Ingoldsby's Irish rents were 'calculated at £1200 a year',[432] less than Robert Molesworth's £2,000 p.a.[433] Both incomes were surpassed by the extraordinary wealth of Speaker William Conolly, who 'by 1715 was among the richest men in Ireland'.[434] 'A contemporary estimate of Conolly's income was £12–13,000 per annum, but at the time of his death in 1729 Primate Boulter thought it might be nearer £17,000 per annum, and his Irish estates alone were estimated to be worth £300,000.'[435] Robert Molesworth overextended himself financially in order to create the very personal and highly ambitious gardens of Breckdenston. In contrast, Richard and Henry Ingoldsby do not appear greatly to have altered what they found. The Carton garden remained that of a typical provincial nobleman at the turn of the seventeenth century, who favoured an Anglo-Dutch style of garden in preference to a more French-Italianate continental model. The plants Henry bought for the Carton gardens are those that one would expect to find in a conservative walled garden design of the 1720s. The remainder of the demesne was devoted to farming, particularly the rearing and breeding of cattle. Unlike Breckdenston, no evidence exists of a grand garden design, and Henry Ingoldsby does not appear to have had any canal or landscaping projects. He admired English gardening more for its practical achievements than for any aesthetic advances. Henry's emphasis is that of the plantsman, a Dutch characteristic, and the new gardener was employed principally for his pruning skills and his knowledge of the correct composition of flower borders. The Glashrooneen river enclosed his 'gardens', and he rented out the land beyond. These gardens have none of the breadth or ambition of Molesworth, or Conolly's vision. Both Sir Richard Ingoldsby and the Earl of Tyrconnell had soldiered in the Low Countries and the gardens they encountered when abroad probably influenced their landscaping endeavours at home. There is no evidence to conclude that the Ingoldsbys altered the Duke of Tyrconnell's Anglo-Dutch gardens in any substantial way or that they found

Fig. 51

Anon., *Stradbally, Co. Laois*, c.1740.

its design at all distasteful. As the intermediate owners between the great titled families of Talbot and Fitzgerald, the Ingoldsby family knew their place.

The French garden style employed a great scale and favoured the use of formal avenues for effect. It promoted elaborate *parterres de broderie* and was considered to be generally more expensive and less productive than the Dutch. The early Carton landscape followed the general pattern of provincial English gardening by retaining the grass parterres, the productive fruit trees, and the simple walls, terraces and walks, which defined it structurally. Topiary, which evidently survived at Carton, was considered particularly unfashionable by the 1730s when it was very much associated with the Dutch style of gardening. 'The fussiness in small scale of these Dutch-style gardens in England was at the centre of Pope's attack on their most visible feature, topiary.' A Catholic and a Tory, 'he shared the party's hatred or distrust of the Dutch nation, so we may have here a case of a politically coloured perspective'.[436] A comparison of Carton with the garden depicted in the painting of Stradbally, Co. Laois, in about 1740 reveals Carton's late adherence to the Dutch tradition, which was regarded as thoroughly provincial by this time in England (Fig. 51). The painting depicts a grotto, a gazebo, stepped grass terraces and early examples of curved water channels and garden paths in its lower left-hand corner. These Italianate features were derived from contemporary interpretations of the gardens of the ancients, and from sixteenth-century Italian villa gardens. Breckdenston and Castletown enthusiastically accommodated such features into their respective gardens while Carton did not. Any comparison of the Baylie and Mooney plan of 1744 with other aristocratic gardens of the time indicates that the demesne and gardens of Carton were entirely too small, modest and unfashionable for the great aristocratic family of Fitzgerald. The alteration and extension of the Carton landscape was necessary if Carton was to become the Kildares' principal residence.

The garden and its boundaries were central to the national iconography of Holland; the Dutch arms bore the device of a lion rampant guarding a fertile fenced garden. A tradition of boundary-making is endemic in the Netherlands, where much of the physical geography can be described as man-made. The laying out of marks or signs of ownership on the landscape is simpler on virgin territory and the accumulation of religious and moral importance to those markings more easily invented. 'The period between 1550 and 1650, when the political identity of an independent Netherlands was being established, was also a time of dramatic physical alteration of its landscape.'[437] The Dutch tradition employed a rigorous and symbolic geometry that did not have to manipulate the surrounding geography in order to create the impression that the estate was an organic extension

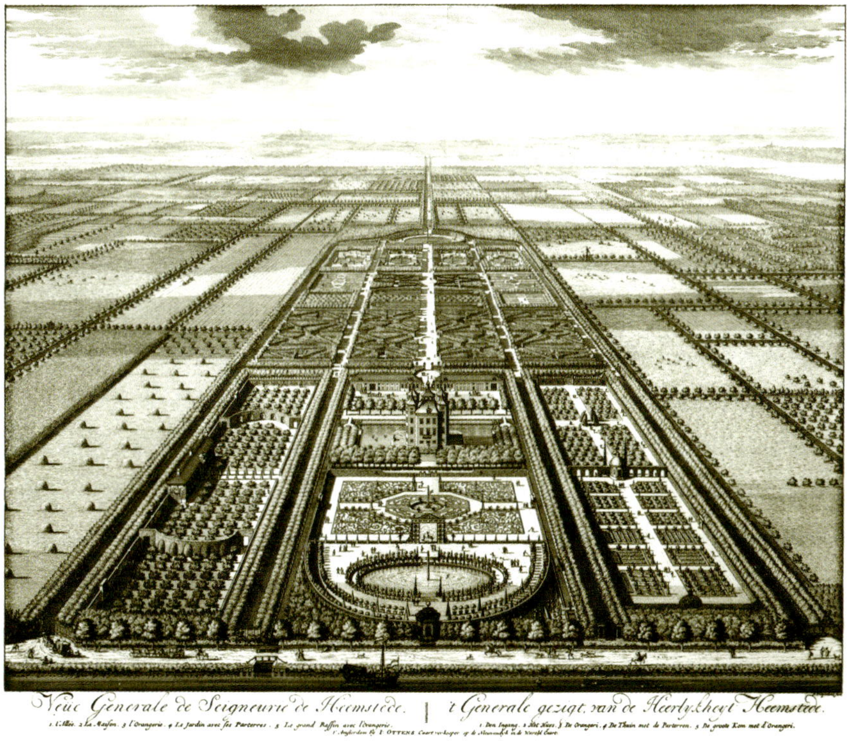


Fig. 52
Daniel Stoopendaal (1672–1726) naar Isaac de Moucheron (1667–1744), *Vogelvlucht van de Heemstede*.

Fig. 57
Thomas Roberts, *The Bridge in the Park*, c.1770.

afford to refuse the Duke of Leinster's offer of £1,000 on landing if only he would go to Ireland, excusing himself on the grounds that he had not finished England'.[461] Both paintings suggest that the Ryewater was widened by constructing artificial islands. The effect of a lake was achieved by carefully positioning the islands to split the flow of water and thus make it wider overall, although the result could hardly be described as a genuine lake (Fig. 57). James Kildare had visited 'Lord Thomond's, where there is a pretty stone bridge & a River laid out by Mr. Brown', in 1766, concurring with general opinion that it was a 'pretty place'. He reassured his wife, who had been studying 'a Model of the little Bridge', that no 'Waters or Bridges' could put him 'out of conceit with the pritty Rye, as you say I should call it, instead of the poor Rye'.[462] The adjective 'poor' implies that James was not yet happy with the river's landscaping and that he was only too aware of the difficulties posed by its successful alteration into a Brownian lake landscape. Searching for reassurance from his wife's more confident taste, he also wondered 'how the bridge was liked' by some of Carton's visitors. Public approval of their landscaping projects was evidently desirable.

The undulating and varied topography of the Ryewater valley was very suitable for the new eighteenth-century fashion in landscape design. The turfed, rolled and manicured lawns of the Anglo-Dutch garden were replaced by the gently sloping ground of *The Bridge in the Park*, and armies of grazing animals replaced armies of gardeners. Broadleaf trees dotted the parkland and the upright forms of specimen junipers and other shrubs were confined to the islands. The Rocque demesne plan of 1760 with its clumps, perimeter belt and broad sweeps of parkland

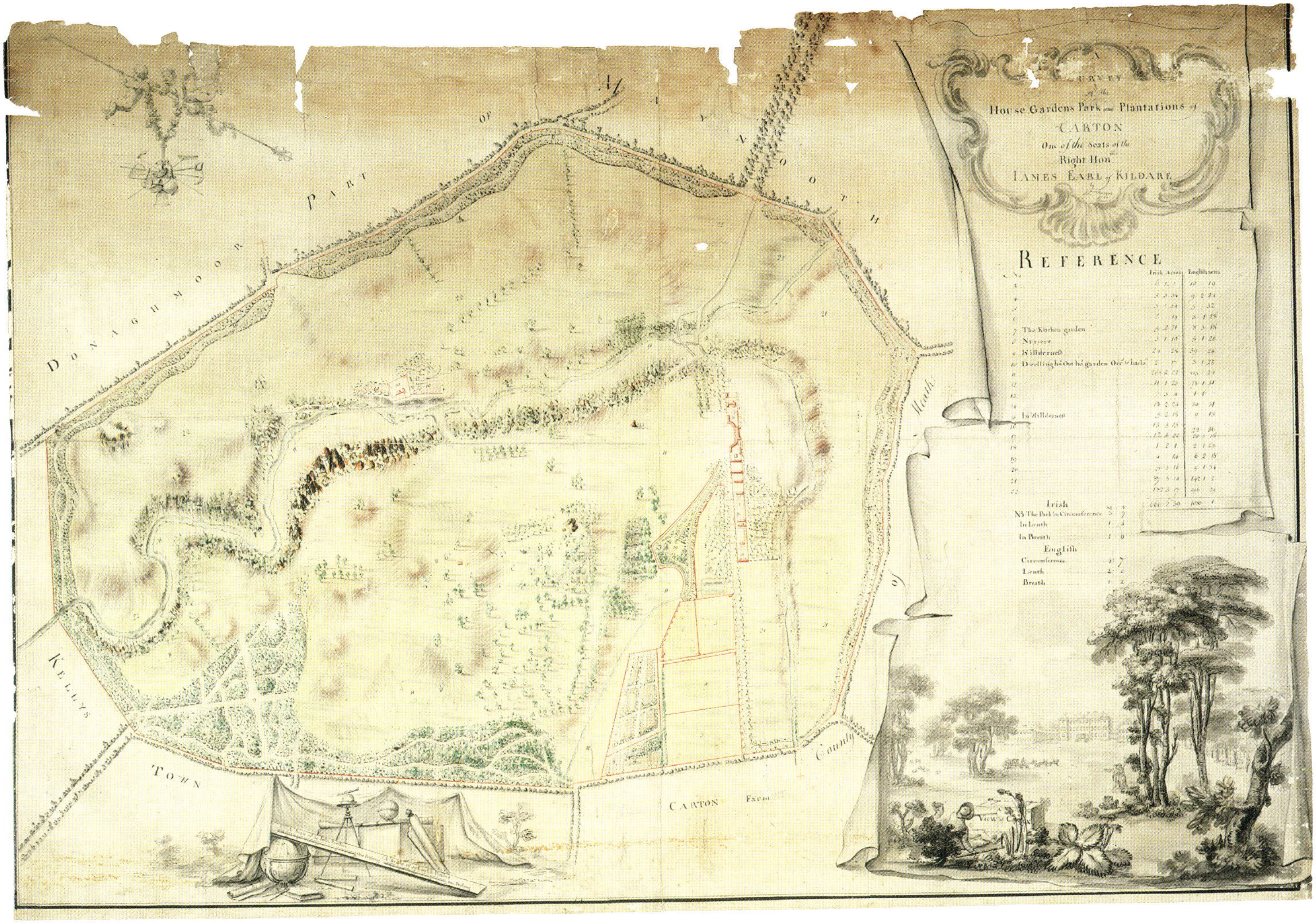


Fig. 58
John Rocque, *A Survey of the demesne of Carton in the County of Kildare Seat of His Grace James Duke of Leinster*, 1760.

described the Carton landscape at the height of Brown's influence (Fig. 58). The prospect mount depicted in the 1744 Baylie & Mooney map, unlike the canals and fishponds of the same period, had not yet been completely erased. A small vignette painting in the lower right-hand corner of Rocque's map captured an image of the changing landscape. Charmingly informal, the guardian shepherdess at its centre hints at a bucolic and pastoral future. Ghosts of the former landscape remain in the vestigial straight line of a formal avenue in the lower right-hand corner, and a coach and six progress boldly through the vast expanses of parkland without an avenue's guidance (Fig. 59). Some of these errant avenue lime trees remain in the landscape today, accommodated into the parkland landscape as specimen trees, or in the clumps (Fig. 60). The river's width broadened slightly near Waterstone cottage where three small islands punctuated its flow. The planting of the perimeter belt was evidently well advanced and the map suggests that an area southeast of the house was planted with an elongated and undulating central space reminiscent of Brown's great Grecian Valley at Stowe.

Fig. 59
Vignette detail from John Rocque, *A Survey of the demesne of Carton in the County of Kildare Seat of His Grace James Duke of Leinster,* 1760.

Henry and Lady Caroline Fox, Emily's brother-in-law and sister, visited Carton in 1750. James Kildare wrote to Henry Fox immediately after their departure to say that he had 'bespoke the cut stone for to mark the battlements of the Bridge' as Fox had 'desired to have it', but that it would not 'be all done till Christmas', which would do, as 'the Road is not to be finish'd till Spring'.[463] Construction had certainly commenced by 1766 when James Kildare was concerned that he had 'not heard that the Stone Bridge is going on well'.[464] Two surveys of the Ryewater valley were commissioned in 1763, entitled *Levels of the Rye River thro' Carton Park* and *Section thro' the Vale where the Bridge is to be Built at Carton,*[465] probably from Captain Vallencey, a military surveyor.[466] A sight-line drawn from a small figure standing on the front steps of Carton House in *Section thro' the Vale* was designed to intersect with both the balustrade of the bridge and the proposed new level of the approach road on the far side. The specified location of 'the old River, with level of the Ryewater in June' reveals that the route of the river was altered when the bridge was built. The calculation for cuts through the landscape's existing profile revealed how arduous any alterations to the Ryewater's banks would be. The gradient between the house and the river was so substantial that large amounts of earth would have to be moved to make any appreciable alteration to the topography. Such ambitious remoulding of the land's natural gradient again suggests Brown's influence. A letter of 1768, which referred to the river being 'finished' in that year, implied that the information the Vallencey surveys had supplied was acted upon.[467] A survey of 1788, still in Carton House and commissioned by William, then second Duke of Leinster, of *Sections of the Ground in Front of Carton House,* indicates where a 'former cut' had been made, probably when the bridge was constructed.

Fig. 60
1995 photograph of two old lime trees in the south park, probable remnants of Carton's radiating avenues.

Subsequent developments at Carton diverged more and more from Brown's landscaping style. The great tree-belts and clumps, which are still partially extant, followed Brown's choice of 'predominantly hardwoods – elms, oak or beeches, according to locality, and many ashes and limes – with a mixture of Scotch fir and larches, and usually a few cedars sited to give special emphasis'.[468] Brown was 'more conservative in his use of new species than his predecessors', and his 'work ... would not have been possible without' their work, 'both in botanical importation and experimentation and in planting out'.[469] Many of these predecessors, including Peter Collinson, the Dukes of Richmond, Charles Hamilton and Henry Fox were extensively consulted about the planting of Carton. Their advice on the parkland's planting design, where Brown's influence is generally at its most powerful, must have lessened the influence of Brown's aesthetic. James visited Warwick Castle (where Brown had been at work since 1744)[470] in 1766, where he 'liked everything very much' but remarked that the river was 'a large one in comparison to my own Rye'.[471] The earth-moving required to flood the Ryewater and create a Brownian lake proved either physically or financially impossible; this then placed the adoption of a completely Brownian approach to the landscape's design in doubt. Alternatively, or arising from this situation, Emily and James became more interested in developing a more personal landscaping style which empathized with Carton's natural environment. Influence and advice for these developments they found elsewhere.

Fig. 61

Thomas Roberts, *The Sheet of Water*, c.1770.

become 'too vain' she bemoaned 'the shape of the island in its present state', which was 'not pretty'. It was 'rising so much above the water' and needed 'that grace and easy pretty turn'[481] James had accomplished elsewhere. Thomas Roberts's painting of the newly completed sheet of water in about 1770 described a very different landscape to that portrayed in his other paintings of Carton (Fig. 61). Peter Collinson's style is evident in the shrubberies in the picture, which carefully deploy the new evergreens and exotics. Emily and James walk to their boat, rather than ride through the landscape in a carriage. The two servants diligently hauling a heavy roller laboriously maintain the manicured lawns and gravel walks. Unlike in the other paintings, specimen conifers can be easily identified, and the new kitchen garden walls have not yet been screened with new planting. The island manipulates scale, as the narrowing channels of water to either side create an illusion that the overall width remains constant as they recede around its mass. This creates an impression of depth and distance. At

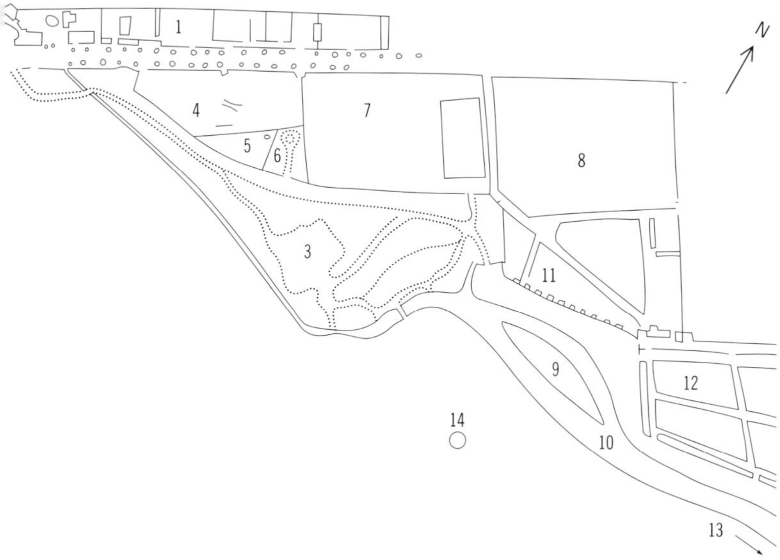


Fig. 62
Drawing of the sheet of water area from Bernard Scalé, *A Survey of the Demesne of Carton in The County of Kildare Seat of His Grace James Duke of Leinster*, 1769.
The map has been badly water-damaged.

1. The House, Offices
2. ?
3. The Shrubbery
4. Lumber Yard
5. Laundry Yard
6. Flower Garden
7. Reservoir Paddock
8. Paddock
9. Island
10. New River
11. Melon Ground and Hothouses
12. Kitchen Garden
12. Kitchen Garden
13. Direction of dam on Old Carton stream
14. Ice House

the end nearest the great house, the visitor's understanding of the water's extent and source was deliberately confused. These factors suggest that the sheet of water was a rococo pleasure-garden. The duke and duchess had wandered from the aesthetic and practice of parkland design to indulge the rococo fascination for the miniature, the horticultural and the whimsical.[485]

Carton's new ice house and kitchen garden both needed a generous supply of water and inconspicuous locations. The old ice house was situated by the Ryewater, where it disrupted the new approach route and the views towards the house from Thomas Ivory's bridge (Fig. 57). The water levels of both the Glashrooneen and Ryewater rivers were far below that of the house, and bringing water up from either river would have required hydraulic machines of some complexity. William Richards redesigned the house entrance area in 1758 and paid particular attention to the surface and foul water drainage systems.[486] A rectangular reservoir located southeast of the house collected the 'skywater' (rainwater) from the house and service yards (Fig. 62). But this reservoir fed by 'skywater' could not provide an adequate supply of water for a large kitchen garden or sufficient ice for an ice house. Only by diverting the Old Carton stream could sufficient water for the reservoir, the kitchen and the ice house be provided. Richards's reservoir and drainage systems were probably constructed first. The stream from Old Carton was then dammed and diverted into a channel to annexe this much more reliable source, and a far greater volume of water (Fig. 63). With this in place, the kitchen garden was constructed and stocked with fruit trees, vegetables and other plants. The sheet of water was in turn completed, in order to supply the new ice house with ice. Bernard Scalé's map documented the finished landscape of the sheet of water in 1769 (Fig. 62). A meandering walk was laid out around its full extent, with carefully landscaped sloping banks, and an artificial island to create multiple and changing views. The shrubbery was re-landscaped to accommodate views of the new piece of water and a flower-garden was planted north of the shrubbery. A Chinese bridge over the new rivulet led out into the Brownian parkland beyond, and further planting softened the new kitchen garden walls. The sheet of water enclave was separated from the parkland by a water channel and ha-ha. As Molesworth had discovered to his cost with the canal at Breckdenston, predicting the finished level of incoming water into a man-made water feature was either inaccurately done or left wholly to chance. The reservoir controlled the level of the sheet of water, a most important factor in its aesthetic success, and excess water from the rooftops topped up the reservoir level when the Old Carton source was low. Alternatively, when the level of the Old Carton stream was too high, the reservoir was used as an overflow tank. Thus the development of this whole area was rendered logical and derivative, and indicates that the design was not only determined by aesthetic effect.

O L D C A R T O N
Oldcarton
C A T H E R I
Carton
Reservoir
Pond
Boat Ho.
C A R T O N D E M E S N E
The Cottage
Bride's Well
Maynooth Gate
Gate
Dublin Gate
Donaghmore Church
B
R
Y
B L A
L P A R K

Henry Fox advised James Kildare 'to sow and plant with great variety, and mix foreign trees with the natives', as they required 'no more care than common trees, and some of them are fine forest trees too'.[487] Emily's brother George also thought that the Kildares should 'plant evergreens around' their 'park wall, as well as other trees, because they are so pretty in winter'.[488] Emily and James's conifer plantations near the Kellystown gate were also influenced by the planting schemes that Collinson developed with his fellow enthusiasts. The general emphasis placed on the introduction of exotics to the Carton landscape reveals both Collinson's influence and the ease with which he managed to procure such specimens for his friends. An 1872 edition of the *Journal of Horticulture and Cottage Gardener* suggests, however, that the great conifer-planting recommended by Collinson and Fox either took place on a smaller scale than the letters suggest or did not survive. The article reveals that by 1872 there were 'but a small proportion of evergreen trees about Carton' with 'some fine specimens of Silver Fir, especially on the slip [sheet] of water'.[489] Much of the recommended evergreen planting may only have been carried out at the Sheet of Water (Fig. 63).

Emily visited the great woodland garden of Cassiobury, Hertfordshire, the seventeenth-century forest landscape of the Earl of Essex, in June 1757.[490] The creation of 'a landscape garden out of woodland' at Cassiobury had 'not only anticipated the recommendations of Addison and Pope and Stephen Switzer, but the practice of such forest gardens as Bathurst's Cirencester, Bingley's Bramham, and even Charles Hamilton's Painshill'. The park was 'a sort of *forêt ornée,* a garden created out of and through productive woodland that also anticipated the *fermes ornées* of Philip Southcote and William Shenstone in the next century'.[491] Emily had also visited Painshill in the month before her visit to Cassiobury. She found that 'nothing was ever so lovely as Mr. Hamilton's park', and thought that her husband 'would admire it', as it had been 'vastly improved'[492] since he had last seen it. Charles Hamilton had 'joined forces with Collinson to advise Henry Fox', and his involvement with Holland Park dated from the 1750s, when a 'regular correspondence between Fox and Collinson on flowers, plants and trees' began.[493] Fox probably introduced Emily and James Kildare to Charles Hamilton, and an important letter of 1750 proves that Hamilton was directly involved in the alteration of the Carton landscape. Lord Kildare wrote to Henry Fox in 1750 that he was 'vastly obliged to Mr. Hamilton for his directions how to lay the Ground to Grass' having 'read it more than once, and shall again and again'.[494] The physical similarities between Hamilton's great garden of Painshill and Carton are more striking than those between Carton and Holland House. At Carton and Painshill existing rivers were dammed to create lakes, and artificial islands were constructed both to shield each lake's terminus and to confuse the onlooker's perception. Hamilton was particularly gifted in the manipulation of scale, and such techniques were certainly used to design Carton's sheet of water. Michael Symes has tried to explain this strange talent: 'Hamilton created illusions at Painshill, where both the lake and the wild wood gave the impression of being larger than they were, so he knew how to manipulate scenery, shapes and plantings to make much of a small area.'[495] Both Carton and Painshill were also highly eclectic in their choice of building styles. They each had a Chinese bridge, and Carton's Brideswell, which lies on the Ryewater's southern bank beyond Waterstone cottage, is almost

Fig. 63
First edition Ordnance Survey map of Carton, Co. Kildare, 1837.

an exact replica of a similar feature at Painshill. Hamilton may also have influenced the landscaping of the Ryewater river valley. At Painshill 'a broad river, issuing from a lake, passes under a bridge of five arches near the outlet, then directs its course towards the wood, and flows underneath it'.[496] This is reminiscent of Thomas Roberts's *The Bridge in the Park,* which depicts Thomas Ivory's five-bay bridge (Fig. 57). The avenues of conifers depicted in the Kellystown plantation at Carton's southeastern edge on the first edition Ordnance Survey map (Fig. 63) suggest the romantic conifer landscape of Painshill's alpine valley, which, like Carton, has a prospect tower (Fig. 64). As one of the first planted and designed romantic and sublime landscapes, it may have inspired a similar interpretation of the lower Ryewater, which then acquired rocks, natural bowers and conifer plantations. The Painshill shrubberies are reminiscent of those at Carton, being more ornate and elaborate than any Brown would have laid out. Charles Hamilton approved of flowers, and a flower-garden was included on the Bernard Scalé map of the demesne in 1769 (Fig. 62). James once sent 'fifty tuberoses and twenty-four narcissus roots'[497] to his wife, and other family members were often asked to send flowers.

Fig. 64
1996 photograph of the alpine valley at Painshill Garden, Surrey.

Interest in *forêt* gardens and exotic tree planting eventually waned, to be replaced by water features and cottages; yet the continuous planting of trees was a management necessity on any great demesne. Emily wrote of her pleasure at 'seeing ten men thickening up that part of the plantation between the Dublin and the Nine Mile Stone Gate with good, tall, shewy-looking trees – elm and ash'. There were, however, 'still quantities of holes not filled' and she suspected that Jacob Smith, the gardener, had 'dug more than he will get trees to fill this winter . . . to satisfy' their 'impatience'[498] in 1762. Another letter informed her husband that the new seeds had arrived, but she feared that the 'walnuts and chestnuts' were spoilt, which was 'vexatious'.[499] Louisa visited Carton in 1771 to find Emily 'very busy clearing out some plantations',[500] and they sometimes enjoyed 'sauntering about the Nursery'.[501] 'A vast number of trees . . . from Carton, about 1,500',[502] were planted in Emily's new suburban villa garden at Frescati, Blackrock, Co. Dublin, in 1775. If such a number could be spared from the Carton nursery, that nursery, and the park it served, must have been in a thriving condition.

The influence of Collinson, Hamilton, Fox and the Duke of Richmond on the form of the Carton landscape is important. The emphasis these collectors placed on fine specimens, good plantsmanship and the gradual development of a landscape's design explains Carton's estrangement from Brown and subsequent adoption of a rococo, francophile and picturesque sensibility. Plant collectors naturally embraced the concept of a useful and beautiful landscape, being instinctively concerned with successful horticulture and arboriculture. The experimental possibilities of flower-gardens, shrubberies and American gardens were important appendages to their landscape gardens. The *forêt ornée* moved the emphasis away from the purist aestheticism of Brown and towards a more

Fig. 65
William Ashford, *Carton, Seat of the Duke of Leinster*, 1779.

utilitarian, productive and scientific way of making the landscape. Emily's later precocious developments at Frescati stem in part from the gentlemen arboriculturists' rich precedent.

> *On the Waterstown townland was a thatched house with out-offices, in which dwelt an old gentleman named Richard Nelson, who was allowed to live on in the new demesne until his death occurred some time previous to the year 1769. His dwelling-house was then kept up as an ornamental cottage.*[503]

The acquisition of the Waterstone townland enabled Emily to create her own cottage landscape, which was situated downstream on the Ryewater from the Ivory bridge, beyond the three islands. Rocque's survey of 1760 listed

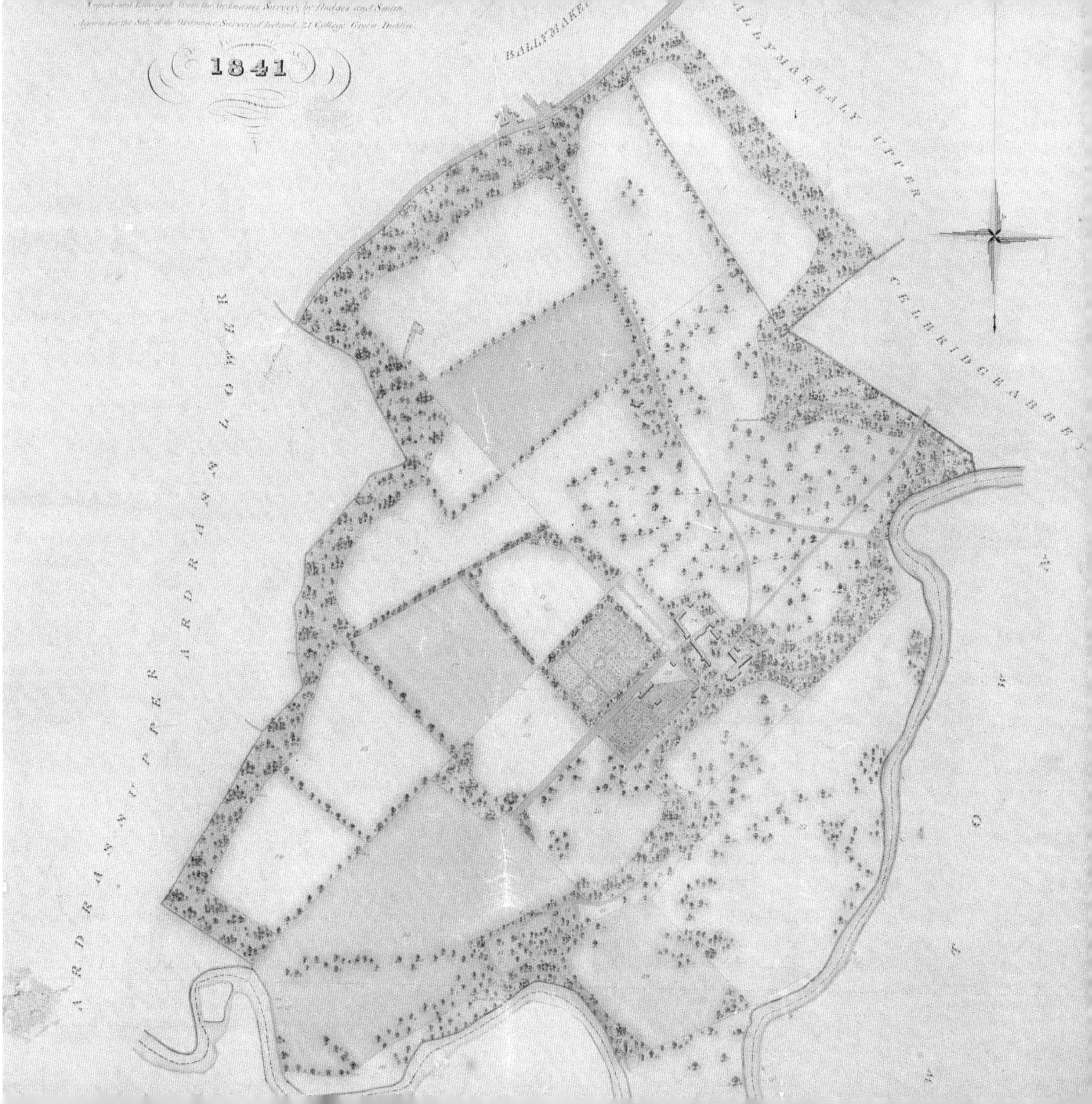
Agents for the Sale of the Ordnance Survey of Ireland, 21 College Green Dublin.
1841
BALLYMAKE
BALLYMAKEALY UPPER
CELBRIDGEABBEY
ARDRASS LOWER
ARDRASS UPPER

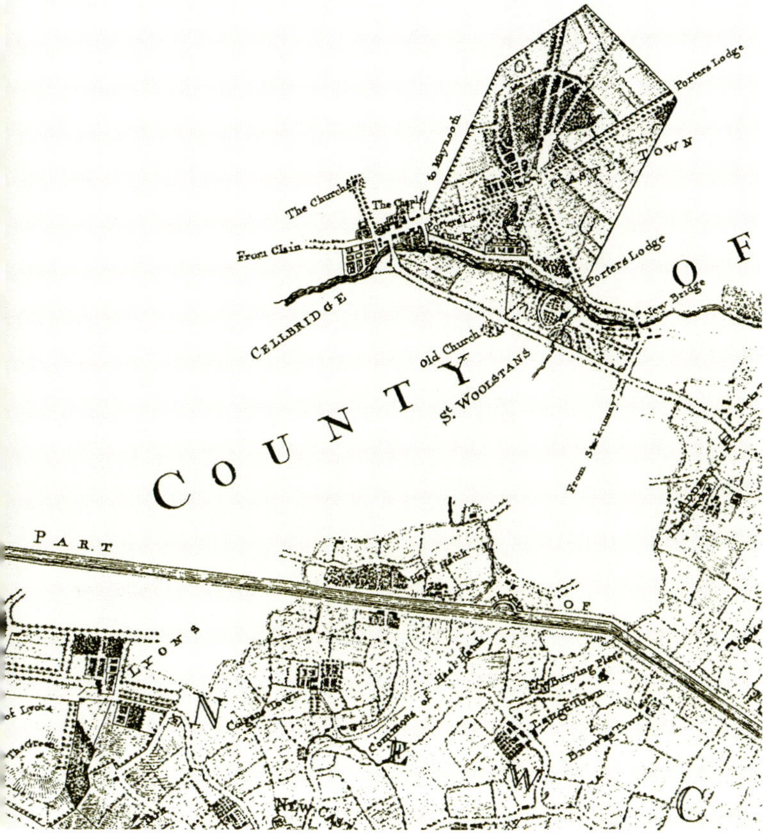


Fig. 73
John Rocque, *Map of the County of Dublin*, 1760. Detail of Castletown and Lyons demesnes.

Clements was Conolly's tenant, and 'leases as well as regulating much of the rural economy, regulated – often in considerable detail – the most important relationships of the social hierarchy'.[535] Once Robert Clements had married safely away from the Fitzgerald extended family, a close friendship between the families of Castletown, Carton and Killadoon could be established, and many letters describe social visits between the three estates. Louisa even proposed in 1786 that Sarah and her family 'might sleep at Killadoon'[536] when there was no room for them at Castletown.

Killadoon is situated upstream on the Liffey from Castletown along the southwestern approach road to Celbridge from Clane (Fig. 22). The estate originally reflected its owners' status as tenant landlords, with the house forming one side of a service courtyard. Scalé and Richards's survey map of 1765 described a functional farm landscape with little land devoted to pleasure-gardens and landscaping features (Fig. 71). A large part of the low-lying demesne, always threatened by flooding, was drained by a long ha-ha running west–east through the land south of the house. The lawns it protected took advantage of the southern view of the Liffey and the distant prospect of the hill of Lyons. An elementary curvilinear approach route led to the house from the east, and a shrubbery walk wound past the picturesque ruin of the old church, which had been carefully retained. A small formal garden lay adjacent to the western gable of the house and a 'new garden' and kitchen garden completed the landscaping programme (Fig. 71). The present Killadoon House was constructed to replace the older house in about 1779 (Fig. 70). Like the house it replaced, the new entrance front also addressed the service courtyard, an unusual setting for a three-storey, five-bay Georgian house of some architectural pretensions, and still in keeping with the design of a farmhouse (Fig. 72). Robert Clements was created Baron Leitrim in 1783, Viscount Leitrim in 1793 and Earl of Leitrim in 1795. The demesne was gradually transformed into a designed landscape worthy of the family's advancement (Fig. 72). New fields were acquired to the north in order to develop an alternative and longer approach route from that direction and the demesne was also extended into the northwestern countryside. The shrubbery walk was extended as far as the riverside and then to a summerhouse, and the small formal garden became a large pleasure-garden. All of the land south of the house fronting onto the Liffey and surrounding the eastern approach routes was carefully incorporated into the designed landscape. Rectilinear field boundaries disappeared and belts and clumps of trees were planted. Building types consistent with a great demesne – a cottage,

Fig. 72
First edition Ordnance Survey map of Killadoon, Co. Kildare, 1841. Detail.

a boathouse and a summerhouse – were constructed at suitably scenic sites, and the kitchen garden was enlarged (Fig. 72). As the structure of the landscape became more hierarchic, another service courtyard was built north of the existing one. The courtyard close to the house became a transitional space between the new service yard and the house itself, and its trees and shrubs separated the decorative from the productive landscape. The formal signs of the great noble demesne – the tree belt, the multiple approach routes, the lodges and the pleasure buildings – gradually appeared. Once they had achieved aristocratic status, the Clements family created a demesne to express that achievement.

Fig. 74
Lyons: Entrance Front from J.P. Neale, *Views of the Seats of Noblemen and Gentlemen in England, Wales, Scotland and Ireland*; 1825.

Lyons House and demesne is situated south of the Liffey from Carton and Castletown. During the late eighteenth century its baroque garden was transformed into an ambitious landscape garden. The landscaper Browne worked to develop the first garden at Lyons,[537] and in 1760 Rocque depicted a house approached by formal avenues and surrounded by a walled courtyard, walled gardens, formal planting beds and geometric *bosquets* of trees (Fig. 73). In 1796 Nicholas Lawless, subsequently Baron Cloncurry, bought the old house and the lands of Lyons from Michael Aylmer for £37,450.[538] Born a Catholic, Lawless had made his fortune by marrying the widow of his employer, a Dublin merchant. He soon constructed a new Palladian house at Lyons, designed by an architect named Grace (Fig. 74).[539] In order to develop a new entrance route, he enlarged the demesne northwards to the Grand Canal. The old straight entrance avenue from the west, like the Dunboyne avenue at Carton, was demoted to lead to the kitchen garden, estate farm and service areas, which were located in the vicinity of the old house complex. John Roe's map of 1796 distinguished between the 'old demesne' and the 'new demesne' to indicate what lands Lawless had bought to enlarge the older Aylmer estate (Fig. 76). It would have been logical to purchase this land with the future site of the house in mind, and the new house with its front and back lawns and eastern fields were all sited on the newly acquired land. By retaining the old house complex Lawless avoided the expense of constructing another kitchen garden, as it could easily operate within the old walled enclosures. The new house took advantage of the estate's southern view of the Hill of Lyons, which contrasts with the great northern open vista of softly undulating hills and neighbouring great houses.

The position of the house also enabled it to take advantage of its oblique relation to the two dominant prospect points: the church and castle ruins of the old Aylmer stronghold southeast of the garden façade and the Conolly folly northwest of the entrance façade. Nicholas Lawless's son Valentine wrote expressly from

Fig. 75
1998 photograph of the ruin vista from the interior of Lyons.

Rome in 1804 to veto any 'clump to hide the old house'. Such planting would be 'useless as it must hide the old church which I wish to see especially when the old house is thrown down'.[540] The ruins still provide a prospect from the garden front of Lyons (Fig. 75). Unlike the demesnes of Castletown, Carton and Killadoon, Lyons contained no water interest, an unacceptable situation in the eighteenth century. The great artificial lake appeared on John Roe's map of 1796 (Fig. 76). It was created by damming or diverting a water source which entered the demesne at its western end, and Valentine Lawless included a drawing of his own in a letter of 1803 to show how the drainage of the lawn between the pond and the house was to be organized.[541] In 1803 Mr Kelly, the chief overseer, wished to drain the pond completely because he believed that 'the damp of the house proceeded from it'. Cloncurry retorted that he 'would sooner pull down the house than drain it'.[542] Thomas Ryan, his agent, was pointedly reminded that 'the planting ... and draining are the two most necessary improvements of a demesne'.[543] The sophistication demonstrated in adapting the old house complex is somewhat diminished by the awkward alignment of hill, lake and house, and by the artificial character of the lake, whose man-made origins were never successfully disguised.

The older patterns of landscape design are more readily observed in the demesnes of the minor and less wealthy gentry. This was due in part to discrepancies in wealth. Demesnes of intermediate scale, where the owners' circumstances led them to maintain a farm-like character, retained that subtle restraint that many theorists of the landscape garden, and in particular of the *ferme ornée,* sought to promote. Killadoon is an example of what can be achieved when the house and landscape are tweaked and pruned over time, and many of Louisa and Emily's interventions at Carton and Castletown attempted to achieve its quiet nonchalance. The received structure of the great noble demesne was not easily manipulated. Unlike the structural reorientation of the Carton landscape in the 1740s and the mid-1800s, the alterations to Killadoon refocused the landscape by a series of minimal interventions for maximum effect. Killadoon also attempted, unlike the other houses, to unite the older tradition of enclosed rectilinear space with the wide embrace of Palladianism. Its new house was probably built on the site of the house it replaced and in the vicinity of the much older churchyard, which was also retained. The new house at Lyons was sited in an area far removed from the older Aylmer landscape, which allowed the Lawless family to use the older landscape as a prospect for the new house, and a landscaped location for the service yards and kitchen garden. At Castletown and Carton the new

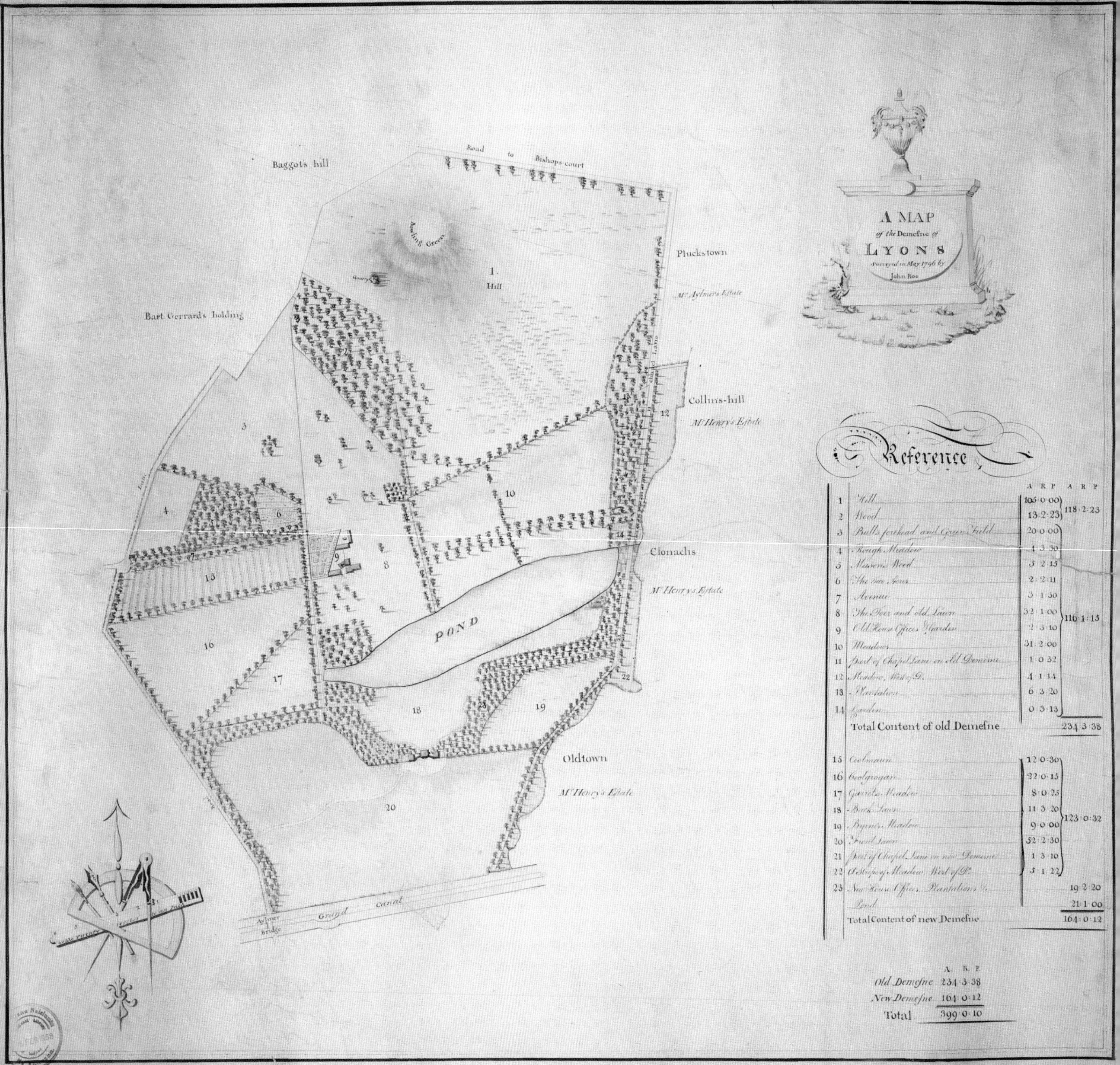
A MAP
of the Demesne of
LYONS
Surveyed in May 1796 by
John Roe
Road to Bishops court
Baggots hill
Bowling Green
Quarry
1 Hill
Pluckstown
Mr. Aylmers Estate
Bart Gerrard's holding
Collins-hill
Mr. Henry's Estate
Clonachs
Mr. Henry's Estate
POND
Oldtown
Mr. Henry's Estate
Aylmer Bridge
Grand Canal
Reference
A R P A R P
1 Hill 105:0:00 } 118:2:23
2 Wood 13:2:23
3 Bull's forehead and Green Field 20:0:00
4 Rough Meadow 1:3:30
5 Mason's Wood 5:2:15
6 The Five Acres 2:2:11
7 Avenue 3:1:30
8 The Deer and old Lawn 32:1:00 } 116:1:15
9 Old House Offices & Garden 2:3:10
10 Meadows 31:2:00
11 Part of Chapel Lane on old Demesne 1:0:32
12 Meadow, West of D. 4:1:14
13 Plantation 6:3:20
14 Garden 0:3:13
Total Content of old Demesne 234:3:38
15 Coolmaun 12:0:30
16 Coolgragan 22:0:15
17 Garret's Meadow 8:0:25
18 Back Lawn 11:3:20
19 Byrne's Meadow 9:0:00 } 123:0:32
20 Front Lawn 52:2:30
21 Part of Chapel Lane on new Demesne 1:3:10
22 A Stripe of Meadow, West of Do. 5:1:22
23 New House Offices Plantations & 19:2:20
Pond 21:1:00
Total Content of new Demesne 164:0:12
A. R. P.
Old Demesne 234:3:38
New Demesne 164:0:12
Total 399:0:10

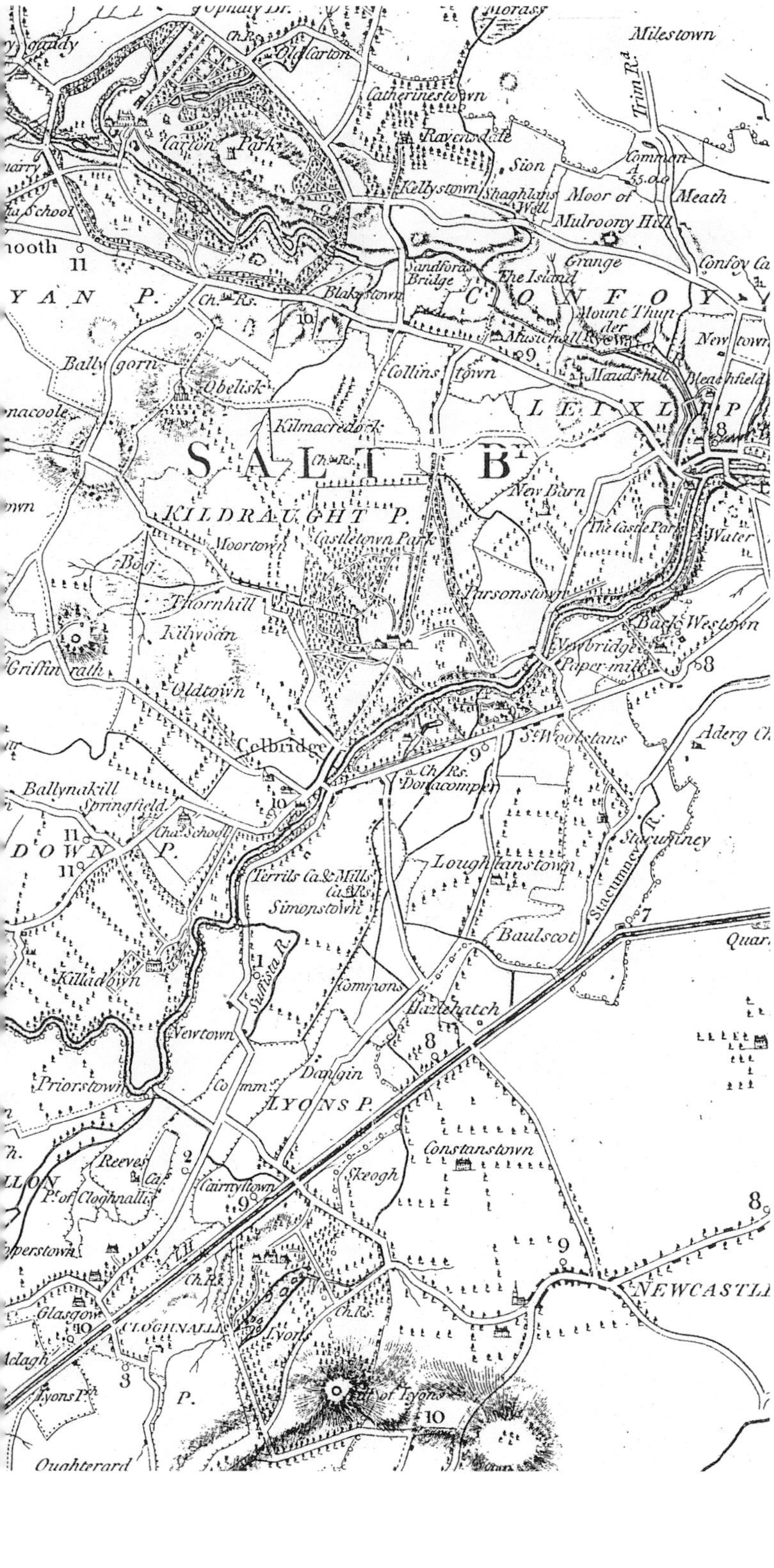


Palladian houses were sited either over (at Carton) or beside (at Castletown) the older dwelling and gardens, which were substantially demolished or completely redesigned. Areas within the demesne could then be developed in the *ferme ornée* style, but the great demesne structure of estate town, walls, avenues, walks, prospects, lawns and other accumulated design features could not be so quickly adjusted.

Fig. 77

James Taylor, *Map of the county of Dublin*, 1783. Detail of Killadoon, Lyons and Castletown demesnes.

Fig. 76

John Roe, *A Map of the Demesne of Lyons*, May 1796.

Chapter 4

# The School at Frescati

Fig. 78

William Ashford, *Landscape with Carriage and Horses*, 1781.

*No matter if I am interrupted by hedges and ditches, I take my park on my back, and I carry it elsewhere.*[544]

Jean-Jacques Rousseau

In 1766 Emily and James Fitzgerald, first Duke and Duchess of Leinster, decided to purchase the house and lands of Frescati in the seaside suburb of Blackrock, Co. Dublin, to serve as an educational establishment for their nine children (Fig. 79).[545] The acknowledged therapeutic effects of sea-bathing probably influenced their decision to take a property so close to the sea, which was not particularly fashionable at the time, and Caroline Fox wondered whether Emily had managed to 'grow reconciled to the sea prospect?'[546] The Fox estate at Kingsgate in Kent was close to the seaside and Caroline had recommended sea-bathing to Emily in 1764.[547] Seaside gardening was difficult, as trees and shrubs planted 'in the shelter of walls and the house grows, tho' but slowly', while 'elms and other trees that are planted do very well till they get high up enough for the sea wind to cut them at the top, when they grow ragged'.[548] The idea of a nearby sea prospect was relatively novel and promoted a new form of landscape aesthetic that drew its inspiration from the improvement and ornamentation of the seashore and aspect. Breckdenston and Leinster House both enjoyed a sea prospect, but not at such proximity to the house and gardens.

In 1762 Emily had written that she particularly disliked tablecloths decorated with 'all those ugly sort of patterns in squares without meaning'.[549] If she attached 'meaning' to tablecloths, in design matters of greater import, such as those of her house and landscape, she must certainly have demanded that some meaning lay behind their composition. The pedagogical and revolutionary theories she developed at Frescati presented her with the opportunity to develop such meaning in her designs, which Carton and Leinster House had evidently begun to lack. In 1762 Caroline Fox had 'just finished Rousseau's *Sur L'Education*'[550] (*Émile*), which contained 'more paradoxes, more absurdities and more striking pretty thoughts in it than in any book' she had 'ever read that he did not write'.[551] Shortly afterwards she sent Emily a copy[552] and proceeded to include some of Rousseau's precepts, which she considered 'very wholesome',[553] in the education of her children. When her initial enthusiasm had worn off five years later, she thought Rousseau 'undoubtedly right in some things', but also 'very dangerous, so very destructive of all principles hitherto held sacred both moral and religious'.[554] She had, however, converted Emily, who was so enamoured of his books that she decided that Rousseau himself should become her children's teacher. Mary Delany recounted with wonder in 1766 that Emily had indeed offered Rousseau 'an elegant retreat *if he would educate her children!*', expressing the general misgivings of Irish landed society at such an action and writing that she differed 'widely from her ladyship, and would rather commit that charge to a downright honest parson . . . as far as to religious principles'.[555] Drawn into the debate by her sisters, Louisa agreed that there was much to be 'learnt out of it [*Émile*] for the use of children', but thought that it was also 'wild and impossible'.[556] Rousseau did not come to Ireland and the position of tutor was eventually offered to William Ogilvie, a Scot.

Fig. 79
Frescati House. Photograph of the ruined garden front before the house was demolished to make way for the Frescati shopping centre.

Distinct chidren's spaces were apparent at Carton and Castletown by this time, and Waterstone and the Batty Langley lodge became centres for children's activities within both demesnes. Sarah made a specific 'little garden for the children' at Castletown in 1775.[557] The respect Emily received for her prolific childbearing achievements and the evident lack of such achievement in Louisa's life seems to have engendered in the latter a constant desire for children's companionship. In 1784 Louisa legally adopted Emily Napier, her sister Sarah's daughter, and the Castletown landscape started to acquire a more educational and child-orientated cast from that date onwards. The exodus of both families to Blackrock suggests that Emily and Louisa found it difficult to create a successful educational environment at either their demesnes or their city residences. The families were never free from the critical comments of the press when in town, nor from their benevolent responsibilities as aristocrats and model landlords in the countryside. Blackrock's suburban seaside location proved ideal for the educational and theatrical ambitions of both families, while Rousseau's radical pedagogical theories could be more actively promoted away from Leinster House, Carton and Castletown, where previous generations had been conservatively educated in the aristocratic tradition. Rousseau carefully blurred the definition of property for educational purposes. He found that 'the demon of property spoils everything he lays hands upon', and to counteract his influence Rousseau took 'possession of every open space' to become 'their owner', and to 'wander among them at will'. Fruit was 'free to those who walked in the orchard', and the gardener should 'neither count it nor gather it'.[558] The young student's geography began 'with the town he lives in and his father's country house, then the places between them, the rivers near them, and then the sun's aspect and how to find one's way by its aid'. He was encouraged to make 'his own map, a very simple map, at first containing only two places; others may be added from time to time, as he is able to estimate their distance and position'.[559] The young Fitzgeralds were not to be orientated by their principal aristocratic residences of Carton and Leinster House but by the natural landscape of Blackrock. Enclosed by high walls and gates, the property boundaries of the great city and country residences could not be rendered ambiguous. The unformed seaside suburb was much more indistinct and flexible.

Louisa Conolly, who maintained that she did 'detest a Town and wish to live as little as possible in them',[560] soon acquired a neighbouring property in Blackrock. The house the Conollys bought in 1768 was 'a little tidy, neat place delightfully situated' and close to 'those sort of places the being so near is vastly pleasant'.[561] It came, of course, with 'a pretty little garden . . . to make the going there much pleasanter',[562] with 'only a hedge' between the property and Frescati. For people accustomed to gardens of a thousand acres, this spatial relationship was 'so near,

Culvert or Tunnel
Flooded
Ladies Bathing Place
at
High Tides
Culvert or Tunnel
Westfield Ho.
Peafield Baths
Ruby Lodge
Gate Lodge
Peafield Ho.
Foot Br.
Black Rock Station
Elm Cliff
Fairy Hill
Fort Lisle
Gentlemens' Bathing Place
Ladies Bathing Place
Pembroke Ho.
Peafield Terrace
Lisalea
Fitzwilliam Lodge
Albion Ho.
Gate Lodge
Herbert Terrace
Frescati
Turrets
Bathing Place
Church
School Ho.
Maretimo
Wooden Br.
Brook Lawn
Herbert Lodge
Pembroke Lodge
R.C. Chapel
Black Rock
Nunnery Cottage
Laburnum Lodge
Black Rock Dispensary
Carysfort Cottage
School Ho.
Laburnum Lodge
Anne Villa
Wood View
Sydney Lodge
Holly Court
Nunnery
Dove Ho.
Castle Byrn
Prospect Ho.
White Hall School
Anglesey Ho.
Bellview Cottage
NEWTOWN BLACKROCK
Rosemount Cot.
Brookfield Place
Prince Edward Terrace
Gate Lodge
Gravel Pit
Mont Pelier Place
ROCKFIELD
Carysfort

that 'tis like being in the same house'.[563] The childless Louisa became involved in her young nephews' and nieces' education, and her house became an extension of the Frescati complex. By 1762, 'all hopes' that Louisa had held 'of breeding' had been extinguished and she could 'not expect it [pregnancy] now to be sure'. She wrote that she was 'mortified' by her inability to bear children.[564] In a society that frequently valued women according to this ability, the extent of her 'mortification' must have been great. Aristocratic men frequently married to form political and economic alliances, and a childless marriage deprived descendants of these intended connections. Louisa acquired the child-bearing and child-rearing experiences she had lost by caring for her sisters' children. She never excluded herself from parenting issues, writing from Blackrock in 1778 that it was 'reckon'd wholesome to have four or five Children, & if you reflect on it, those Women that bear Children, & give suck, must be in a much more natural state that those that don't'.[565]

Louisa considered Frescati 'a sweet pretty little neat house which my Sister is making very comfortable every Day, nothing fine on account of the Brats'.[566] William, Marquess of Kildare, was 'very glad' that his mother had 'bought that place at the Blackrock', because it would 'always be of use' and 'very comfortable when the two wings are built'.[567] A boundary belt of trees was planted, shrubberies and decorative planting encircled the house, and a lodge signalled Frescati's entrance on the Blackrock road (Fig. 80). A 'pin alley' was laid out, 'the place was swarming with young birds, but particularly Blackbirds and Thrushes . . . as tame as Chickens'.[568] William Ashford's painting, *Landscape with Carriage and Horses,*[569] which looks southeastwards towards the spire of Dún Laoghaire (Kingstown), depicts this lodge and those of the neighbouring houses (Fig. 78). The lodges followed each other in rapid succession, as the land areas of the villas they announced were much smaller than those of the great countryside demesnes. The numerous travellers on the road declared it a main thoroughfare to Dublin city, yet the sheep indicated that Blackrock retained some of its rustic traditions.

In February 1768, Louisa and Emily 'spent the most comfortable day at the Blackrock . . . out with the workmen planting, and making neat little fences'.[570] The land immediately surrounding the house was designed and laid out to teach the rudiments of horticulture and gardening, and the children visited seed-suppliers to learn the management and economy of flower and vegetable cultivation. Agriculture was considered 'the earliest and most honourable of the arts',[571] and gardening the simplest way to teach basic economics. The 'foundation' for understanding the 'exchange of industry, that of commerce in the exchange of commodities' and 'that of banks in the exchange of money', was 'laid in early childhood with the help of Robert the gardener'.[572] William Ogilvie, as the children's tutor, was responsible for the 'farm at the Blackrock',[573] and for implementing Emily's curriculum at Frescati. 'Every instant' that the children were not occupied by schoolwork was 'employed in digging, or working in the Garden, running and playing with Night[m]are and Carlos [the ponies] or feeding and nursing the white Bantam chickens'.[574]

Fig. 80
First edition Ordnance Survey map of Blackrock, Co. Dublin, depicting Frescati and Maretimo, 1843.

*In the morning, Business and Bathing as usual till nine – Lady Louisa allways rides after bathing . . . at nine they go to Lady Louisa's for breakfast . . . after they come to Business and continue . . . till 1 or ½ an hour after, when we work and play and dress 'till three when we go to Lady Louisa's to dine. Lady Louisa and Miss Waring generally walk in the forenoon in the Gardens but we are then in the heart of our Business, I made it a rule never to go near them . . . after dinner they play and bathe till five, when we go to Business. Lady Louisa and Miss Waring go out in the one horse chaise at half an hour after seven or thereabouts and we go in again to Tea and Supper & stay near an hour, then we come home all, they go to bed and I settle to read, Lady Louisa sups, But I declined being of that party, as it would lose me all the evening.*[575]

Fig. 81
Carton. The dairy interior.

The fields were meticulously kept for productive purposes, their fences maintained and the children instructed in the natural rhythms of mowing and reaping. Emily liked to see the children occupied with the farming activities when she visited, and Ogilvie took particular 'care' that she should 'have the pleasure of seeing the little haymakers at work'.[576] 'Every kind of rural labour' was promoted at Frescati as an educational principle.[577] Sometimes 'hard at work drawing gravel and digging up ramps',[578] the children also constructed weirs, dams and fences to teach them the principles of manual labour, civil engineering and mechanics. With the 'children scattered about the fields at a distance from their fathers, mothers, and other children' they could 'practice at making themselves heard at a distance', an asset for future politicians and public speakers.[579] Of 'all the pursuits by which a man may earn his living, the nearest to a state of nature is manual labour; of all the stations that of the artisan is least dependent on fortune'.[580] The trade Rousseau selected for his pupil was 'that of a carpenter',[581] and Lord Edward Fitzgerald constructed 'two benches in the most shady parts' of his garden at Aubigny 'with boards under them to keep dear Mother's feet from feeling any damp from the ground'.[582]

Frescati was rapidly stocked with flowers, and it was not long before it supplied flowers for Leinster House. 'Two large hampers of flower roots – a thousand bunches of Daffodils & Narcissus & two hundred and fifty wall flowers' were despatched by Ogilvie in the early 1770s.[583] The flower-garden 'embodied a concept central to Rousseau's thoughts of the simple natural life . . . that flowers should serve a moral purpose, that they should uplift as well as give pleasure'.[584] The children accompanied Ogilvie on trips to nurserymen, and these trips occasioned long letters to the duchess on the best ways of making compost and frames for cultivating more flowers.[585] Ogilvie was particularly occupied with the Frescati lawns and he sent the duchess 'the dimensions of

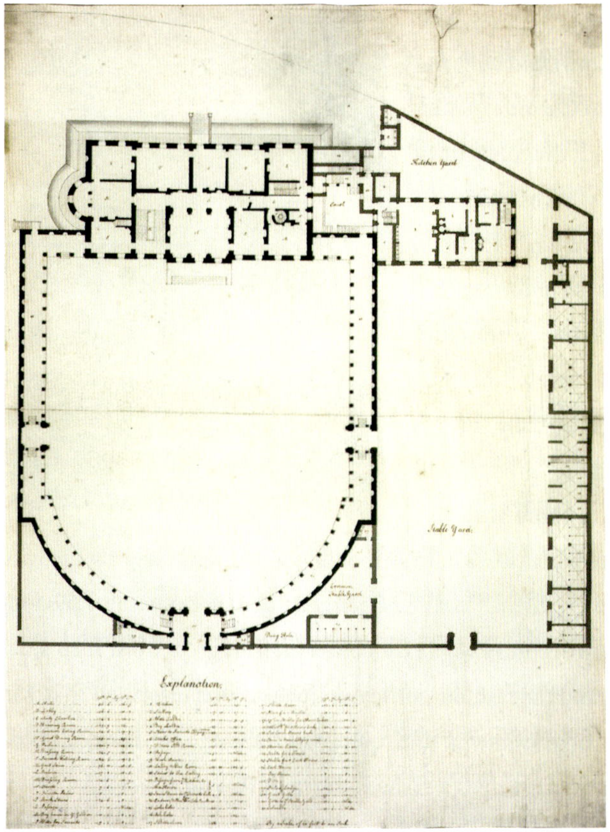

Fig. 82
Richard Castle,
*General Plan of Leinster House and Offices*, c.1745.

a roller . . . five feet long, and the thicker the better'.[586] He kept Emily informed of such seemingly prosaic matters as the condition of the fields and the best manner of improving them,[587] and Lord Edward worked hard in the fields 'picking off the weeds' to make 'a great many bonfires of them'.[588] The children bathed in the sea every day for the good of their health, even though they sometimes found 'the lower places there so very dirty'.[589]

The three elder Lennox sisters were generally acquainted with French culture from their frequent visits to France. Caroline Fox 'dined and supped very frequently at their villas', during her visits, and claimed to be generally '*au fait* of their way of life in the country'. She considered their houses 'in general excellent; no people ever studied or succeeded so well in enjoying all the conveniences of life as the French do'.[590] Great French houses and gardens were discussed with other members of the extended family, and they all visited the Lennox family's French estate of Aubigny, where the landscape was deemed 'pretty enough for a sporting country'.[591] Two of Caroline's letters described visits to Marly and Lunéville, the latter being a most influential garden in the development of the French picturesque gardening tradition: 'We stayed half a day at Limeville [Lunéville] to see old Stanislaus's palace and gardens, all in disorder since his death.'[592] The proportion of French books in both Carton and Castletown libraries is notable, and Thomas Conolly's subscription to a number of French newspapers suggests that the other branches of the family did likewise.[593] Among the Anglo-Irish Ascendancy, the Leinster and Conolly families were in a unique position to understand and imitate the nuances of French culture. Their direct experience of the French landscaping tradition, and their endeavours to remain informed of cultural and political events in France, enabled them to interpret French traditions in the Irish environment.

Rousseau rebelled against formal or 'high' architecture, and 'would not go and build a town in the country or erect the Tuileries at the door of my lodgings' but would construct instead 'a little cottage, a white house with green shutters'. The farm, cottage and dairy designs at Carton, Castletown and Frescati were also consciously informal, and eager to announce their separation from the city. Rousseau's intention to change the 'numerous temples of

Fig. 89
Jean-Michel Moreau,
*Illumination du parc de Versailles a l'occasion des fêtes du mariage du dauphin avec l'archiduchesse Marie-Antoinette le 19 mai 1770.*

A painting by Jean-Michel Moreau depicts such an illumination in the garden of Versailles on the occasion of the Dauphin's marriage to Marie-Antoinette in 1770 (Fig. 89). The Castletown illuminations were of course smaller in scale, but the painting does convey how the character of the gardens could be changed and used at night-time with the aid of torches and candles. The tradition of holding illuminations in woods is a particularly French one, and 'the very function of a French garden, as a site for fêtes and other entertainments, suggests a traditional connection between theatre and garden'.[664] Another French fascination was the dairy, and the dairy at Castletown was used as a theatre:

> *The weather has been so fine this last week that we have breakfasted and dined in the Dairy – your dear Animals have dined with us, three of those days and this afternoon the Screens were brought out upon the Grass opposite the Dairy, where they performed in Dumb shew, the story of the Child stole out of the Cradle, Fanny was the Fairy and looked so like Mrs Ponsonby . . . Emmy had painted their faces with Red to a degree of Horror.*[665]

Louisa's interest in the theatre developed partly because she was not a lover of music, which was a popular entertainment in the great country houses. She wrote to Sarah from Goodwood, where 'entertainments' had been taking place, that she 'never found' that she 'could like Italian music . . . owing to some fault in the formation' of her ear which heard sounds 'differently from what they do other people'.[666] A letter to Thomas Conolly bemoaned the 'good deal of music' at Goodwood, where boredom led her to hope that 'in time' she would 'grow to like music

Fig. 90
George Barret, *View on the River Dargle, Co. Wicklow.*

better'.[667] Louisa was much more interested in the composite artistic pleasures of stage and garden. She considered music, without the attendant muses of dance, art and literature, greatly lacking in entertainment.

Emily's description of a professional Dublin drama called *A Trip to the Dargil,* performed in 1762, is particularly intriguing in its relevance to landscape theory and design. The play was set in the river valley of the Dargle in Co. Wicklow, which became a prime tourist site for enthusiasts of the picturesque, a movement which eventually excluded both Castletown and Carton from the contemporary tourist guide books (Fig. 90). The Powerscourt waterfall was, and still is, one of the landscape features of Powerscourt demesne, and Arthur Young found that 'this horrid precipice, the pointed bleak mountains in view, with the roar of the water, all conspire to raise one great emotion of the sublime'.[668] Emily found that the play 'was mighty ill executed', but thought that the stage set of the 'Water Fall was the prettiest thing I ever saw, much beyond that at the Opera, and so like that at Powerscourt, that you actually fancy yourself in the very place'.[669] As a naturally occurring phenomenon, the Powerscourt waterfall's popularity increased when the taste for sublime landscape took hold. It was painted by the foremost landscape painters and reproduced in contemporary books of views and early tour guides (Fig. 91). The charms of Powerscourt's waterfall were indirectly advertised and promoted by using its painted reproduction on the stage. The stage set, by portraying this particular scene, promoted a particular landscaping style to the Dublin theatre audience. The theatre became an early travel guide or agent, and tourism was a close indicator of the movement of contemporary taste. *A Trip to the Dargil* is an early example of the Irish interpretative experience. Lord Powerscourt, owner of the Powerscourt demesne through which the Dargle ran, was a close friend of the Conolly and Leinster families. He participated in the theatricals at Castletown, and a 1775 letter of Louisa's included the plot of a play, *The Humours of the Gallery*, by Robert Jephson, and a list of the cast members that included the second Duke and Duchess of Leinster, Louisa and Thomas Conolly, and Lord Powerscourt. Powerscourt demesne advertised and promoted the beauties of Co. Wicklow, and the presentation of its landscape attractions on stage encouraged the audience to perceive the various sites as natural theatres.

Fig. 91
*George Barret the Elder,*
*A View of Powerscourt Waterfall c.*1760.

The theatrical interpretation of landscape also affected the interior decoration of these great houses.[670] At Lyons House nearby, the walls of the foyer rooms to the famous central painted room were painted with vignettes of the Dargle and other prime Wicklow picturesque sites. The visitor progressed from the imaginary landscapes of the central painted room to the painted landscapes of 'real' sites (one of which was the Dargle) and then to the real Kildare landscape outside the windows.[671] The interior decoration of the room not only defined the physical location of Lyons demesne, 'it was cultural and proprietorial as well, creating a setting for the lives of this noble dynastic line'.[672] Russborough House, further upstream along the Liffey, also contained a spectacular painted room of landscapes. The resonance between the vignettes of Apollo and the muses in Castletown's long gallery and Apollo's hovel, and the lake statues outside, also suggested the manipulation of real and imaginary space.

Fig. 92
Photograph of the central painted room at Lyons House.

Fig. 93
Roundel depicting the Salmon Leap on the Liffey, Lyons House.

Lord Cloncurry's patronage of the painter Gaspar Gabrielli led to the creation of the painted room at Lyons House with its six panels of imaginary pastoral antique scenes (Fig. 92).[673] These sought to establish the house at the centre of a rural neo-classical arcadia. In the adjoining room three circular overdoor panels depict three local waterfalls: the Poolaphuca and Powerscourt waterfalls in Wicklow and the Liffey Salmon Leap (Fig. 93). The neighbouring dining room once contained two great murals of the bays of Naples and Dublin.[674] The painted room's six panels depict the times of the day, and their position within the room reflects the passage of the sun past the south façade of Lyons house (Fig. 94).[672] The *Dawn* and *Day* panels are thus situated on the eastern wall of the room, with *Twilight* and *Night* on the western wall. The northern wall faces the three opening windows, and *Morning* is placed by the east wall and *Evening* by the west. The panel *Evening* (Fig. 95), which is located on the axis of symmetry of the house, was based on the painting *Il Molino* by Claude Lorraine.[676] Beyond the three windows, which echoed the tripartite design of each wall plane, lay a landscape of rolling grass with a central lake and a distant ruin. The painted landscape's structure reflected that which existed in reality, before the addition of the Victorian parterre (Fig. 75). Entering the painted room from the west, one passed the Powerscourt and Leixlip Salmon Leap waterfalls and under the Poolaphuca waterfall to move from the real landscapes of the roundels to the imaginary ideal landscapes of the panels:

> *In the Palladian villa the positioning of the frescoes, their framing and relationship with the views of the external landscape, suggest that this utopian perspective is to be projected outwards from the villa. The conscious occlusion of the real and painted landscapes suggests that the harmony and perfection represented in the latter actually existed in the former.*[677]

At Lyons a similar dialogue takes place between imaginary classical Claudian scenes of the painted room, the real painted scenes of the Irish picturesque tour and the landscape of Lyons itself. The dialogue created between the 'real' and 'imaginary' views was intended to reconcile both the beautiful and the economic aspects of Cloncurry's villa landscape. A comparative dialogue was also conducted between the painted 'real' landscape of Italy (Naples) and that of Ascendancy Ireland (Dublin) in the dining room, which sought to compare the greater landscape of the

Presbyterianism, had visited Lady Arbella's garden at Peafield Cliff in 1783, which he found 'one of the pleasantest spots':

> *Everything in miniature; on one side . . . a little meadow and a greenhouse with a study (which she calls her chapel) hanging over the sea, between these is a broad walk leading down almost to the edge of the water, along which runs two narrow walks commanding the quay, one above the other.*[746]

Wesley's description suggests the ease with which this landscape was transformed into a public pleasure-garden, where miniaturization was typically employed to compress and intensify the spatial experience. The Henrys sold the property in 1762 to Lord Lisle, who renamed it Fort Lisle, and in 1793 Lord Lisle's daughter sold it to a Mr Mayne, 'who called it Vauxhall Gardens and opened it to the public as a hotel and tavern'.[747] Edward and Pamela Fitzgerald were still in residence at Frescati and, as the area's most notorious and noble citizens, must have contributed to Blackrock's growing reputation as both a radical and an aristocratic milieu. Blackrock became 'a great social centre and the residence or resort of many distinguished people' and the Vauxhall Gardens became 'for a time, a favourite place of public amusement':[748]

> *The house is furnished with everything in season – bowers, grottoes, interspersed through dark shady walks – make the garden truly romantic, and the effect the music has on the sea, which flows at the foot of the garden, can be better imagined than expressed.*[749]

Pamela Fitzgerald's *soi-disant* father, the Duc d'Orléans, had turned the Palais Royal complex in central Paris 'into the most spectacular habitat for pleasure and politics in Europe'. By 1785 it had 'succeeded in bringing the raw and Rabelaisian popular culture right to the heart of Paris' and, as 'the private domain of the Orléans' family', it was 'virtually safe from patrol by the police and it exploited this freedom to the utmost'. Simon Schama has suggested that the subversive potential of this new space helped to develop thoughts of revolution:

> *Were les enfants de paradis closely related then, to les enfants de la patrie? It is hard to know whether the social commingling apparent in theatre audiences and amidst the strollers in the pleasure gardens may be taken as an accurate indicator of the collapse of rank in old-regime France.*[750]

The 'enthusiasm for ballooning' which the Leinster family had encouraged on the front lawn of Leinster House was 'a remarkable phenomenon' as 'such large assemblies of people had never before occurred and were novelties in themselves'. The egalitarian space created by the spectacle rendered the front lawn of Leinster House, like that

Fig. 99
Mallary, *Lady Pamela Fitzgerald*, c.1800.

of the Palais Royal, 'completely beyond the control of the authorities'.[751] Dublin, as the centre of Ascendancy power, where the resident 'court' did not remove to an Irish Versailles, and possessed of a long-established police and informer network, perhaps could not indulge a permanent site of this kind in the city-centre. Fitzwilliam's designs for Merrion Street and Square 'all but obliterated the experience of an urban space and its reading as a theatre of life'. The opportunity presented by the open space in front of Leinster House for a 'natural theatre of display' was thwarted by Fitzwilliam's subsequent development of a railed garden 'which you enter to escape the presence of the city'.[752] The language of the revolutionary festival did not wish to escape from the city, it desired to commingle the vocabulary of country, city and garden in order to create a theatrical event. Thus perhaps it is not surprising that the late eighteenth-century pleasure-garden was situated in suburban Blackrock, the home of revolutionaries and their revolutionary families. Pamela Fitzgerald's proclaimed relation to the Duc d'Orléans was generally known, as was the entire family's francophile tendency, and Edward Fitzgerald's revolutionary partner and friend, Valentine Lawless, second Lord Cloncurry, occupied the adjacent Maretimo. Following the rising of 1798, Blackrock became part of its mythology, and this gave rise to such dubious stories as that which claimed that Thomas Paine, the author of *The Rights of Man*, had visited Blackrock 'to offer French aid'.[753] Early nineteenth-century descriptions of Blackrock depict a tragic landscape steeped in the memory of a more glorious era and perhaps also of the futile rebellion of 1798:

> *The Black Rock, one of the most ruinous suburbs of the metropolis, is a collection of deserted lodging houses and bathing villas . . . The gaiety and respectability of the village have passed away, and the autumnal tinge on its deserted gardens and shrubberies, is in melancholy but correct keeping with its fallen fortune.*[754]

Louisa Conolly's close acquaintance with the radical Fitzgerald family led her, if not to sympathize with them, at least to consider the egalitarian and natural society their gardens sought to represent. After Thomas Conolly's death in 1806, the landscape of Castletown acquired a more utilitarian and economic aspect, which arose in part from his legacy of debts. Louisa devoted much of her energy and resources to projects for the greater community. The new church she constructed within Castletown demesne near the Celbridge gate opened in 1806. Her Free School opened in 1814 on the site of Thomas Conolly's kennels, and in 1820 she opened her Industrial School. Louisa appears to have designed the school herself, and a Mr Grant 'promised to make me another visit' in 1820 'to see and consider the plan of my school, whether it is likely to answer or not'. She meant 'then to dedicate my winter to my School, which I opened about two months ago & have met with more encouragement than I expected'.[755] As a charter school already existed in Celbridge, to which the Conolly family paid a hefty subscription each year, these activities proclaimed her serious interest in pedagogy. Louisa even wrote a behavioural code for the children in support of co-denominational education:

*Finally, no disrespectful word,*
*Touching Religion, shall be spoken*
*By the Protestants, to Catholics,*
*Or from Catholics, to Protestants.*[756]

The school also demonstrated her benevolent compassion for the poor, which she considered the 'first care of the Rich'.[757] Memories of the school she had helped to create forty years earlier at Frescati must have flooded back. Unlike Emily, Louisa was never naïve about or uninterested in the position of the Anglo-Irish Ascendancy, and she regularly provided her powerful brother, the Duke of Richmond, with assessments of the Irish political environment. She also possessed a lucid understanding that her family's status was partly due to their religion. Whatever sympathies she may have had for the 'rights of man' were expressed by the application of her energy to those areas she knew most about – design, management and education.

Chapter 5

# The Grand Tourist

Fig. 100

Jonathan Fisher, *Scenery of Ireland*, London 1795:

Plate 'Poula Poucka, on the River Liffey'. Detail.

Published articles and guidebooks created an identity for the troubled country both in England and further afield. The re-orientation of Carton House expressed the Irish aristocracy's diminished identity, both from their own perspective and that of their public, in the nineteenth century. It was a time when 'the country gentry of old time lived in a rarefied social air: dotted apart on their stations up the mountain they looked down with imperfect discrimination on the belts of thicker life below . . . not at ease in the perspective and chilliness of that height'.[802] As 'the belts of thicker life' became more complex, and the relations between city and country, farmer, merchant and landowner more clearly those of a capitalist rather than of a natural order, the 'imperfect discrimination' of the gentry became problematic and potentially dangerous. Carton's nineteenth-century accumulation of decorative detail and boundary consumed the pastoral dream and the country house came to express little of the ideal of hospitality and generosity to which great-house culture had once subscribed. 'The farmlike way of gardening' was destroyed by the popularity of the sublime, the reality of Ireland's misery and the new myopia of the landlord within his demesne.

During the nineteenth century, the demesne came publicly to express the overt economic and social power of the landowning class:

> *Because of the well-established obsession with landlord–tenant relations, and the events of 1879–82, the whole issue of Irish land came to be viewed exclusively in terms of ownership and occupation. Against the drama of evictions and agrarian crime, the minutiae of agricultural improvement and rural organization seemed dull; against the contending claims of landlords and tenants, the claims of other groups – landless labourers, taxpayers, and city people who wanted access to the land – seemed less pressing.*[803]

As W.E. Vaughan has argued, landlordism was merely replaced by smaller units of privately owned land:

> *Public control was limited to the modestly exercised powers of the Land Commission; the landlords as centres of power were not replaced; farming became confined to those who inherited land, with some exceptions; physical access even to stretches of beach became a matter of private arrangement. Thus despite the Land League's campaign, the 'land for the people' did not lead to the establishment of great national forests, to areas of common land, or even to public footpaths.*[804]

The opportunity to adopt or exploit an existing heritage and tradition of landscape design was lost. Irish people no longer demanded, anticipated or created a designed environment. The reductive process naturally resulted in the impoverishment of twentieth-century spatial and environmental design. This has become particularly evident in the Irish suburb and countryside, where the unappreciated demesne landscape was to be found and where there is no civic authority prepared to ensure a civilized environment.

Fig. 109 Carton.
Aerial photograph taken from the southwest looking across Thomas Ivory's bridge to the new nineteenth-century approach route around the family graveyard.

Epilogue

# The Obelisk on the Horizon

Fig. 110
Photograph from the St. Enda's school year book of a mythological play being performed in the grounds.

Robert Molesworth's gardens at Breckdenston set a course for a narrative of improvement through Irish gardening history. The landscape he promoted seems aggressively capitalist in the context of the nervous vulnerability of early eighteenth-century Ireland, and his enthusiasm for removing the footprints of earlier generations motivated more by the mentality of the conquering colonist than by economic good sense. Jonathan Swift, however, admired the 'farmlike way of gardening' Molesworth adopted and found its improving 'Air of Freedom' the only landscaping ideal to set against the futile pastoral dreams of Dublin's suburbia. Speaker Conolly also recognized that the language of improvement served both to ameliorate and to mask the reality of the Irish countryside, and the expansionist mentality of Whig improvement was perpetuated by his heirs. Castletown's Gothic walk promoted the provenance of the Conolly family's wealth by establishing a dialectic between the improved Gothick of the Batty Langley lodge and the ancient gothic of St Wolstan's ruins.

At nearby Carton, Emily and James, first Duke and Duchess of Leinster, were less inspired by the political nuances of improvement than by the pleasure of exploring diverse landscaping ideas. They created a designed landscape with the guidance of acknowledged gardening experts and Carton was nonchalantly transformed into a rococo landscape, with Philip Collinson and Charles Hamilton in attendance rather than Capability Brown. Louisa Conolly and Emily, Duchess of Leinster, also enjoyed the illusionist lifestyle of the *cottage* and *ferme ornée*; and the theatres of Carton and Castletown suggest a radical restructuring of social tradition. The interpretation of landscape as a pedagogical tool encouraged a critical observation of the city, the great estate and the suburb, and each environment's educational value was carefully estimated. The families abandoned the regimented setting of the urban town house and square, and the prescribed customs of the country house and demesne, for the flexible anonymity of the modern suburb. Frescati's pedagogical landscape encouraged a love of liberty in its young charges, and the nascent nationalism of the romantic idiom helped to bring revolution to the suburbs of Blackrock and the valleys of Kildare. Dublin's suburban landscape took some of the French Revolution's spatial ideas and distilled them to reveal a perceived connection between gardening, pedagogy and revolution. This subversive tradition of cottage gardening continued into the twentieth century, when Patrick Pearse, revolutionary and educationalist, created a garden at St Enda's school in south Co. Dublin.[805] This school garden was inspired by the egalitarian cottage garden, and the curriculum included hours of gardening in the school's kitchen garden. The food produced by the pupils fed and funded the school. Plays were performed for the public in suitably mythological locations among the Celtic Revival follies, and the Aedhireacht festival, complete with symbolic pageants and sports, communicated the school's ideology to the wider world (Fig. 110).

The Liffey valley, the seaside of Frescati and Breckdenston, and the foothills of the Dublin mountains (St Enda's) consciously imitated other places and other times. The associative character of the landscape garden with its series of connected but incomplete references was uniquely adapted to this process. In suburbia, traditional definitions of town and country lost their meaning and the language developed in their stead served to fill this void. None of these gardens was created for propaganda alone, and their analysis informs both eighteenth-century social history and the technology and tradition of gardening culture. Their stories chart the theoretical and practical heritage of Irish landscape design, as each sought to change and improve the Irish environment. The Whig narrative of improvement exposed the moral issues that lie at the core of landscape development, particularly in a country where the absence of improvement has proved apocalyptic. The collective Irish mentality, which is unable to divorce the interpretation, understanding and appreciation of historic landscapes from a moral judgement placed upon those who created them, is an ironic inheritance from the narrative of improvement these gardens explored. It now encourages their destruction, as the vista of 'improvement', when seen through the prism of a planner/developer's Claude glass, interprets shopping malls, housing estates, hotels and golf courses as the modern 'rights of man'.

The history of the tour is critical for understanding the modern interpretation of landscape because it carefully categorized some localities as exceptionally and 'naturally' beautiful. Contemporary planning theory also advocates that a landscape may be perceived, interpreted and judged in an abstract manner by qualified persons. If the picturesque had the ability to be subversive, either overtly in the manner of the 'Catholic' tours of property confiscated during the plantations, or through encouraging the amoral interpretation of art, it was inordinately successful in its aim. The picturesque style, without the subversive content, has become the status quo, proving most genial to the modern mind interested in psychological effect rather than balanced improvement. The ideal of the 'natural' and untouched landscape is in part responsible for the current apathy towards wasteland, and other debased landscapes which are unimproved and underused. Perhaps with the revival of interest in ethical and healthier farming practice, the modern eye will regard the landscape in a way more receptive to the apparatus of improvement than to the emotional pleasures of sheer cliffs, scenic forests and thunderous waterfalls. Arthur Young might inspire a new generation of travel writers to explore the physical structure of the countryside, armed with a definition of beauty as that which affects the whole consciousness and not merely the emotive imagination. Jonathan Swift's incandescent rage at the inappropriate untruth of the Irish pastoral may again attract a following, and some measure of Augustan rigour may be applied to the overwhelming sentimentality of 'building in the landscape'.

The history of the demesne documents the development of Irish landscape interpretation. The tourism that demesne culture encouraged has indirectly created the modern heritage-site and national park. Its categorization of landscape has profoundly affected the methodology of the planning process and determines the pattern of future spatial development. It has also affected the manner in which we perceive cities, as the definition of landscape counters that of the city. If Ireland's designed landscape heritage is to benefit the greatest possible number of people, landscape can no longer signify merely private ownership. Irish society should learn to value and control communal ownership, public land and open space, and to demand the quality of environment achieved in the past. Demesne landscape examined the Irish countryside's adaptation for both use and beauty, and the scale and confidence of its endeavours to change the landscape are noteworthy, as are the areas of expertise upon which it drew to establish a critical and intellectual base.

Carton and Castletown demesnes are still linked across a broad expanse of Kildare countryside by the Conolly obelisk. The eleven-year-old Lord Gerald Fitzgerald of Carton wrote in 1862: 'We went in the double car with Mama, we first went to the Wonderful Barn and then to Castletown, we went by the river first, and then we saw the house, there is a big stuffed bear in the hall, we are just behind the obelisk.'[806] Today, the great house élite has mostly been replaced by a golfing, business, tourist élite; few local people are able to enjoy the Irish demesne and its pleasures, just as it is difficult to imagine Lord Walter Fitzgerald relishing the prospect of a walk around a golf course. This route starts and ends at the opposing oblique eighteenth-century viewpoint of Castletown from Carton, where it lies 'just behind the obelisk', somewhat elevated and slightly to the left. There are many ways to make a garden and many more ways to use a garden. We only have to remember them.

# Appendices

## Castletown Account Books, Book 1762–1767

**1763** Robert Quin–Seedsman. p. 123

| | | |
|---|---|---|
| *Mar 12th* | *To Mignionett seed* | |
| | *To French Marigold seed* | |
| | *To African do.* | |
| | *To Princes feather* | |
| | *To one Bass Matt* | |
| *May 27th* | *To 6 Scythe stones* | |
| | *To 3 " stones Paid July 20th* | *£0,11,8,5* |
| *Oct 24th* | *To 70 fine double Rose coloured Hyacinths* | |
| | *To 70 do. bleu do.* | |
| | *To 70 do. double white do.* | |
| | *To 100 Narcissus polyanthus* | |
| | *To 1 Box* | |

**1764**

| | | |
|---|---|---|
| *Jan 5th* | *To 4 Rose acacias[?]* | |
| | *To 2 Dog Tuberose Roots Paid Sept. 3rd* | *£8,16,10* |

**1763** Daniel Bullen, p. 131

| | | |
|---|---|---|
| *Nov 14th* | *To 50 Phylerea15s* | |
| | *Two Franquillas* | *2s2d* |
| | *To 2 Double Peaches* | *3s* |
| | *6 Striped Sycamores* | *9s* |
| | *10 Red Cedars* | *1,7,1* |
| | *2 Flowering Ash* | *3s* |
| | *6 three-thorn'd acacias* | *9s* |
| | *6 Catalpas* | *13s* |
| | *6 red berry-bearing honeysucles* | *6s6d* |
| | *2 Coronilla* | *1s1d* |
| | *20 Mesereons? 1* | *0s10d* |
| | *2 scarlet Horse Chestnuts* | *5s5d* |
| | *6 Agnus Castus* | *13s* |
| | *2 Velvett roses* | *2s2d* |
| | *2 York & Lancaster* | *2s2d* |
| | *2 Blush province* | *2s2d* |
| | *2 Mase? province* | *4s4d* |
| | *2 Red* | *2s2d* |
| | *2 Blush Belgian* | *2s2d* |
| | *2 Childing* | *1s1d* |
| | *2 Maidens Blush* | *2s2d* |
| | *2 White Monthly* | *2s2d* |
| | *2 White Damask* | *2s2d* |
| | *2 Striped Monthly* | *2s2sd* |
| | *2 Dutch ?* | *2s2d* |
| | *2 Musk* | *4s4d* |
| | *2 Cluster* | *1s1d* |
| | *2 Pennsylvania* | *1s1d* |
| | *2 Burnett leaved* | *1s1d* |
| | *Paid Oct 21st, 1764* | *£7,12,9* |

**1763** Alex Montgomery

| | | |
|---|---|---|
| *Dec. 12th* | *To 5 bundles of Trees form London delivery* | *£4,8,11* |

**1762** John Phelan, p. 186, 189

*– usual vegetables, tools, see typical list below*

**1763** John Phelan

| | |
|---|---|
| *Feb 11th* | *1 Garden wyre Riddle* |
| | *2 garden Lines* |
| *Sept 24th* | *2 Scarlet Geraniums* |
| | *2 Potts fo balm of Gilea* |
| | *a Baskett* |
| *Oct 29th* | *50 Double Dutch Hyacinths* |
| | *20 Persian Iris* |
| | *A band box* |
| *Nov 4th* | *4 double dwarf flowering Almonds* |
| | *1 perfumed Cherry* |
| | *2 tacamatac [?]* |
| | *24 Arbutus* |
| | *10 female Dogwood* |
| | *6 shining flav'd Laurustinus?* |
| | *8 Diff. Altea Frutex* |
| | *6 Catalpas* |
| | *1 barbanovis?* |
| | *1 Cockspur Thorn* |
| | *6 Moss? province Roses* |
| | *1 Yellow berried Thorn* |
| | *1 Scarlet flowering Maple* |
| | *1 Agnus Castus* |
| | *40 Junipers* |
| | *8 Lucca Brooms* |
| | *2 Staff [?]* |
| | *6 German Tamarisk* |
| | *1 Bansfar [?] Indigo* |
| | *12 Weymouth Pines* |
| | *21 Double Hyacinths* |
| | *A band box with do.* |
| | *1 Jesuits bark* |
| | *1 Double virgins Bower* |
| | *2 Arbor Judas* |
| | *1 Toxicodendron* |
| | *1 Double Sweet Briar* |
| | *1 Lazarole* |
| | *6 Standard Almonds* |
| | *2 Potts Balm Giled* |
| | *1 Gold Strip'd Alaternus* |
| | *1 Silver do.* |
| | *1 olive leav'd do.* |
| | *2 Potts fo Double Nasturtium* |
| | *2 New England Sumachs* |
| | *1 White Cluster or Mush. Rose* |
| | *1 Carolina Kidney Bean Tree* |
| | *1 Myrtle leaved Sumach* |
| | *1 carolina Guelder Rose* |
| | *1 White Persian jasmine* |
| | *2 Iris Utaria* |
| | *1 Pesiploca* |
| | *1 Scarlet Geranium* |
| | *1 Horseshoe do.* |
| | *1/4 100 Narcissus Polyanthus* |
| | *2 Basketts* |

Typical kitchen garden account of John Phelan's Seedsman dated 27 January 1766 from Book 1762–1767:

*5 lbs of Shaftburgh Onion*
*4 lbs of long orange Carrott*
*3 lbs of Salmon Radish*
*2 lbs of Dutch Swelling Parsnip*
*1 lb of London Leek*
*6 lbs of – Celery*
*6 lbs of White Coss Lettuce*
*6 lbs of Cabbage Lettuce*
*4 lbs of Italian Collyflower*
*4 lbs of White Collyflower Broccoli*
*4 lbs of Purple Flowering Broccoli*
*2 ozs of Dutch Green Savoy*
*1 oz sweet Bazill*
*5 oz Curled Endive*
*2 oz Dutch Red Cabbage*
*4 ozs Spanish Gardoon*
*2 ozs Scorzonera*
*1 lb Early Green Turnip*
*4 Pruning Knives*
*4 Garden Rakes*
*2 Garden Lines*
*1/2 Dozen Scythes*
*2 Dozen Large Dutch Bass Matt??*
*3 quarts large Dutch shallots*
*20 lbs early Charlton pease*
*20 lbs Golden Hotspur*
*8 lbs Spanish marotts?*
*8 lbs Blue Rouncival*
*20 lbs Glory of England*
*8 lbs Dwarf Marrow*
*8 lbs Early Magazon Beans*
*1 oz long prickly cucumber*
*1 oz green Turkey cucumber*
*Spanish Tomatoes seed*

## Castletown Account Books, Book 1767–1775

**1766** John Phelan, p. 99 (For the North)

| | | |
|---|---|---|
| | *To 62? of Beech Mast* | *6s* |
| | *3 ozs of Scoth Firr* | *2s2d* |
| | *3 ozs of Spruce do.* | *2s2d* |
| | *42 ts? Furze seed* | *4s* |

**1766** John Phelan, Seedsman, p. 99 Acct book 67–75?

*Jan 27th* *5 lbs of Shaftburgh Onion*
*4 lbs of long orange Carrott*
*3 lbs of Salmon Radish*
*2 lbs of Dutch Swelling Parsnip*
*1 lb of London Leek*
*6 lbs of – Celery*
*6 lbs of White Coss Lettuce*
*6 lbs of Cabbage Lettuce*
*4 lbs of Italian Collyflower*
*4 lbs of White Collyflower Broccoli*
*4 lbs of Purple Flowering Broccoli*
*2 oz of Dutch Green Savoy*
*1 oz sweet Bazill*
*5 oz Curled Endive*
*2 oz Dutch Red Cabbage*
*4 ozs Spanish Gardoon*
*2 ozs Scorzonera*
*1 lb Early Green Turnip*
*4 Pruning Knives*
*4 Garden Rakes*
*2 Garden Lines*
*½ Dozen Scythes*
*2 Dozen Large Dutch Bass Matt??*
*3 quarts large Dutch shallots*
*20 lbs. early Charlton pease*
*20 lbs Golden Hotspur*
*8 lbs Spanish marotts [?]*
*8 lbs Blue Rouncival*
*20 lbs Glory of England*
*8 lbs Dwarf Marrow*
*8 lbs Early Magazon Beans*
*1 oz long prickly cucumber*
*1 oz green Turkey cucumber*
*Spanish Tomatoes seed*
*1 oz Spanish ramlas?*
*1 small watering Pott with a long spout*
*A large chest with Seeds* *£13,14,0*

Other kitchen garden accounts very similar to the one above on the:

**1766** Dec 17th
**1767** Feb 5th
**1767** June 16th
**1770** June 20th, 25th, Oct 13th, Nov 3rd, Nov 20th
**1771** Feb 9th, Mar 23rd, Dec 28th
**1772** Jan 29th
**1773** Feb 4th

**1767** (for the North)

| | | |
|---|---|---|
| | *3 lbs of Walnutts* | *1s6d* |
| | *3 lbs of Chestnutts* | *1s6d* |
| | *2 lbs Oak acorns* | *8d* |
| | *2 lbs Beech Mast* | *1s8d* |
| | *4 lbs Philbork* | *1s6d* |
| | *1 Pint Hornbeam* | *2s* |
| | *A box & cord* | *1s2d* |

**1770** (for the Blackrock) July 28th

*3 ozs Shafburgh Onion*
*¼ oz Cabbage & Dutch brown lettuce mixt.*
*8 ozs Yorkshire cabbage 1 to 1 oz sugar loaf*
*1 oz prickly Spinach*
*½ oz Collyflower*
*1 oz green Turnip*
*½ m Garden 6 Naills*

**1771** Daniel Bullen, p.349

| | | |
|---|---|---|
| *Sept 18th & 19th to* | | |
| | *50 Junipers* | *0,12,6* |
| | *50 red Cedars* | *2,14,2* |
| | *50 Portugall Laurells* | *2,14,2* |

**1772**

| | | |
|---|---|---|
| *Mar 5th* | *38 Pears* | *1,18,0* |
| | *15 Dwarf Apricots* | *1,12,0* |
| | *8 standard Apricotts* | *0,1,8* |
| | *2 Standard Plums* | *0,3,0* |
| | *3 Dwarf Plums* | *0,3,0* |
| | *64 Apples* | *0,12,0* |
| | *Paid May 28th '72* | *6,9,8* |

**1773**

| | | |
|---|---|---|
| *Sept 14th* | *To 2 hundred Scotch Firs* | *3,0,0* |
| *Sept 17th* | *To 500 do.* | *7,10,0* |
| *Sept 30th* | *To 50 do.* | *0,15,0* |
| *Nov 30th* | *To 5 red Cedars* | *0,5,5* |
| | *To 140 Apples* | *3,10,0* |
| | *To 13 Pears* | *0,13,0* |
| | *To 6 dwarf Nectarines* | *0,10,0* |
| | *6 Standard Nectarines* | *0,19,6* |
| | *8 Apricotts* | *0,12,0* |
| | *18 dwarf Peaches* | *1,10,0* |
| | *18 standard Peaches* | *2,18,6* |
| | *7 dwarf Cherrys* | *0,7,7* |
| | *8 standard Cherrys* | *0,13,4* |
| | *2 standard Plums* | *0,3,0* |
| | *24 Mass roses* | *2,12,0* |
| | | *£25,19,4* |

+ standard kitchen garden orders for following dates:

**1774** Jan 6th (p. 516)
**1775** Jan 21st also implements

**1774** Daniel Bullen, p. 516

| | | |
|---|---|---|
| *Feb 22nd* | *16 standard Pears* | *1,4,4,* |
| | *8 standard Cherrys* | *1,12,0* |
| *Apr 8th* | *2 Matts* | *0,2,2* |
| | *30 Scotch Firr* | *10,0,0* |
| | *20 Weymouth Pine* | *10,1,0* |

p. 526

| | | |
|---|---|---|
| *Nov 24th* | *32 standard Peaches and Nectarines* | *10,8,0* |
| | *26 dwarf Peaches and nectarines* | *7,0,10* |
| | *4 Peaches* | *0,6,8* |
| | *13 Cherrys* | *0,14,1* |
| | *1 Plumb* | *0,1,0* |
| | *27 dwarf Pears* | *1,7,0* |
| | *50 Roses in sorts* | *2,3,0* |
| | *12 Apples* | *0,6,0* |

**1775**

| | | |
|---|---|---|
| *Jan 21st* | *2 ozs Sweet Pease* | |
| | *35 sorts of flower seed* | |
| | *5 sorts do.* | |
| *Nov 5th* | *(for the Shrubery)* | |
| | *1 Splashing Hook* | |
| | *1 Bill Hook* | |
| | *6 Pruning knives* | |
| | *1 English Ax* | |
| | *1 Pruning saw* | |
| | *1 Chisell* | |
| *Feb 24th* | *(for ditto)* | |
| | *4 ozs Candytuft* | *0,2,0* |
| | *1 oz best Rose Larkspurs* | *0,2,0* |
| | *4 ozs Annuall Stock* | *0,2,0* |
| | *1 lbs of Sweet Pease* | *0,3,0* |
| | *(for the farmer)* | |
| | *¼ Hundred Red Clover* | |
| | *¼ hundred Trefoyle* | |
| | *Sack* | |
| | *(for the Gardener)* | |
| | *6 Persian Cyclamens* | |
| | *6 Spring Cyclamens* | |
| | *103 Lead Lables for the uale?? trees* | |

**1774** Carters to Dublin, p. 543

*Nov 23rd* *1 Cart Trees*

**1775** Carters to Dublin, p. 543

*Jan 2nd* *1 Cart Trees*
*Apr 27th* *1 Cart Kildare??*

## Castletown Account Books, Book 1775–1781

**1775** Daniel Bullen, Book 2, p. 137

| | | |
|---|---|---|
| *Nov 6th* | *To 1 oz Mignionett* | |
| | *To 2 ozs of mix'd Larkspur* | |
| | *To 1 oz Strip'd Convul … ? Minor* | |
| | *To 1 oz Pink* | |
| | *To 4 sorts Stock* | |
| | *To 2 oz mix'd Stock* | |
| | *To 1 oz Annual Stock* | |
| | *To 4 ozs Mixt Sweet Pea* | |

**1776**

| | | |
|---|---|---|
| *Mar 19th* | *To 4 ozs Scotch Firrs* | *4s* |
| | *To 4 ozs of Spruce* | *8s* |
| | *To 2 ozs of Larch* | *2s* |
| | *To 2 ozs of Weymouth Pines* | *8s* |
| *Nov 18th* | *To 2 Dozen Double red Rose Hyacinths* | |
| | *" " " white do.* | |
| | *" " " blue do.* | |
| | *" " " white do.* | |
| | *To 12 " " dutch jonquills* | |
| | *To 4 " " Narcissus Polyanthus* | |

**1776** Accounts (Green book)?

| | | |
|---|---|---|
| *Apr 29th* | *A freight of plants from Portugal* | *£0,12,7.5* |

**1779** Benjamin Simpson – new seed supplier for the kitchen garden, p. 358, p. 360

| | | |
|---|---|---|
| | *To carnation* | *£0,1,1* |
| | *To sweet pease and yellow lupins* | *£0,3,0* |
| *Feb 3rd* | *To flower seeds* | *£0,13,6.5* |
| | *To 6 Catherine Peaches* | *£0,9,9* |
| *March 5th* | *To 1 lb best Asparagus* | *£0,12,0* |
| *Mar 8th* | *To 1 Peek of English Potatoes* | *£0,2,2* |
| *Mar 31st* | *To 2 lbs strong Tobacco for Hot Houses* | *£0,6,6* |
| *Mar 11th* | *To 2 ozs of Pine Aster* | *£0,3,0* |
| | *To 4 ozs of Cluster Pine* | *£0,4,0* |
| | *To 1 oz Weymouth Pine* | *£0,2,6* |
| | *To 4 ozs Larch* | *£0,4,0* |
| | *To 4 ozs Scotch Firr* | *£0,4,0* |
| | *To 4 ozs Spruce Firr* | *£0,4,0* |
| | *To 4 ozs Silver Firr* | *£0,4,0* |
| | *To Red Cedar Berrys* | *£0,2,0* |
| | *To Spanish Broom* | *£0,2,6* |
| | *To Cypress* | *£0,2,0* |
| | *To China Arbor Vitae* | *£0,2,0* |
| | *To 1 lb Arbutus* | *£1,2,9* |
| *Paid Aug 3rd 1779* | | |
| | *By Mayrath* | *£6,9,9* |
| | *By Lane* | *£26,8,8* |
| | *By Simmonds* | *£5,2,6* |
| *Apr 27th* | *To 2 white Nectarine Trees* | *£1,2,9* |
| | *To 22 standard Peaches and Nectarines* | *£2,19,7* |
| | *To 4 dwarf do.* | *£0,6,6* |
| | *To 2 dozen Tuberoses* | *£0,8,0* |
| | *To ½ oz Mignionett* | *£0,1,0* |
| | *To 2 lbs strong Tobacco for Stoves* | *£0,6,6* |
| | *To 2 bass Matts for packing Trees* | *£0,2,2* |

*This on Sept 6th, 1780 By my Lady's Draft on Mr Coane* *£32,19,9.5*

## Castletown Account Books, Book 1781–1790

1781 Benjamin Simpson, p. 131, Book 1781–

| | | | |
|---|---|---|---|
| | *Nov 17th* | *To 400 Hornbeams* | |
| | | *To 300 do.* | *£7,10,0* |
| 1782 | | | |
| | *Jan 25th* | *To 49 Double Dutch Hyacinths* | *£1,12,8* |
| | *Feb 21st* | *To 16 new kinds of Gooseberry Trees* | *£1,14,8* |
| | *Apr. 17th* | *To 4 oz Double Rose Larkspur* | *£0,8,0* |
| | | *To 2 oz of 4 fine new kinds* | *£0,6,0* |
| | | *To ½ Pint of fine new Scarlet Pease* | *£0,2,0* |
| | | *To 3.5 Pint sweet Pease* | *£0,3,0* |
| 1783 | | | |
| | *Feb 14th* | *To 2 ozs Mignionette* | |
| | | *To 2 ozs French Scarlet Stock* | |
| | | *To 8 then -? of Stock* | |
| | | *To 3 ozs Scarlet sweet Pea* | |
| | | *To 9 ozs other sweet Pea* | |
| | | *To 2 ozs sweet bazile* | |
| | *Mar 23rd* | *To 2 Bottles of Filax? seed* | |
| | | *To 3 ? of American do.* | |
| | *Shrubbery accounts separate Tools –* | | *£5,7,5* |
| 1786 | Ben Simpson | | |
| | *July 3rd* | *4oz Mignionett* | |
| | *Sept 3rd* | *On Andrew Flood's acct.* | |
| | | *On the farm acct.* | |
| | | *On the Garden acct.* | |

Carters

| | | |
|---|---|---|
| 1781 | | |
| | *Nov 27th* | *1 cart Trees* |
| | *Nov 30th* | " " |
| 1782 | | |
| | *Dec 5th* | *1 cart Plants* |
| 1783 | | |
| | *Apr 1st & 2nd* | *1 Cart Rock with Plants* |
| | *Oct 1st* | *Seeds* |
| 1784 | | |
| | *Feb 17th* | *Seeds* |
| 1785 | | |
| | *July 6th* | *Tyles for Cottage* |
| 1786 | | |
| | *Jan 27th* | *Seeds* |
| | *Apr. 28th* | *Seeds* |
| | *May 4th* | *Garden seeds* |
| 1787 | | |
| | *Jan 6th* | *Garden seeds* |
| | *Jan 23rd* | " " |
| | *Apr 10th* | *For the garden* |

Mss. 3939, TCD, Tradesmen's accts. Bk. 1

*no. 289* *Castletown, Aug 16th 1779*
*'… By William McBride … £2,14,0 for 4 ? of Flowers'*

*no. 985* *Dublin, Apr 25th 1782*
*'£3,2,3 … for split pease and mustard … Benj. Simpson'*

*no. 147* *Castletown, Oct 18th 1784*
*'£1,4,0 … for 2 dozen of Arbutus plants … John Sutherland'*

*no. 153* *Castletown, Aug 14th 1784*
*'£1,0,0 … for two Clives? of Goosburys … George Coyle'*

Mss. 3940, TCD, Tradesmen's accts. Bk. 2

*no. 97* *Dublin, 20th Dec 1792*
*'£30,17,5 … seeds for the Garden at Castletown … Benj. Simpson'*

*no. 286* *Dublin, 25th Jan 1794*
*'£19,3,8 … for my Bill of plants and shrubs … Sarah Simmonds'*

Mss. 3941, TCD, Tradesmen's accts. Bk. 3

*no. 159* *C., 1st Oct 1796*
*'£10,7,5 … for Trees and Flower Roots … Thos. Thompson'*

*no. 127* *Dublin, 3rd June 1798*
*'£53,17,10 … for Farm Bill: £33,4,5;*
*Kit. Garden: £6,10,2.5;*
*Pleasure ground: £8,1,11.5;*
*House: £1,16,9;*
*Bird Seeds: £4,4,6 … Benj Simpson'*

*no. 8* *C., 25th Aug 1798*
*'… £26,6,4.5 … trees: 5,11,5;*
*Firrs: 0,5,5;*
*Ditching 23,3,0;*
*Potatoes: 16,1,7.5;*
*WaterCuts: 1,4,10.75 … Matthew Ging'*

*no. 35* *C., 16th Nov 1799*
*'£1,15,11.5 … Planting Firr Quick nd making a Walk as per Bill … Finly Black'*

*no. 72* *Dublin, 21st Feb 1800*
*'£79,3,7 … Benj. Simpson'*

*no. 160* *Dublin 15th Oct 1800*
*'£26,13,0 for 82 Pine Plants at 6/6 … Benj. Simpson Jnr.'*

*no. 162* *C., 10th Nov 1800*
*'£2,17,5 … a Bill of Green House Plants bought by Miss Emily Napier..? Bryan'*

*no. 163* *C., 29th Dec 1800*
*'£3,8,3 for Two Orange Trees … D. Bryan'*

*no. 274* *C.,*
*Garden Seeds £11,7,6 … John Lane*

*no. 321*
*Pine Plants £16,8,3*

*no. 98* *C., 27th June 1801*
*'£7,2,6 for Green House Plants … D.Bryan'*

*no. 144* *C., 8th June 1801*
*'£13,18,6 … my Bill for Trees Flower Roots … Thos Thompson … (This I am not to charge as I got credit for his rent)'*

*no. 109* *?, 1802*
*? Flower Roots … 12s 25.5d*

Ms. 3962, TCD, Exps. 1792–1797

| | | | |
|---|---|---|---|
| 1792 | | | |
| | *Dec 20th* | *To Benjamin Simpson, his bill of seeds for the garden to 1st of May* | *96,45,0,0* |
| 1793 | | | |
| | *Dec. 25th* | *To Mr. John Simmonds, a Bill for Plants and Shrubs from Collinstown* | *286,19,3,8* |
| 1793 | | | |
| | | *Tradesmen's Bills* | |
| | | *Six Barrels of Seed Pease* | *7,7,9* |
| | | *Benjamin Simpson Seedsman* | *65,12,1* |
| | | *Mrs. Simmonds, for Shrubs & c.* | *19,3,8* |
| 1795 | | | |
| | *Jan 3rd* | *Benjamin Simpson bill* | |
| | | *Farm bill* | *19,8,1.5* |
| | | *Garden* | *0,1,4* |
| | | *Shrubbery* | *0,6,6* |
| | | *Ben Simpson (Seedsman) 3 bills* | *74,19,2.5* |
| 1795 | | | |
| | | *Tradesmen's Bills* | |
| | | *To Mr. Simpson (seedsman)* | *69,1,9* |
| 1796 | | | |
| | *Jan 23rd* | *Benjamin Simpson, his Bills to 1st May 1795* | |
| | | *Kitchen Garden* | *28,19,4* |
| | | *Farm Seeds* | *23,10,4.5* |
| | | *Shrubbery* | *7,7,6.5* |
| | | *B.S. bills to 1st Nov 1795* | |
| | | *K.G.* | *0,9,2* |
| | | *Farm* | *1,19,10* |
| | | *Shrubbery* | *6,15,6* |
| 1797 | | | |
| | *April …* | *To Mr. Murphy (seedsman) as pr Bill* | *10,11,3* |
| | | *Ben Simpson* | |
| | | *Garden* | *21,8,5* |
| | | *Farm* | *21,8,10.5* |
| | | *Plantation of Shrubbery* | *6,13,8* |
| | *To Mr. Thompson for Flower Roots* | | *1,3,9* |

## Castletown Account Books, Book 1767–1785

**1767** Thomas Kavanagh – Ironmonger

| | | |
|---|---|---|
| *July 30* | *1 Garden Spade* | 0,4,0 |
| | *1 Rake* | 0,1,2 |
| | *1 Pushing Hoe & 1 Chopping do.* | 0,2,10 |
| | *1 Pair fo garden Shears* | 0,3,6 |
| | *1 small Hoe* | 0,0 |
| | *1 Watering Pott* | 0,5,5 |
| | *1 Dung fork & Handle* | 0,2,0 |
| | *1 Scythe & Stone* | 0,2,0.5 |
| | *1 garden Hammer* | 0,1,4 |
| | *4 Handles for the Rake and Hoes* | 0,1,4 |

**1772** Implements (for the Town Garden)

*1 Scythe & 1 Scythe stone*
*1 English garden spade*
*1 garden rake*
*1 small garden flower rake*
*1 garden hoe*
*1 Dutch hoe*
*1 weeding spudd*
*1 Prong fork*
*6 handles for the above Tools*
*3 Rings for 3 of the above handles*
*1 scythe sned??*
*To the smith for fixing the scythe to the spade & handles to the tools*
*1 scythe pipe*

**1775** Daniel Bullen, p. 516

*Nov 5th* *(for the Shrubery)*
*1 Splashing Hook*
*1 Bill Hook*
*6 Pruning knives*
*1 English Ax*
*1 Pruning saw*
*1 Chisell*

Ms 3940, T.C.D., Nov 28th 1785–24th Dec. 1795,
Trdsmen's accts. Bk 2

*no. 61* *Castletown, 10th May 1786*
*'… £7,7,10.5 … Glass and Basketts for the Kitchen Garden'*

*no. 262* *Dublin, 7th April 1790*

*'Received from Thos Conolly, Esq; by Lady Louisa Conolly the Sum of £0,8,1.5 Sterling, for a Garden Engine, at 7sh/yd minding a Tambour Screw in full of all Demands … Geo. Cartland'*

*no. 152* *Dublin, 9th Oct 1795*
*'… £0,18,5 … for four Basket work flower Pots, in Queens Ware and a box …'*

*no 99* *C., 1st April 1795*
*'£1,7,9.5 … my bills for Garden Baskets … John Lane'*

*no. 150* *Dublin, 23rd Dec 1802*
*'£43,4,11 Tiles & garden Potts. J. Foxall'*

# Notes

## Introduction

1 T. Reeves-Smyth, 'Demesnes', in F.H.A. Aalen, K. Whelan and M. Stout, *Atlas of the Irish Rural Landscape* (Cork, 1997), p. 197.
2 Desmond Guinness and the Knight of Glin, 'The Conolly Folly: A Case for Richard Castle', *Bulletin of the Irish Georgian Society*, vol. 6, no. 4, October-December 1963, p. 63.
3 Tom Williamson, *Polite Landscapes: Gardens and Society in Eighteenth-Century England* (Stroud and Maryland, 1995), p. 65.
4 ibid., p. 1.
5 Maurice Craig, *The Architecture of Ireland* (Dublin, 1982), p. 248.

## Chapter 1

6 R. Molesworth to L. Molesworth, 12 July 1709, N.L.I., P 3752.
7 Breckdenston is also known as Brackenstown or Brackdenstown. The form used throughout this book is that used by Robert Molesworth in his personal correspondence: Breckdenston.
8 R. Molesworth to L. Molesworth, 25 March 1690, N.L.I., P 3752.
9 R. Molesworth to L. Molesworth, undated, N.L.I., P 3752.
10 Edward Malins and the Knight of Glin, *Lost Demesnes* (London, 1976), p. 16: from Robert Molesworth to Lord Coningsby, 1719, P.R.O.N.I., Ms. D 628/82/2.
11 R. Molesworth to L. Molesworth, 13 October 1716, N.L.I., P 3752.
12 R. Molesworth to L. Molesworth, 17 June 1718, N.L.I., P 3752.
13 R. Molesworth to L. Molesworth, 12 July 1709, N.L.I., P 3752.
14 Edward Malins and the Knight of Glin, *Lost Demesnes* (London, 1976), p. 16.
15 R. Molesworth to L. Molesworth, 12 July 1714, N.L.I., P 3752.
16 D.A. Chart (ed.), Clements Mss., *Historic Manuscripts Commision Report on Various Collections,* vol. 8 (1913), p. 315.
17 R. Molesworth to J. Molesworth, 5 March 1722/23, N.L.I., P 3753.
18 R. Molesworth to J. Molesworth, 27 February 1721/22, N.L.I., P 3753.
19 R. Molesworth to L. Molesworth, 7 January 1720, N.L.I., P 3752.
20 R. Molesworth to L. Molesworth, 14 March 1721, N.L.I., P 3752.
21 R. Molesworth to L. Molesworth, 14 March 1721, N.L.I., P 3752.
22 R. Molesworth to L. Molesworth, 17 June 1718, N.L.I., P 3752.
23 R. Molesworth to L. Molesworth, 16 May 1721, N.L.I., P 3752.
24 Weston St John Joyce, *The Neighbourhood of Dublin* (Dublin, 1971), p. 316.
25 R. Molesworth to L. Molesworth, undated, N.L.I., P 3752.
26 R. Molesworth to L. Molesworth, 13 October 1716, N.L.I., P 3752.
27 J. Tichborne to R. Molesworth, 23 July 1710, N.L.I., P 3753.
28 Edward Malins and the Knight of Glin, *Lost Demesnes* (London, 1976), p. 16: Robert Molesworth to Lord Coningsby, 1719, P.R.O.N.I., Ms. D 628/82/2.
29 R. Molesworth to L. Molesworth, 12 July 1709, N.L.I., P 3752.
30 R. Molesworth to L. Molesworth, 13 October 1716, N.L.I., P 3752.
31 R. Molesworth to L. Molesworth, 3 May 1712, N.L.I., P 3752.
32 R. Molesworth to L. Molesworth, 13 October 1716, N.L.I., P 3752.
33 R. Molesworth to L. Molesworth, 25 February 1714, N.L.I., P 3752.
34 R. Molesworth to L. Molesworth, 10 November 1695, N.L.I., P 3752.
35 R. Molesworth to L. Molesworth, 2 November 1709, N.L.I., P 3752.
36 R. Molesworth to L. Molesworth, 19 November 1709, N.L.I., P 3752.
37 R. Molesworth to L. Molesworth, 19 January 1719, N.L.I., P 3752.
38 R. Molesworth to L. Molesworth, 12 April 1707, N.L.I., P 3752.
39 R. Molesworth to L. Molesworth, 16 May 1721, N.L.I., P 3752.
40 R. Molesworth to L. Molesworth, 13 October 1716, N.L.I., P 3752.
41 R. Molesworth to L. Molesworth, 23 March 1721, N.L.I., P 3752.
42 R. Molesworth to L. Molesworth, 16 May 1721, N.L.I., P 3752.
43 George Cartwright to R. Molesworth, 19 February 1723, N.L.I., P 3753.
44 R. Molesworth to L. Molesworth, 11 June 1707, N.L.I., P 3752.
45 R. Molesworth to L. Molesworth, 13 October 1716, N.L.I., P 3752.
46 R. Molesworth to L. Molesworth, 25 February 1714, N.L.I., P 3752.
47 R. Molesworth to L. Molesworth, 7 June 1703, N.L.I., P 3752.
48 R. Molesworth to L. Molesworth, 18 February 1720, N.L.I., P 3752.
49 R. Molesworth to L. Molesworth, 16 March 1721, N.L.I., P 3752.
50 R. Molesworth to L. Molesworth, 19 January 1718/1719, N.L.I., P 3752.
51 R. Molesworth to L. Molesworth, 16 May 1721, N.L.I., P 3752.
52 R. Molesworth to L. Molesworth, 7 January 1720, N.L.I., P 3752.
53 R. Molesworth to L. Molesworth, 12 July 1709, N.L.I., P 3752.
54 R. Molesworth to L. Molesworth, 12 July 1709, N.L.I., P 3752.
55 D.A. Chart (ed.), *Clements Mss.,* p. 328: J. Molesworth to R. Molesworth, 10 December 1721.
56 R. Molesworth to L. Molesworth, 19 January 1719, N.L.I., P 3752.
57 R. Molesworth to L. Molesworth, 25 February 1714, N.L.I., P 3752.
58 R. Molesworth to L. Molesworth, 16 May 1721, N.L.I., P 3752.
59 R. Molesworth to L. Molesworth, 3 May 1712, N.L.I., P 3752.
60 R. Molesworth to L. Molesworth, 8 April 1710, N.L.I., P 3752.
61 R. Molesworth to L. Molesworth, undated, N.L.I., P 3752.
62 R. Molesworth to L. Molesworth, 7 January 1720, N.L.I., P 3752.
63 Simon Thurley (ed.), *The Privy Garden at Hampton Court Palace* (London, 1995), p. 45.
64 R. Molesworth to L. Molesworth, 7 June 1704, N.L.I., P 3752.
65 R. Molesworth to L. Molesworth, 3 May 1712, N.L.I., P 3752.
66 D.A. Chart (ed.), *Clements Mss.,* p.328: J. Molesworth to R. Molesworth, 10 December 1721.
67 R. Molesworth to L. Molesworth, 14 March 1721, N.L.I., P 3752.
68 R. Molesworth to L. Molesworth, 8 April 1710, N.L.I., P 3752.
69 D.A. Chart (ed.), *Clements Mss.,* p. 328: J. Molesworth to R. Molesworth, 10 December 1721.
70 R. Molesworth to L. Molesworth, 12 July 1709, N.L.I., P 3752.
71 R. Molesworth to L. Molesworth, 28 March 1696, N.L.I., P 3752.
72 R. Molesworth to L. Molesworth, 8 April 1710, N.L.I., P 3752.
73 R. Molesworth to L. Molesworth, 25 May 1714, N.L.I., P 3752.
74 Stephen Switzer, *The Practical Kitchen Gardiner* (London, 1727), pp. 11–12.
75 R. Molesworth to L. Molesworth, 13 October 1716, N.L.I., P 3752.
76 John Tichborne to R. Molesworth, 23 July 1710, N.L.I., P 3753.
77 R. Molesworth to L. Molesworth, 8 August 1709, N.L.I., P 3752.
78 R. Molesworth to L. Molesworth, 16 July 1712, N.L.I., P 3752.
79 R. Molesworth to L. Molesworth, 16 July 1712, N.L.I., P 3752.
80 R. Molesworth to L. Molesworth, 12 July 1707, N.L.I., P 3752.
81 R. Molesworth to L. Molesworth, 3 May 1712, N.L.I., P 3752.
82 R. Molesworth to L. Molesworth, 7 August 1704, N.L.I., P 3752.
83 R. Molesworth to L. Molesworth, 25 February 1714, N.L.I., P 3752.
84 Edward Malins and the Knight of Glin, *Lost Demesnes* (London, 1976), p. 16: Robert Molesworth to Lord Coningsby, 1719, P.R.O.N.I., Ms. D 628/82/2.

85 R. Molesworth to L. Molesworth, 12 July 1709, N.L.I., P 3752.
86 R. Molesworth to L. Molesworth, 29 November 1712, N.L.I., P 3752.
87 D.A. Chart (ed.), *Clements Mss.*, p. 275, undated.
88 R. Molesworth to L. Molesworth, 19 January 1719, N.L.I., P 3752.
89 R. Molesworth to L. Molesworth, undated, N.L.I., P 3752.
90 R. Molesworth to L. Molesworth, 19 January 1719, N.L.I., P 3752.
91 W.A. McCutcheon, *The Industrial Archaeology of Northern Ireland* (New Jersey, 1984), p. 248.
92 R. Molesworth to L. Molesworth, 12 July 1709, N.L.I., P 3752.
93 R. Molesworth to L. Molesworth, 18 November 1710, N.L.I., P 3752.
94 R. Molesworth to L. Molesworth, 29 November 1712, N.L.I., P 3752.
95 R. Molesworth to L. Molesworth, 18 November 1710, N.L.I., P 3752.
96 R. Molesworth to L. Molesworth, undated, N.L.I., P 3752.
97 R. Molesworth to L. Molesworth, 18 May 1717, N.L.I., P 3752.
98 Stephen Switzer, *An Introduction to a General System of Hydrostaticks & Hydraulics, Philosophical & Practical* (London, 1729), p. 323.
99 ibid., p. 319.
100 ibid., p. 317.
101 R. Molesworth to L. Molesworth, 18 May 1717, N.L.I., P 3752.
102 R. Molesworth to L. Molesworth, 12 June 1709, N.L.I., P 3752.
103 R. Molesworth to L. Molesworth, 2 February 1712, N.L.I., P 3752.
104 R. Molesworth to L. Molesworth, 8 July 1710, N.L.I., P 3752.
105 R. Molesworth to L. Molesworth, 13 October 1716, N.L.I., P 3752.
106 George Cartwright to R. Molesworth, 27 February 1722, N.L.I., P 3753.
107 R. Molesworth to L. Molesworth, 23 June 1713, N.L.I., P 3752.
108 R. Molesworth to L. Molesworth, 29 November 1712, N.L.I., P 3752.
109 R. Molesworth to L. Molesworth, 23 June 1713, N.L.I., P 3752.
110 R. Molesworth to L. Molesworth, 27 December 1720, N.L.I., P 3752.
111 R. Molesworth to L. Molesworth, 25 May 1714, N.L.I., P 3752.
112 R. Molesworth to L. Molesworth, 13 October 1716, N.L.I., P 3752.
113 L. Molesworth to R. Molesworth, 12 June 1714, N.L.I., P 3753.
114 R. Molesworth to L. Molesworth, 25 May 1714, N.L.I., P 3752.
115 R. Molesworth to L. Molesworth, 28 March 1719, N.L.I., P 3752.
116 George Cartwright to R. Molesworth, 19 February 1722, N.L.I., P 3753.
117 R. Molesworth to L. Molesworth, undated, N.L.I., P 3752.
118 George Cartwright to R. Molesworth, 19 February 1722, N.L.I., P 3753.
119 R. Molesworth to L. Molesworth, 7 April 1720, N.L.I., P 3752.
120 R. Molesworth to L. Molesworth, 27 December 1720, N.L.I., P 3752.
121 R. Molesworth to L. Molesworth, 27 December 1720, N.L.I., P 3752.
122 D.A. Chart (ed.), *Clements Mss.*, pp. 328–9: J. Molesworth to R. Molesworth, 10 December 1721.
123 ibid. pp. 328–9: J. Molesworth to R. Molesworth, 10 December 1721.
124 ibid., p. 328–9.
125 R. Molesworth to L. Molesworth, 16 May 1721, N.L.I., P 3752.
126 R. Molesworth to L. Molesworth, 12 June 1714, N.L.I., P 3752.
127 R. Molesworth to L. Molesworth, 16 May 1721, N.L.I., P 3752.
128 George Cartwright to R. Molesworth, 19 February 1722, N.L.I., P 3753.
129 R. Molesworth to L. Molesworth, 16 May 1721, N.L.I., P 3752.
130 R. Molesworth to J. Molesworth, 27 February 1722, N.L.I., P 3753.
131 R. Molesworth to J. Molesworth, 20 October 1722, N.L.I., P 3753.
132 John Dixon Hunt and Peter Willis (eds.), *The Genius of the Place: The English Landscape Garden 1620–1820,* p. 162: from Stephen Switzer, 'Appendix', in *Ichnographia Rustica* (1742), iii.
133 Caroline Robbins, *The Eighteenth-Century Commonwealthman: Studies in the Transmission, Development & Circumstance of English Liberal Thought from the Restoration of Charles II until the War with the Thirteen Colonies* (Harvard, 1959), p. 5.
134 ibid., p. 8.
135 ibid., p. 6.
136 See Raymond Williams, *The Country and the City* (London, 1973); Ann Bermingham, *Landscape and Ideology* (Berkeley, 1986).
137 J.C.D. Clark, English Society 1688–1832: *Ideology, Social Structure and Political Practice during the Ancien Régime* (Cambridge, 1986), p. 14: J.H. Plumb's widely acclaimed statement of the view that the early eighteenth century witnessed 'The Triumph of the Venetian Oligarchy'.
See also C.D.A. Leighton, *Catholics in a Protestant Kingdom: A Study of the Irish Ancien Regime* (Dublin, 1994), p. 22.
138 Denis Cosgrove, *Social Formation & the Symbolic Landscape* (London, 1984), p. 122.
139 R. Bentmann and M. Mueller, *The Villa as Hegemonic Architecture* (International Inc., 1992), p. 39.
140 R.F. Foster, *Modern Ireland 1600–1972* (London, 1988), p. 106.
141 Denis Cosgrove, *Social Formation & the Symbolic Landscape,* p. 107.
142 See T.C. Barnard, 'Gardening, Diet and "Improvement" in Later Seventeenth-Century Ireland', *Journal of Garden History,* 1990, vol. 10, no. 1, pp. 71–85.
143 Toby Barnard, 'Public and Private Uses of Wealth in Ireland, c.1660–1760', in Jacqueline Hill and Colm Lennon (eds.), *Luxury and Austerity* (Dublin 1999), p. 67.
144 Robert Molesworth, *Some Considerations for the Promoting of Agriculture and Employing the Poor* (Dublin, 1723).
145 ibid., p. 6.
146 ibid., p. 5.
147 ibid., p. 3.
148 ibid., p. 10.
149 ibid., p. 5.
150 Christine Casey, 'Eighteenth Century Architecture in Ireland: A Bibliographical Approach' (unpublished Ph.D. thesis, Trinity College Dublin, 1992), Introduction.
151 ibid., p. 69.
152 Stephen Switzer, *An Introduction to a General System of Hydrostaticks & Hydraulics, Philosophical & Practical* (London, 1729), frontispiece.
153 R. Molesworth to J. Molesworth?, 27 February 1722, N.L.I., P 3753.
154 Christine Casey, 'Eighteenth Century Architecture in Ireland: A Bibliographical Approach' (unpublished Ph.D. thesis , Trinity College Dublin, 1992), p. 67.
155 Phillipstown, King's County, was later changed to Daingean, Co. Westmeath, its current name.
156 R. Molesworth to L. Molesworth, 16 July 1712, N.L.I., P 3752.
157 Robert Molesworth, *Some Considerations for the Promoting of Agriculture and Employing the Poor,* p. 5.
158 R. Molesworth to L. Molesworth, 24 June 1704, N.L.I., P 3752.
159 R. Molesworth to L. Molesworth, 9 July 1709, N.L.I., P 3752.
160 R. Molesworth to L. Molesworth, undated, N.L.I., P 3752.
161 For the opposing Tory and Whig ideas of landscape development, see Nigel Everett, *The Tory View of Landscape* (London, 1994).
162 R. Molesworth to L. Molesworth, 8 April 1710, N.L.I., P 3752.
163 R. Molesworth to L. Molesworth, 3 May 1712, N.L.I., P 3752.
164 R. Molesworth to L. Molesworth, 13 November 1710, N.L.I., P 3752.
165 R. Molesworth to L. Molesworth, 23 June 1713, N.L.I., P 3752.

166 D.A. Chart (ed.), *Clements Mss.,* p. 369: R. Molesworth to L. Molesworth, 3 May 1724.
167 R. Molesworth to L. Molesworth, 7 June 1704?, N.L.I., P 3752.
168 John Dixon Hunt and Peter Willis (eds.), *The Genius of the Place: The English Landscape Garden 1620–1820,* p. 162: from Stephen Switzer, 'Appendix', in Ichnographia Rustica (1742), iii.
169 Stephen Switzer, *The Practical Kitchen Gardiner* (London, 1727), p. A3.
170 Edward Malins and the Knight of Glin, *Lost Demesnes* (London, 1976), p. 16: from Robert Molesworth to Lord Coningsby, 1719, P.R.O.N.I., Ms. D 628/82/2.
171 Edward Mc Parland, 'The New Junta for Architecture', in T. Barnard, and J. Clark (eds.), *Lord Burlington, Architecture, Art & Life* (London, 1995), p. 160: from Lord Molesworth to Lord Stanhope, Kent Archives Office, u1590/c9/35.
172 ibid., p. 161.
173 Anthony Ashley Cooper, third Earl of Shaftesbury, *The Late Earl of Shaftesbury's Letters to the Rt. Hon. Lord Robert Molesworth* (London, 1721), p. 26.
174 Edward Mc Parland, 'The New Junta for Architecture', in T. Barnard, and J. Clark (eds.), *Lord Burlington, Architecture, Art & Life* (London, 1995), p. 163.
175 Edward Mc Parland, *Public Architecture in Ireland 1680–1760* (Yale, 2001), p. 11.
176 Caroline Robbins, *The Eighteenth-Century Commonwealthman,* p. 8.
177 John Dixon Hunt, *Garden & Grove: The Italian Renaissance Garden in the English Imagination: 1600–1750* (Princeton, 1986), pp. 182–3.
178 E. Klein Lawrence, *Shaftesbury and the Culture of Politeness: Moral Discourse and Cultural Politics in Early Eighteenth-Century England* (Cambridge, 1994), p. 124.
179 ibid., p. 204.
180 'Paper full of Corrections and additions by Lord Shaftesbury on Plantations to be altered and renewed in his estate, under five headings, dated April, 1707', Public Record Office Shaftesbury Papers Series 5, Catalogue page 188 [PRO 30/24/20/133b] from David Leatherbarrow, 'Character Geometry and Perspective: The Third Earl of Shaftesbury's Principles of Garden Design', *Journal of Garden History,* vol. 4, no. 4, 1984, p. 354.
181 ibid. pp. 354–5.
182 D.A. Chart (ed.), *Clements Mss.,* p. 245: 18 February 1710, London, Richard Molesworth to his mother, the Hon. Mrs Molesworth.
183 R. Molesworth to L. Molesworth, 18 February 1720, N.L.I., P 3752.
184 D.A. Chart (ed.), *Clements Mss.,* p. 349: R. Molesworth to J. Molesworth, 20 October 1722.
185 ibid., p. 356: 5 March 1722/23, R. Molesworth to J. Molesworth.
186 Caroline Robbins, *The Eighteenth-Century Commonwealthman* (1959), p. 94.
187 D.A. Chart (ed.), *Clements Mss.,* p. 329: J. Molesworth to R. Molesworth, 10 December 1710.
188 ibid., p. 329: J. Molesworth to R. Molesworth, 10 December 1710.
189 Jonathan Swift, *The Drapier's Letters to the People of Ireland against rec. Wood's Halfpence* (Oxford 1935), p. 117, ed. Herbert Davis.
190 ibid., p. 108.
191 Carole Fabricant, *Swift's Landscape* (Notre Dame and London, 1995), p. 54.
192 Jonathan Swift, quoted in Oliver Ferguson, Jonathan Swift & Ireland (1962), p. 81.
193 Carole Fabricant, *Swift's Landscape,* p. 103: (C, 3: 493); *The Correspondence of Jonathan Swift,* 5 vols., ed. Harold Williams (Oxford, 1963–5).
194 ibid., p. 163.
195 ibid., p. 55.
196 Carole Fabricant, *Swift's Landscape,* p. 148: Fabricant states that Swift, 'in the poem *An Epistle upon an Epistle,* ...manages to turn a description of Delany's elegant villa into a playfully expressed but nonetheless serious comment on the follies of political patronage and the perils of financial improvidence'; p. 134: 'She writes that the verses *"A Pastoral Dialogue between Richmond-Lodge and Marble Hill"* and *"Dr. Swift to Mr. Pope, While he was writing the 'Dunciad'"* ... undermine or reverse the situations and relationships upon which the country-house ideal depends.'
197 ibid., p. 54.
198 ibid., p. 15.
199 ibid., p. 13.
200 ibid., p. 151.
201 ibid., p. 152.
202 ibid., p. 152: from Jonathan Swift, *An Epistle upon an Epistle.*
203 R. Molesworth to J. Molesworth, 27 February 1722, N.L.I., P 3753.
204 Robert Molesworth, *Some Considerations for the Promoting of Agriculture and Employing the Poor,* p. 11.
205 John Dixon Hunt and Peter Willis (eds.), *The Genius of the Place, The English Landscape Garden 1620–1820,* p. 152: from Stephen Switzer, 'Appendix', in *Ichnographia Rustica* (1742), iii.
206 R. Molesworth to J. Molesworth, 5 March 1722/23, N.L.I., P 3753.
207 R. Molesworth to J. Molesworth, 5 March 1722/23, N.L.I., P 3753.
208 Michael Brown, *Francis Hutcheson in Dublin, 1719–1730* (Dublin, 2002), p. 44.
209 ibid., p. 50.
210 Toby Barnard, 'Public and Private Uses of Wealth in Ireland, c.1660–1760', in Jacqueline Hill and Colm Lennon (eds.), *Luxury and Austerity* (Dublin, 1999), p. 72.
211 ibid., p. 71.
212 R. Molesworth to L. Molesworth, 12 July 1707, N.L.I., P 3752.
213 Stephen Switzer, *The Practical Kitchen Gardiner* (London, 1727), p. 47.
214 R. Molesworth to L. Molesworth, 8 July 1710, N.L.I., P 3752.
215 R. Molesworth to J. Molesworth, 20 October 1722, N.L.I., P 3753.
216 L. Molesworth to R. Molesworth, 19 April 1700, N.L.I., P 3753.

## Chapter 2

217 Lena Boylan, 'The Conollys of Castletown: A Family History', *Bulletin of the Irish Georgian Society,* vol. 11, no. 4 (1968), p. 4.
218 ibid., p. 14.
219 *Collins English Dictionary* (1979): messuage: a dwelling house together with its outbuildings, curtilage, and the adjacent land appropriated to its use.
220 Lena Boylan, 'Castletown and its Owners, Parts 1 & 2', *Bulletin of the Irish Georgian Society,* 1968, p. 5.
221 This area has been calculated from the c.1768 demesne plan of Castletown, N.L.I., Ms. 16.H.14 (11). The area is totalled at 389.1.35 Irish acres = c.666 English acres.
222 Edward Mc Parland, 'The New Junta for Architecture', in T. Barnard and J. Clark, (eds.), *Lord Burlington, Architecure, Art & Life* (London, 1995), p. 163.
223 R. Molesworth to L. Molesworth, 18 May 1717, N.L.I., P 3752.
224 D.A. Chart (ed.), *Clements Mss.,* p. 315: Alessandro Galilei to John Molesworth, 13 June 1721, Florence.
225 Edward Malins and the Knight of Glin, *Lost Demesnes* (London, 1976), p. 16.
226 ibid.
227 Lena Boylan, 'Skeaghgutta or Thornhill', *The Celbridge Charter,* no. 141, May 1985, pp. 10–11.
228 Castletown Account Book, 1767–1775, Bryan Kavanagh's account, 23 January 1773, I.A.A. Uncatalogued Conolly Papers.
229 Castletown Account Book 1775–1781, Bryan Kavanagh's account, 1778, I.A.A. Uncatalogued Conolly Papers.
230 Brian Fitzgerald (ed.), *Correspondence of Emily, Duchess of Leinster,* 3 vols. (Dublin, 1949), vol. 1, p. 145: E. Kildare to J. Kildare, 2 December 1762.

231 Castletown Account Book 1767–1775, 30 April 1774, p. 506, I.A.A. Uncatalogued Conolly Papers.
232 ibid., Bryan Kavanagh's account, 19 February 1774.
233 ibid., 10 August, 15 September, 31 October 1770.
234 ibid., 19 August 1769, p. 292.
235 Edith Mary Johnston-Liik (ed.), *History of the Irish Parliament 1692–1800* (Belfast, 2002), vol. 3, p. 478.
236 K. Conolly to J. Bonnell, 27 November 1732, Dublin, N.L.I., P.C. 434.
237 K. Conolly to J. Bonnell, 14 May 1736, Dublin, N.L.I., P.C. 434.
238 K. Conolly to J. Bonnell, 6 March 1738, Dublin, N.L.I., P.C. 434.
239 K. Conolly to J. Bonnell, 1 August 1738, Dublin, N.L.I., P.C. 434.
240 Lady Ann Conolly to Lord Strafford, 3 January 1733, B.L. Add. Ms. 22,228, N.L.I., P 527.
241 Lady Ann Conolly to Lord Strafford, 8 November 1733, B.L. Add. Ms. 22,228, N.L.I., P 527.
242 See Patrick Eyres, 'Hearts of Oak, Commerce, Empire and the Landscape Garden', *New Arcadian Press,* nos. 35 and 36 (1993), and Simon Schama, *Landscape and Memory* (London, 1995), pp. 135–74.
243 Simon Schama, *Landscape and Memory* (London, 1995), p. 163.
244 Brian Fitzgerald (ed.), *Correspondence of Emily, Duchess of Leinster,* 3 vols. (Dublin, 1949), vol. 1, p. 145: E. Kildare to J. Kildare, 2 December 1762.
245 The area of the woodland extant in c.1768 is itemized on the demesne map of that date (Fig. 27).
246 Arthur Young, *A Tour in Ireland, 1776–1779,* 2 vols., 5th edn. (Shannon, 1780, 1970), vol. i, p. 31.
247 Lady Ann Conolly to Lord Strafford, 5 May 1734, B.L., Add. Ms. 22,228, N.L.I., P 527.
248 Lady Ann Conolly to Lord Strafford, 5 May 1734, B.L., Add. Ms. 22,228, N.L.I., P 527.
249 K. Conolly to J. Bonnell, 6 March, 1738, Dublin, N.L.I., P.C. 434.
250 N. Pevsner, *The Buildings of England,* 46 vols. (Harmondsworth, 1951–74), vol. Yorkshire West Riding, p. 548.
251 Edith Mary Johnston-Liik, *History of the Irish Parliament 1692–1800,* vol. 3, p. 479.
252 L. Conolly to S. Bunbury, née Lennox, January 1776, Castletown Letter Transcripts, Uncatalogued Castletown Papers in the care of Mrs Lena Boylan.
253 Ann Margaret Kelleher, 'The Long Gallery of Castletown House', *Bulletin of the Irish Georgian Society,* vol. 22, 1979, p. 34.
254 ibid., p. 36.
255 Castletown Account Book 1762–1767, Daniel Conolly's account, 31 October 1763, I.A.A. Uncatalogued Conolly Papers.
256 Personal account books of Tom Conolly, 1770, T.C.D., Ms. 3964, 1767–1770.
257 Castletown Account Book 1767–1775, William Golding's account, 24 December 1767, I.A.A. Uncatalogued Conolly Papers.
258 L. Conolly to S. Bunbury, née Lennox, 22 January 1772, I.A.A. The Irish Georgian Society's Uncatalogued Conolly Letters.
259 L. Conolly to S. Bunbury, née Lennox, 26 April 1777, I.A.A. The Irish Georgian Society's Uncatalogued Conolly Letters.
260 Castletown Account Book 1781–*c.*1790, John Coates' account, from November 1st 1783 to May 1st 1784, I.A.A. Uncatologued Conolly Papers.
261 Castletown Account Book 1762–1767, Daniel Conolly's account, 14 April 1764, I.A.A. Uncatologued Conolly Papers.
262 Castletown Account Book 1761–1767, Will Kearin's account, 23 May 1763, I.A.A. Uncatologued Conolly Papers.
263 L. Conolly to S. Lennox, 16 March 1765, I.A.A. The Irish Georgian Society's Uncatalogued Conolly Letters.
264 L. Conolly to S. Lennox, 17 September 1764, I.A.A. The Irish Georgian Society's Uncatalogued Conolly Letters.
265 Arthur Young, *A Tour in Ireland, 1776–1779,* vol. 1, p. 30.
266 This view is at present almost concealed by the mature trees, but would have been clearly visible in the eighteenth century from selected view-points.
267 Brian Fitzgerald (ed.), *Correspondence of Emily, Duchess of Leinster,* 3 vols., vol. 3, p. 408: L. Conolly to E. Kildare, 7 August 1794.
268 Micheal Symes, *The English Rococo Garden* (Princes Risborough, Buckinghamshire, 1991), p. 62.
269 L. Conolly to S. Lennox, undated, I.A.A. The Irish Georgian Society's Uncatalogued Conolly Letters.
270 L. Conolly to S. Lennox, 2 October 1778, I.A.A. The Irish Georgian Society's Uncatalogued Conolly Letters.
271 Castletown Account Book 1775–1781, p. 192: Edward Byrnes's account, 28 July 1778, I.A.A. Uncatalogued Conolly Papers.
272 ibid., p. 380: Richard Jenkinson's account, 1780.
273 L. Conolly to S. Lennox, 17 August 1776, I.A.A. The Irish Georgian Society's Uncatalogued Conolly Letters.
274 Brian Fitzgerald (ed.), *Correspondence of Emily, Duchess of Leinster,* 3 vols., vol. 3, p. 408: Emily, Marchioness of Kildare, to James, Marquess of Kildare, 7 December 1762.
275 William Gilpin, *Observations on Several Parts of Great Britain, particurlarly the Mountains and Lakes of Cumberland and Westmoreland, relative chiefly to Picturesque Beauty Made in the Year 1772* (London, 1808), 2 vols., vol. 2, p. 122.
276 A.M. Lewin Robinson (ed.), *The letters of Lady Anne Barnard to Henry Dundas from the Cape and Elsewhere* 1793–1803 (Cape Town, 1973), p. 7. I am indebted to Desmond Fitzgerald, the Knight of Glin for this reference.
277 L. Conolly to S. Lennox, 5 May 1767, I.A.A. The Irish Georgian Society's Uncatalogued Conolly Letters.
278 L. Conolly to S. Bunbury, née Lennox, 25 May 1768, I.A.A. The Irish Georgian Society's Uncatalogued Conolly Letters.
279 I.A.A. Uncatalogued Conolly Papers.
280 Dean Bernard to Mr Glascock, Dublin, 8 April 1796, I.A.A. Uncatalogued Conolly Papers: 'Some time ago Mr. Warburton called on me by your desire with the purchase deeds for that piece of ground Mr. Conolly rents from me; I signed them and he carried them away with him.' This piece of ground is presumably that of the earlier indenture.
281 I am indebted to Mrs Lena Boylan for this information. She did not succeed and this right of way is still in existence.
282 Thomas Whateley, *Observations on Modern Gardening* (Dublin, 1770), p. 93.
283 ibid., p. 95
284 The term 'Gothick' denotes the eighteenth-century pastiche style. The use of 'gothic' denotes authentic medieval ruins. Capitalization of 'gothic' as in 'Gothic Revival' or 'Gothic Walk' is used as an umbrella term and may indicate an amalgamation of both.
285 Castletown Account Book 1767–1775, p. 292: Bryan Kavanagh's account, 25 November 1769, I.A.A. Uncatologued Conolly Papers.
286 Castletown Account Book 1781–c.1790, p. 369: John Coates' account, 1784, I.A.A. Uncatalogued Conolly Papers.
287 Barbara Jones, *Follies and Grottoes* (London, 1989), p. 221.
288 The existing ruin's footprint of 4.15m by 3.2m (13' 8" x 10' 6") is somewhat smaller than Louisa's design.
289 L. Conolly to S. Lennox, 19 November 1778, I.A.A. The Irish Georgian Society's Uncatalogued Conolly Letters.
290 Castletown Account Books, Book 1775–1781, p. 444: John Coates' account, May to October 1781, I.A.A. Uncatologued Conolly Papers.
291 ibid., p. 306: Richard Jenkinson's account, 1 November 1778 to 1 May 1779, p. 306.

292 L. Conolly's personal account book, 8 May 1771, T.C.D. Ms. 3960.
293 Charles Mc Intosh, *The Book of the Garden* (London, 1853), pp. 500, 504.
294 Castletown Account Book 1775–1781, p. 306: Richard Jenkinson's account, I.A.A. Uncatologued Conolly Papers.
295 ibid., p. 372: Thomas Tilbury's accounts, 1779.
296 Castletown Account Book 1781–1790, p. 459: John Coates' accounts, 1786, I.A.A. Uncatologued Conolly Papers.
297 Brian Fitzgerald (ed.), *Correspondence of Emily, Duchess of Leinster,* 3 vols., vol. 3, p. 243: L. Conolly to E. Kildare, 5 December 1776, Castletown.
298 David Stewart, 'Political Ruins, Gothic Sham Ruins and the '45', *Journal of the Society of Architectural Historians,* vol. 55, no. 4, December 1996, p. 400.
299 Horace Walpole, *The History of the Modern Taste in Gardening* (New York, 1995), p. 55.
300 David Stewart, 'Political Ruins, Gothic Sham Ruins and the '45', p. 400.
301 Miscellaneous letters (undated), I.A.A. The Irish Georgian Society's Uncatalogued Conolly Letters.
302 W.S. Lewis (ed.), *Horace Wadpole's Correspondence,* vol. 39 (London, 1974), p. 72, vol. 7 (London, 1939), pp. 38, 451.
303 W.S. Lewis (ed.), *Horace Wadpole's Correspondence,* vol. 37 (London, 1974), p. 428.
304 M.J. Charlesworth, 'The Wentworths – Family and Political Rivalry in the English Landscape Garden', *Garden History, The Journal of the Garden History Society,* vol. 14, no. 2, p. 131.
305 L. Conolly to S. Lennox, 19 August 1759, Wentworth Castle, I.A.A. The Irish Georgian Society's Uncatalogued Conolly Letters.
306 S. Copley and P. Garside (eds), *The Politics of the Picturesque* (1994), p. 71.
307 ibid., p. 69.
308 ibid., p. 75.
309 I am indebted to Desmond Fitzgerald, the Knight of Glin, for bringing this painting to my notice.
310 David Stewart, 'Political Ruins, Gothic Sham Ruins and the '45', p. 408.
311 Uvedale Price, *Sir Uvedale Price on the Picturesque:* with *An Essay on the Origin of Taste, and much original matter, by Sir Thomas Dick Lauder* (London, 1846), p. 366.
312 William Gilpin, *Observations on Several Parts of Great Britain, particularly the Mountains and Lakes of Cumberland and Westmoreland, relative chiefly to Picturesque Beauty Made in the Year 1772* (London, 1808), 2 vols., vol. 2, p. 122–3.
313 Thomas Whateley, *Observations on Modern Gardening,* p. 94.
314 L. Conolly to S. Bunbury née Lennox, 25 May 1768, I.A.A. The Irish Georgian Society's Uncatalogued Conolly Letters.
315 L. Conolly to S. Lennox, 22 March 1759, I.A.A. The Irish Georgian Society's Uncatalogued Conolly Letters.
316 Castletown Account Book 1761–1767, p. 105: Isaac Annesley's account, I.A.A. Uncatologued Conolly Papers.
317 L. Conolly to S. Bunbury, née Lennox, 23 June 1764, I.A.A. The Irish Georgian Society's Uncatalogued Conolly Letters.
318 Louisa Conolly to Sarah Bunbury, née Lennox, 29 June 1764, I.A.A. The Irish Georgian Society's Uncatalogued Conolly Letters.
319 Louisa Conolly to Sarah Lennox, 16 June 1761, I.A.A. The Irish Georgian Society's Uncatalogued Conolly Letters.
320 Louisa Conolly to Sarah Napier, née Lennox, 10 June 1795, I.A.A. The Irish Georgian Society's Uncatalogued Conolly Letters.
321 Louisa Conolly to Sarah Napier, née Lennox, undated, I.A.A. The Irish Georgian Society's Uncatalogued Conolly Letters.
322 Louisa Conolly to Sarah Bunbury, née Lennox, 28 May 1772, I.A.A. The Irish Georgian Society's Uncatalogued Conolly Letters.
323 L. Conolly to S. Bunbury, née Lennox, 30 August 1772, I.A.A. The Irish Georgian Society's Uncatalogued Conolly Letters.
324 Batty Langley's *Gothic Architecture Improved by Rules and Proportions* (London, 1747), plate LVII: the plate is marked Batty Langley Invt. 1742.
325 Castletown Account Book 1781–1790, p. 412: John Coates's account, I.A.A. Uncatologued Conolly Papers.
326 ibid.
327 William Chambers, *A Dissertation on Oriental Gardening* (London, 1972), p. 90.
328 Castletown Account Book 1767–1775, p. 349: Daniel Bullen's account, I.A.A. Uncatologued Conolly Papers.
329 Dora Wiebenson, *The Picturesque Garden in France* (Princeton, 1978), explores the popularity of Chambers and Whateley on the Continent.
330 Louisa and Emily's grandfather, the first Duke of Richmond, was the illegitimate son of Charles II and his French mistress Louise de Kéroualle, Duchess of Portsmouth. The Aubigny chateau, which Emily moved to in 1774, came into the Richmond family from Louise de Kéroualle.
331 Brian Fitzgerald (ed.), *Correspondence of Emily, Duchess of Leinster,* 3 vols., vol. 1, p. 494: Lady Caroline Fox to E. Kildare, 12/13 January 1767, Naples.
332 ibid., p. 408, Lady Caroline Fox to E. Kildare, 4 September 1764, Holland House.
333 ibid., p. 130, L. Conolly to Emily, Dowager Duchess of Leinster, 30 April 1775.
334 L. Conolly to S. Bunbury, née Lennox, 15 July 1778, I.A.A. The Irish Georgian Society's Uncatalogued Conolly Letters.
335 Brian Fitzgerald (ed.), *Correspondence of Emily, Duchess of Leinster,* 3 vols., vol. 1, p. 321: L. Conolly to Emily, Dowager Duchess of Leinster, 18 October 1778.
336 Dora Wiebenson, *The Picturesque Garden in France,* p. 99.
337 David Coffin, *The English Garden, Meditation and Memorial* (Chichester, 1994), Introduction.
338 L. Conolly to S. Bunbury, née Lennox, August or September 1762, I.A.A. The Irish Georgian Society's Uncatalogued Conolly Letters.
339 Castletown Account Book 1781–*c.*1790, p. 369: John Coates's account, 1784, I.A.A. Uncatologued Conolly Papers.
340 Castletown Account Book 1767–1775, p. 292: Bryan Kavanagh's account, 30 April 1769, I.A.A. Uncatologued Conolly Papers.
341 L. Conolly to S. Napier, née Lennox, 1 October 1783, I.A.A. The Irish Georgian Society's Uncatalogued Conolly Letters.
342 Tradesmen's Accounts Book 3, no. 163, T.C.D., Ms. 3941.
343 Castletown Account Books 1775–1781 & 1781–1790: Denis Tilbery & Thomas Tilbury's accounts, I.A.A. Uncatalogued Conolly Papers.
344 Castletown Account Book 1767–1775: William Golding's account, 1767, I.A.A. Uncatalogued Conolly Papers.
345 ibid., Bryan Kavanagh's account, April 1770.
346 Tradesmen's Accounts Book 3, no. 98, T.C.D., Ms. 3941.
347 Philip Miller, *The Gardeners Dictionary* (London, 1737), from the section on the Kitchen Garden.
348 Green book of accounts, 19 April 1776, I.A.A. Uncatalogued Conolly Papers.
349 Castletown Account Book 1767–1775, p. 526: Daniel Bullen's account, I.A.A. Uncatologued Conolly Papers.
350 Thomas Whateley, *Observations on Modern Gardening,* p. 85.
351 L. Conolly to S. Bunbury, née Lennox, 25 March 1777, I.A.A. Conolly Letters.

352 Finola O'Kane, 'Mixing Foreign Trees with the Natives: Irish Demese Landscape in the Eighteenth Century', Ph.D. thesis, NUI, 1999, vol. 2/2: Appendix 5: 'Books present in the Castletown and Carton Libraries which may have influenced their development from Castletown Library Catalogue', T.C.D., Ms. 3960, Carton Library Catalogue, NLI, Ms. 14923.
353 John Walker, *Essay on Plantations of Trees presented by John Walker to Lady Louisa Conolly,* 1809, N.L.I., Ms. 15,397.
354 L. Conolly to S. Bunbury, née Lennox, 7 September 1767, I.A.A. The Irish Georgian Society's Uncatalogued Conolly Letters.
355 Brian Fitzgerald (ed.), *Correspondence of Emily, Duchess of Leinster,* 3 vols., vol. 3, p. 23: L. Conolly to E. Kildare, 28 July 1750.
356 William Chambers, *A Dissertation on Oriental Gardening,* p. x.
357 ibid., p. 20.
358 ibid., p. 50.
359 ibid., p. 18.
360 ibid., p. 81.
361 ibid., p. 83.
362 ibid., p. 70.
363 Thomas Whateley, *Observations on Modern Gardening.* The exact edition of the Castletown copy is not recorded in the Castletown Library catalogue: T.C.D., Ms. 3960.
364 ibid., p. 41.
365 ibid., p. 49.
366 ibid., p. 56.
367 ibid., p. 55.
368 ibid., p. 72.
369 ibid., pp. 24–25.
370 Castletown Account Book 1762–1764, p. 134: Aaron Hicholl's account, 17 March 1763, I.A.A. Uncatalogued Conolly Papers.
371 Lena Boylan, 'The Conollys of Castletown', *Quarterly Bulletin of the Irish Georgian Society,* vol. 11, no. 4, p. 43.
372 Brian Fitzgerald (ed.), *Correspondence of Emily, Duchess of Leinster,* 3 vols., vol. 3, p. 410: L. Conolly to E., Dowager Duchess of Leinster, 29 December 1787.
373 ibid., p. 410: L. Conolly to E, Dowager Duchess of Leinster, 29 December 1787.
374 L. Conolly to T. Conolly, 1 October 1796, I.A.A. The Irish Georgian Society's Uncatalogued Conolly Letters.
375 Castletown Account Books 1767–1775: Thomas Kavanagh's account, 30 July 1767, I.A.A. Uncatalogued Conolly Papers.
376 Tradesmen's Accounts Book 2, no. 262, 7 April 1790, T.C.D., Ms 3940.
377 Castletown Account Book 1781–1790, p. 325: John Stokes' account, I.A.A. Uncatalogued Conolly Papers.
378 K. Conolly to J. Bonnell, 18 April 1730, Dublin, N.L.I., P.C. 434.
379 K. Conolly to J. Bonnell, 15 January 1739, Dublin, N.L.I., P.C. 434.
380 K. Conolly to J. Bonnell, 10 August 1742, Dublin, N.L.I., P.C. 434.
381 K. Conolly to J. Bonnell, 10 May 1740, Dublin, N.L.I., P.C. 434.
382 L. Conolly to S. Bunbury, née Lennox, undated, I.A.A. The Irish Georgian Society's Uncatalogued Conolly Letters.
383 L. Conolly to S. Lennox, 1 October 1783, I.A.A. The Irish Georgian Society's Uncatalogued Conolly Letters.
384 L. Conolly to S. Lennox, 10 August 1778, I.A.A. The Irish Georgian Society's Uncatalogued Conolly Letters.
385 L. Conolly to George Napier, 3 October 1820, I.A.A. The Irish Georgian Society's Uncatalogued Conolly Letters.
386 L. Conolly to S. Lennox, 17 May 1768, I.A.A. The Irish Georgian Society's Uncatalogued Conolly Letters.
387 L. Conolly to S. Lennox, 20 August 1778, I.A.A. The Irish Georgian Society's Uncatalogued Conolly Letters.
388 L. Conolly to S. Lennox, 2 October 1778, I.A.A. The Irish Georgian Society's Uncatalogued Conolly Letters.
389 L. Conolly to S. Lennox, 28 December 1778, I.A.A. The Irish Georgian Society's Uncatalogued Conolly Letters.
390 L. Conolly to S. Lennox, 1 October 1783, I.A.A. The Irish Georgian Society's Uncatalogued Conolly Letters.
391 L. Conolly to S. Lennox, May 1774, I.A.A. The Irish Georgian Society's Uncatalogued Conolly Letters.
392 L. Conolly to S. Lennox, 30 July 1776, I.A.A. The Irish Georgian Society's Uncatalogued Conolly Letters.
393 Brian Fitzgerald (ed.), *Correspondence of Emily, Duchess of Leinster,* 3 vols., vol. 3, p. 218: L. Conolly to E., Dowager Duchess of Leinster, 23 August 1778.
394 Personal Account Book of Lady Louisa Conolly, 1766–1775, T.C.D., Ms. 3966.
395 L. Conolly to S. Lennox, 16 July 1761, I.A.A. The Irish Georgian Society's Uncatalogued Conolly Letters.
396 Brian Fitzgerald (ed.), *Correspondence of Emily, Duchess of Leinster,* 3 vols., vol. 3, p. 410: L. Conolly to E., Dowager Duchess of Leinster, 19 December 1787.
397 'Copy to Mr. Burgh about House at Dromoland & changes required pres. From Lady Catherine O'Brien', 1717[?], N.L.I., Folder 1830, Inchiquin Mss.
398 Mrs Catherine O'Brien's account with Sir Edward O'Brien 1719–1722, p. 30, N.L.I., Inchiquin Mss., Ms. 14,369.
399 Patrick Bowe and Keith Lamb, *A History of Gardening in Ireland* (Dublin, 1995), p. 28.
400 Elizabeth Hughes, 'A Book of Reaseat', Four Folders of Miscellaneous Recipes, Folder 1, N.L.I., P.C. 434.
401 L. Conolly to S. Bunbury, née Lennox, 13 June 1778, I.A.A. The Irish Georgian Society's Uncatalogued Conolly Letters.
402 L. Conolly to S. Bunbury, née Lennox, 26 April 1777, I.A.A. The Irish Georgian Society's Uncatalogued Conolly Letters.
403 K. Conolly to J. Bonnell, 24 September, 1739, N.L.I., P.C. 434.
404 Ian Campbell Ross (ed.), *Public Virtue, Public Love: The Early Years of the Dublin Lying-in Hospital, The Rotunda* (Dublin, 1986), pp. 10–11.

## Chapter 3

405 Brian Fitzgerald (ed.), *Correspondence of Emily, Duchess of Leinster,* 3 vols., vol. 1, p. 46: 24 June 1757, Emily Kildare to James Kildare.
406 Lord Walter Fitzgerald, 'Carton', *Journal of the County Kildare Archaeological Society,* vol. 4, no. 1, 1903, p. 5.
407 ibid., p. 12.
408 Arnold Horner, 'Carton, Co. Kildare', *Bulletin of the Irish Georgian Society,* vol. 18, nos. 2 and 3, 1975, p. 49.
409 David Jacques and Jan van der Horst, *The Gardens of William and Mary* (London, 1988), p. 96.
410 ibid., p. 95.
411 Henry Ingoldsby to William Smythe, 21 January 1716, N.L.I., P.C. 445.
412 Lord Walter Fitzgerald, 'Carton', *Journal of the County Kildare Archaeological Society,* vol. 4, no. 1, 1903, p. 12.

413 Toby Barnard, *The Abduction of a Limerick Heiress: Social and Political Relations in Mid-Eighteenth-Century Ireland* (Dublin, 1996), p. 18.
414 Henry Ingoldsby to William Smythe, 3 April 1716, 4 February 1718, 8 February 1724 [2 & 4], N.L.I., P.C. 445.
415 Henry Ingoldsby to William Smythe, 12 November 1723 [4], N.L.I., P.C. 445.
416 Henry Ingoldsby to William Smythe, 18 January 1724 [4], N.L.I., P.C. 445.
417 Henry Ingoldsby to William Smythe, 3 April 1716 [3], N.L.I., P.C. 445.
418 Henry Ingoldsby to William Smythe, 31 December 1724 [4], N.L.I., P.C. 445.
419 Henry Ingoldsby to William Smythe, 19 March 1719 [4], N.L.I., P.C. 445.
420 Henry Ingoldsby to William Smythe, 22 January 1724 [4], N.L.I., P.C. 445.
421 Henry Ingoldsby to William Smythe, 18 January 1724 [4], N.L.I., P.C. 445.
422 Henry Ingoldsby to William Smythe, 8 February 1724 [4], N.L.I., P.C. 445.
423 Henry Ingoldsby to William Smythe, 22 January 1724 [4], N.L.I., P.C. 445.
424 Henry Ingoldsby to William Smythe, 19 March 1724 [4], N.L.I., P.C. 445.
425 Jan Woudstra, 'The Planting of the Privy Garden', in Simon Thurley (ed.), *The Privy Garden at Hampton Court Palace* (London, 1995) p. 44.
426 See Simon Thurley (ed.), *The Privy Garden at Hampton Court Palace* (London, 1995), and David Jacques and Jan van der Horst, *The Gardens of William and Mary* (London, 1988).
427 John Dixon Hunt, 'Reckoning with Dutch Gardens', in 'The Anglo-Dutch Garden in the Age of William and Mary', *Journal of Garden History,* vol. 8, nos. 2 and 3, April–September 1988, p. 53.
428 David Jacques and Jan van der Horst, *The Gardens of William and Mary,* p. 158.
429 ibid., p. 95.
430 John Dixon Hunt, 'Reckoning with Dutch Gardens', in 'The Anglo-Dutch Garden in the Age of William and Mary', *Journal of Garden History,* vol. 8, nos. 2 and 3, April–September 1988, p. 44.
431 Baylie and Mooney, 'Map of Carton Demesne', 1744, N.L.I., Ms. 22,500.
432 Toby Barnard, *The Abduction of a Limerick Heiress: Social and Political Relations in Mid-Eighteenth-Century Ireland,* p. 18.
433 1713 Listing of Irish MPs income. British Library, Additional Ms. 61637, f.3. I am indebted to Dr Toby Barnard for this information.
434 Edith Mary Johnston-Liik, *History of the Irish Parliament 1692–1800,* vol. 3, p. 474.
435 ibid., p. 477.
436 John Dixon Hunt, 'Reckoning with Dutch Gardens', in 'The Anglo-Dutch Garden in the Age of William and Mary', *Journal of Garden History,* vol. 8, nos. 2 and 3, April–September 1988, p. 56.
437 Simon Schama, *The Embarrassment of Riches* (London, 1987), p. 35.
438 John Dixon Hunt, 'Reckoning with Dutch Gardens', in 'The Anglo-Dutch Garden in the Age of William and Mary', *Journal of Garden History,* vol. 8, nos. 2 and 3, April–September 1988, p. 53.
439 R. Molesworth to L. Molesworth, 7 January 1720, N.L.I., P. 3752.
440 Richard Castle, *Essay on Artificial Navigation,* N.L.I., Ms. 2737. This manuscript was once in the Carton library.
441 Christine Casey, 'Eighteenth Century Architecture in Ireland, A Bibliographical Approach' (unpulished Ph.D. thesis, Trinity College Dublin, 1992), p. 207.
442 Richard Castle, *Essay on Artificial Navigation,* N.L.I., Ms. 2737.
443 John Dixon Hunt, 'Reckoning with Dutch Gardens', in 'The Anglo-Dutch Garden in the Age of William and Mary', *Journal of Garden History,* vol. 8, nos. 2 and 3, April–September 1988, p. 56.
444 Arnold Horner, 'Carton, Co. Kildare', *Bulletin of the Irish Georgian Society,* vol. 18, nos. 2 and 3, 1975, p. 102: note 31: Registry of Deeds, Dublin. Memorial 90-461-65674. Ingoldsby to Kildare, Date of Lease 27 January 1738–9.
445 ibid., p. 14. Lord Walter also referred to 'the Original Account Book (at Carton) which gives the expenditure, labourers' wages etc. of the works in progress in 1739'. Unfortunately the whereabouts of the Carton estate accounts are presently unknown.
446 Mary, nineteenth Countess of Kildare, née Mary O'Brien, daughter of William, third Earl of Inchiquin (1693–1780), married Robert, nineteenth Earl of Kildare, on 7 March 1708.
447 Lord Walter Fitzgerald, 'Carton', *Journal of the County Kildare Archaeological Society,* vol. 4, no. 1, 1903, p. 16.
448 Mary, Dowager nineteenth Countess of Kildare, to Emily, twentieth Countess of Kildare, undated, N.L.I., Ms. 629.
449 Mary, Dowager nineteenth Countess of Kildare, to Emily, twentieth Countess of Kildare, 3 October 1778. N.L.I., Ms. 629.
450 Arnold Horner, 'Carton, Co. Kildare', in *Bulletin of the Irish Georgian Society,* vol. 18, nos. 2 and 3, 1975, p. 70.
451 ibid., p. 66.
452 ibid., p. 64.
453 ibid., p. 70.
454 Desmond Guinness and William Ryan, *Irish Houses and Castles* (London, 1971), p. 186.
455 Lord Walter Fitzgerald, 'Carton', *Journal of the County Kildare Archaeological Society,* vol. 4, no. 1, 1903, p. 16.
456 Emily, Duchess of Leinster, to Lady Caroline Fox, undated, British Library, Add. Mss. 51426.
457 Desmond Guinness and William Ryan, Irish Houses and Castles (London, 1971), p. 186.
458 Lord Walter Fitzgerald, 'Carton', *Journal of the County Kildare Archaeological Society,* vol. 4, no. 1, 1903, p. 16: Drawing, *'The Proposed Restoration of the House at Carton by James, 20th Earl of Kildare, in 1762.'*
459 Brian Fitzgerald (ed.), *Correspondence of Emily, Duchess of Leinster,* 3 vols., vol. 1, p. 76: Emily Kildare to James Kildare, 9 May 1759, Brockley Park.
460 ibid., p. 129, James Kildare to Emily Kildare, 11 May 1762.
461 Dorothy Stroud, *Capability Brown* (London, 1950), p. 200. Unfortunately, no reference is given for this quotation.
462 James Kildare to Emily Kildare, 10 June 1766, P.R.O.N.I., T3092/1/4.
463 James Kildare to Henry Fox, 2 August 1750, Carton, British Library, Add. Mss. 51426.
464 James Kildare to Emily Kildare, 10 June 1766, P.R.O.N.I., T3092/1/4.
465 'Section thro' the Vale where the Bridge is to be Built at Carton', June 1763, N.L.I., Ms. 22, 504. The whereabouts of the 'Levels of the Rye River' is unknown to the author.
466 Arnold Horner, 'Carton, Co. Kildare', *Bulletin of the Irish Georgian Society,* vol. 18, nos. 2 and 3, 1975, p. 100.
467 Brian Fitzgerald (ed.), *Correspondence of Emily, Duchess of Leinster,* 3 vols., vol. 3, p. 526: William, Marquess of Kildare, to his mother Emily, Countess of Kildare, 29 June 1768, Turin.
468 Dorothy Stroud, *Capability Brown,* p. 19.
469 D.D.C. Chambers, *The Planters of the English Landscape Garden* (London, 1993), p. 82.
470 Thomas Hinde, *Capability Brown,* The Story of a Master Gardener (London, 1986), p. 38.
471 James Kildare to Emily Kildare, 25 June? 1766, P.R.O.N.I., T3092/1/1.
472 Michael Symes, 'The Hon. Charles Hamilton at Holland Park', *Journal of Garden History,* vol. 3, no. 2, p. 130.
473 D.D.C. Chambers, *The Planters of the English Landscape Garden,* p. 100.
474 Brian Fitzgerald (ed.), *Correspondence of Emily, Duchess of Leinster,* 3 vols., vol. 1, p. 408: Caroline Fox to Emily Kildare, 4 September 1764, Holland House.
475 ibid., p. 412: Caroline Fox to Emily Kildare, 20 September 1764.
476 ibid., p. 408: Caroline Fox to Emily Kildare, 4 September 1764.
477 Penelope Hobhouse, *Plants in Garden History* (London, 1994), p. 208.
478 Brian Fitzgerald (ed.), *Correspondence of Emily, Duchess of Leinster,* 3 vols., vol. 1, p. 46: Emily Kildare to James Kildare, 12 June 1757, Park Place.

479 The paper referred to was not found among the Leinster papers in the N.L.I.
480 D.C.C. Chambers, *The Planters of the English Landscape Garden* (London, 1993), p. 98.
481 Diary of Gerald Fitzgerald subsequently fifth Duke of Leinster 1862–1863 (b. 1851, d. 1893), N.L.I., Ms. 18,852.
482 Brian Fitzgerald (ed.), *Correspondence of Emily, Duchess of Leinster,* 3 vols., vol. 1, p. 76: James Kildare to Emily Kildare, 9 May 1759, Brockley Park.
483 ibid., pp. 105–6: James Kildare to Emily Kildare, 22 August 1761.
484 ibid., p. 150: James Kildare to Emily Kildare, 10 December 1762.
485 See Michael Symes, *The English Rococo Garden,* op. cit.
486 William Richards, *Plan of Carton House and Offices,* 1758, N.L.I., Ms.22,503.
487 Brian Fitzgerald (ed.), *Correspondence of Emily, Duchess of Leinster,* 3 vols., vol. 1, p. 52: Emily Kildare to James Kildare, 21 June 1757, Park Place.
488 ibid., p. 54: Emily Kildare to James Kildare, 24 June 1757.
489 *Journal of Horticulture and Cottage Gardener,* 16 May 1872, p. 407.
490 Brian Fitzgerald (ed.), *Correspondence of Emily, Duchess of Leinster,* 3 vols., vol. 1, p. 52: Emily Kildare to James Kildare, 24 June 1757.
491 Chambers, *The Planters of the English Landscape Garden* (1993), pp. 39–41.
492 Brian Fitzgerald (ed.), *Correspondence of Emily, Duchess of Leinster,* 3 vols., vol. 1, p. 39: Emily Kildare to James Kildare, 31 May 1757.
493 Michael Symes, 'The Hon. Charles Hamilton at Holland Park', *Journal of Garden History,* vol. 3, no. 2, p. 132.
494 James Kildare to Henry Fox, 2 August 1750, Carton, British Library Add. Mss.51426. The location or existence of these directions is not known to the author.
495 Michael Symes, 'The Hon. Charles Hamilton at Holland Park', *Journal of Garden History,* vol. 3, no. 2, p. 133.
496 Quoted in the Painshill guidebook as 'Thomas Whateley, 1770'.
497 Brian Fitzgerald (ed.), *Correspondence of Emily, Duchess of Leinster,* 3 vols., vol. 1, p. 122: Emily Kildare to James Kildare, 14 April 1762.
498 ibid., p. 150: Emily Kildare to James Kildare, 10 December 1762.
499 ibid., p. 156: Emily Kildare to James Kildare, 16 December 1762.
500 L. Conolly to S. Bunbury, née Lennox, 28 August 1771, I.A.A. The Irish Georgian Society's Uncatalogued Conolly Letters.
501 L. Conolly to S. Bunbury, née Lennox, 17 September 1771, I.A.A. The Irish Georgian Society's Uncatalogued Conolly Letters.
502 Brian Fitzgerald (ed.), *Correspondence of Emily, Duchess of Leinster,* 3 vols., vol. 3, p. 139: L. Conolly to Emily, Dowager Duchess of Leinster, 25 June 1775.
503 Lord Walter Fitzgerald, 'Carton', *Journal of the County Kildare Archaeological Society,* vol. 4, no. 1, 1903, p. 18.
504 Lord Walter Fitzgerald, 'Carton', *Journal of the County Kildare Archaeological Society,* vol. 4, no. 1, 1903: W. Steile, *A Map of Waterstown in the Parish of Laraghbrian, Manor of Maynooth and County of Kildare belonging to Mr. Richard Nelson,* 1736.
505 L. Conolly to S. Bunbury, née Lennox, 9 May 1766, I.A.A. The Irish Georgian Society's Uncatalogued Conolly Letters.
506 Brian Fitzgerald (ed.), *Correspondence of Emily, Duchess of Leinster,* 3 vols., vol. 3, p. 129: L. Conolly to Emily, Dowager Duchess of Leinster, 30 April 1775.
507 L. Conolly to S. Bunbury, née Lennox, 25 May 1768, I.A.A. The Irish Georgian Society's Uncatalogued Conolly Letters.
508 Mona O'Rourke, *Transcript of extracts from the Bolger papers relating to building work at Carton House 1815–1825,* I.A.A.
509 *Journal of Horticulture and Cottage Gardener,* 17 February 1863, p. 131.
510 Barbara Jones, *Follies and Grottoes,* p. 156.
511 Stella Tillyard, *Aristocrats: Caroline, Emily, Louisa and Sarah Lennox 1740–1832* (London, 1994), pp. 196–8. In this recent biography of the Lennox sisters the author constructs an elaborate story about the meaning of the cottage's construction and its decoration with shells. It may be that she has some unrevealed source to prove this assertion but, as no footnotes or references are included, she too may be perpetuating the Goodwood myth.
512 Mona O'Rourke, *Transcript of extracts from the Bolger papers relating to building work at Carton House 1815–1825,* 11 August 1821, I.A.A.
513 *Journal of Horticulture and Cottage Gardener,* 17 February 1863, p. 131.
514 Brian Fitzgerald (ed.), *Correspondence of Emily, Duchess of Leinster,* 3 vols., vol. 1, p. 150: Emily Kildare to James Kildare, 10 December 1762.
515 Tom Conolly's Personal Account Book, T.C.D., Mss. 3963: '1766, February 5th, Paid Louisa on account of her Xmas Pin Money: £125,0,0.'
516 Lena Boylan, 'Castletown and its Owners, Parts 1 & 2', *Bulletin of the Irish Georgian Society,* 1968, p. 22.
517 ibid., p. 59.
518 Thomas Conolly's 'List', 4 March 1773, T.C.D., Mss. 3974–3984a, no. 381.
519 Edith Mary Johnston-Liik (ed.), *History of the Irish Parliament 1692–1800,* vol. 3, p. 472.
520 ibid., p. 473.
521 ibid., p. 474.
522 Toby Barnard, 'Public and Private Uses of Wealth in Ireland, c.1660–1760', in Jacqueline Hill and Colm Lennon (eds.), *Luxury and Austerity,* p. 68.
523 Brian Fitzgerald (ed.), *Correspondence of Emily, Duchess of Leinster,* 3 vols., vol. 1, pp. 163–4: Emily Kildare to James Kildare, 23 December 1762.
524 Edith Mary Johnston-Liik (ed.), *History of the Irish Parliament 1692–1800,* vol. 3, p. 149.
525 A.P.W. Malcolmson, *The Pursuit of the Heiress: Aristocratic Marriage in Ireland 1750–1820* (Antrim, 1982), pp. 4, 9–10.
526 Edith Mary Johnston-Liik (ed.), *History of the Irish Parliament 1692–1800,* vol. 3, p. 473.
527 Thomas Conolly to anonymous uncle, 19 November 1786, T.C.D., Mss. 3974–3984a, no. 912.
528 Mark Bence-Jones, *A Guide to Irish Country Houses* (London, 1988), p. 245.
529 Brian Fitzgerald (ed.), *Correspondence of Emily, Duchess of Leinster,* 3 vols., vol. 3, p. 398: L. Conolly to Emily, Dowager Duchess of Leinster, 9 March 1787.
530 A.P.W. Malcolmson, *John Foster and the Politics of the Anglo-Irish Ascendancy* (Oxford, 1978), p. 2.
531 Thomas Conolly to anonymous uncle, 19 November 1786, T.C.D., Mss. 3974–3984a, no. 912.
532 L. Conolly to S. Bunbury, née Lennox, 8 October 1777, I.A.A. The Irish Georgian Society's Uncatalogued Conolly Letters.
533 Brian Fitzgerald (ed.), *Correspondence of Emily, Duchess of Leinster,* 3 vols., vol. 1, p. 71: Emily Kildare to James Kildare, 18 April 1759.
534 ibid., p. 218: Caroline Fox to Emily Kildare, 8 May 1759.
535 C.D.A. Leighton, *Catholics in a Protestant Kingdom, A Study of the Irish Ancien Regime,* p. 118.
536 Brian Fitzgerald (ed.), *Correspondence of Emily, Duchess of Leinster,* 3 vols., vol. 3, p. 391: L. Conolly to Emily, Dowager Duchess of Leinster, 10 December 1786.
537 Patrick Bowe and Keith Lamb, *A History of Gardening in Ireland,* p. 28
538 Peter O'Sullivan (ed.), *Newcastle Lyons, A Parish of the Pale* (Dublin, 1986), p. 139.
539 Patricia Cashen, 'Valentine, Lord Cloncurry and his Collection at Lyons' (unpublished M.A. thesis, U.C.D., 1986), p. 119.
540 Valentine Cloncurry to Thomas Ryan, Rome, 28 April 1804, N.L.I., Ms. 8492 [4].
541 Valentine Cloncurry to Thomas Ryan, Rome, 16 April 1803, N.L.I., Ms. 8492.
542 Valentine Cloncurry to Thomas Ryan, Rome, 19 May 1803, N.L.I., Ms. 8492.
543 Valentine Cloncurry to Thomas Ryan, Rome, 5 April 1803, N.L.I., Ms. 8492.

## Chapter 4

544 Jean-Jacques Rousseau, *Émile* (London, 1995), p. 382.
545 In 1766 Emily had nine children and four more children were born in the next seven years.
546 Brian Fitzgerald (ed.), *Correspondence of Emily, Duchess of Leinster,* 3 vols., vol. 1, p. 521: Caroline Fox to Emily Kildare, 19 September 1767, Holland House.
547 ibid., p. 418: Caroline Fox to Emily Kildare, November 1764.
548 ibid., p. 410: Caroline Fox to Emily Kildare, 8 September 1764, Holland House.
549 ibid., vol. 1, p. 139: Emily Kildare to James, 20 November 1762.
550 The title *Sur l'éducation or Traité d'Education* was used by Rousseau as an alternative title for the novel *Émile.* The book was first published in May 1762 and Caroline must have acquired a very early copy.
551 Brian Fitzgerald (ed.), *Correspondence of Emily, Duchess of Leinster,* 3 vols., vol. 1, p. 336: Caroline Fox to Emily Kildare, 8 August 1762, Kingsgate.
552 The following books by Rousseau were listed in the Carton Library Catalogue, 1874, N.L.I., Ms. 14923, with their dates and places of publication:
*Oeuvres* (London, 1774);
*Oeuvres* (Amsterdam, 1769);
*Nouvelle Heloise* (Amsterdam, 1761);
*Emilius* (London, 1762).
The Castletown Library Catalogue, T.C.D., Mss. 3960, also contained copies of *Émile, La Confession, Lettres de deux Amants and Jean-Jacques Rousseau, Citoyen de Génêve, Collection complête de ses Oeuvres.* Unfortunately the catalogue does not include the dates of publication.
553 Brian Fitzgerald (ed.), *Correspondence of Emily, Duchess of Leinster,* 3 vols., vol.1, p. 343: Caroline Fox to Emily Kildare, 28 September 1762, Kingsgate.
554 ibid., p. 522: Caroline Fox to Emily Kildare, 8 October 1767.
555 Angélique Day (ed.), *Letters from Georgian Ireland, Mary Delaney 1731–1768* (Belfast, 1991), p. 286.
556 L. Conolly to S. Bunbury, née Lennox, 9 October 1771, I.A.A. The Irish Georgian Society's Uncatalogued Conolly Letters.
557 Brian Fitzgerald (ed.), *Correspondence of Emily, Duchess of Leinster,* 3 vols., vol. 3, p. 321: L. Conolly to Emily, Dowager Duchess of Leinster, 23 May 1775, Castletown.
558 Jean-Jacques Rousseau, *Émile,* p. 379.
559 ibid., p. 160.
560 L. Conolly to S. Bunbury, née Lennox, 29 June 1764, I.A.A. The Irish Georgian Society's Uncatalogued Conolly Letters.
561 L. Conolly to S. Bunbury, née Lennox, 14 June 1768, I.A.A. The Irish Georgian Society's Uncatalogued Conolly Letters.
562 L. Conolly to S. Bunbury, née Lennox, 21 June 1768, I.A.A. The Irish Georgian Society's Uncatalogued Conolly Letters.
563 L. Conolly to S. Bunbury, née Lennox, 7 July 1768, I.A.A. The Irish Georgian Society's Uncatalogued Conolly Letters.
564 L. Conolly to S. Bunbury, née Lennox, 27 February, 1762, I.A.A. The Irish Georgian Society's Uncatalogued Conolly Letters.
565 L. Conolly to S. Bunbury, née Lennox, 13 June, 1778, I.A.A. The Irish Georgian Society's Uncatalogued Conolly Letters.
566 L. Conolly to S. Bunbury, née Lennox, 2 February 1768, I.A.A. The Irish Georgian Society's Uncatalogued Conolly Letters.
567 Brian Fitzgerald (ed.), *Correspondence of Emily, Duchess of Leinster,* 3 vols., vol. 3, p. 445: William, Marquess of Kildare to Emily, Duchess of Leinster, 23 December 1766, Naples.
568 William Ogilvie to Emily, Duchess of Leinster, undated, N.L.I., Ms. 623, no. 45.
569 Eileen Black, *A Catalogue of the Permanent Collection 3: Irish Oil Paintings, 1572– c.1830* (Ulster Museum: Belfast, 1991), p. 3: 'An almost identical version of this work, dated 1781, is at Carton, County Kildare, entitled *A Carriage passing Frascati*'.
The compiler of the catalogue finds it 'unlikely' that the painting depicts Frescati. Ashford was commissioned to paint many landscapes for the Leinster family. This, and the fact that the painting was at Carton (where it is unlikely to have been mis-titled), suggest to me that it is more likely to depict Frescati than not.
570 L. Conolly to S. Bunbury, née Lennox, 19 February 1768, I.A.A. The Irish Georgian Society's Uncatalogued Conolly Letters.
571 Jean-Jacques Rousseau, *Émile,* p. 181.
572 ibid., p. 182.
573 Brian Fitzgerald (ed.), *Correspondence of Emily, Duchess of Leinster,* 3 vols., vol. 1, p. 522: Caroline Fox to Emily Kildare, 8 October 1767.
574 William Ogilvie to Emily, Duchess of Leinster, undated, N.L.I., Ms. 623, no. 101.
575 William Ogilvie to Emily, Duchess of Leinster, undated, N.L.I., Ms. 623, no. 37.
576 William Ogilvie to Emily, Duchess of Leinster, undated, N.L.I., Ms. 623, no. 100.
577 Jean-Jacques Rousseau, *Émile,* p. 190.
578 William Ogilvie to Emily, Duchess of Leinster, undated, N.L.I., Ms. 623, no. 21.
579 Jean-Jacques Rousseau, *Émile,* p. 44.
580 ibid., pp. 189–90.
581 ibid., pp. 189–95.
582 Brian Fitzgerald (ed.), *Correspondence of Emily, Duchess of Leinster,* 3 vols., vol. 2, p. 22: Lord Edward Fitzgerald to Emily, Dowager Duchess of Leinster, 22 May 1779.
583 William Ogilvie to Emily, Duchess of Leinster, undated, N.L.I., Ms. 623, no. 35.
584 Michael Symes, The English Rococo Garden, p. 27.
585 William Ogilvie to Emily, Duchess of Leinster, undated N.L.I., Ms. 623, no. 60.
586 Brian Fitzgerald (ed.), *Correspondence of Emily, Duchess of Leinster,* 3 vols., vol. 2, p. 10: Lord Edward Fitzgerald and William Ogilvie to Emily, Duchess of Leinster, 1774.
587 William Ogilvie to Emily, Duchess of Leinster, undated, N.L.I., Ms. 623, no. 67.
588 William Ogilvie and Lord Edward Fitzgerald to Emily, Duchess of Leinster, undated, N.L.I., Ms. 623, no. 51.
589 James, Marquess of Kildare, to Emily, Marchioness of Kildare, 31 May 1766, P.R.O.N.I., T3092/1/3.
590 Brian Fitzgerald (ed.), *Correspondence of Emily, Duchess of Leinster,* 3 vols., vol. 1, p. 431: Caroline Fox to Emily Kildare, 1765.
591 ibid., p. 389: Caroline Fox to Emily Kildare, 21 September 1763, Aubigny.
592 ibid., p. 535: Caroline Fox to Emily Kildare, 12 May 1768, Nancy.
593 Conolly Papers, T.C.D., Ms. 3974–3984a no. 1015.
594 Jean-Jacques Rousseau, *Émile,* p. 30.
595 Desmond Guinness and William Ryan, *Irish Houses and Castles,* p. 190.
596 William Ogilvie to Emily, Duchess of Leinster, undated, N.L.I., Ms. 623, no. 56.
597 William Ogilvie to Emily, Duchess of Leinster, undated, N.L.I., Ms. 623, no. 83.
598 William Ogilvie to Emily, Duchess of Leinster, 5 August 1771, N.L.I., Ms. 623.
599 William Ogilvie to Emily, Duchess of Leinster, undated, N.L.I., Ms. 623, no. 51.
600 William Ogilvie to Emily, Duchess of Leinster, undated, N.L.I., Ms. 623, no. 102.
601 Brian Fitzgerald (ed.), *Correspondence of Emily, Duchess of Leinster,* 3 vols., vol. 1, pp. 406–7: Lady Caroline Fox to Emily, Countess of Kildare, 28 August 1764, Kingsgate.
602 William Ogilvie to Emily Ogilvie, Dowager Duchess of Leinster, 29/30 November 1783, N.L.I., Ms. 624.
603 William Ogilvie to Emily Ogilvie, Dowager Duchess of Leinster, 29/30 November 1783, N.L.I., Ms. 624.
604 William Ogilvie to Emily, Duchess of Leinster, undated, N.L.I., Ms. 623, no. 63.

605 William, second Duke of Leinster, to Emily, Dowager Duchess of Leinster, 19 October 1776, N.L.I., Ms. 616.
606 William, second Duke of Leinster, to Emily, Dowager Duchess of Leinster, 19 October 1776, N.L.I., Ms. 616.
607 Edward Malins and the Knight of Glin, Lost Demesnes (London, 1976), p. 16: from Robert Molesworth to Lord Coningsby, 1719, P.R.O.N.I., Ms. D628/82/2.
608 William, second Duke of Leinster, to Emily, Dowager Duchess of Leinster, 7 June 1775, N.L.I., Ms. 616.
609 Niall Mc Cullough, *Dublin, an Urban History* (Dublin, 1989), p. 70.
610 K. Conolly to J. Bonnell, 28 May 1734, Dublin, N.L.I., P.C. 434.
611 Jean-Jacques Rousseau, *Émile,* p. 30.
612 William Ogilvie to Emily, Duchess of Leinster, 11 May 1786, N.L.I., Ms. 625.
613 Jean-Jacques Rousseau, *Émile,* pp. 5–6.
614 Maria Edgeworth and Richard Lovell Edgeworth, *Essays on Practical Education,* 2 vols. (London, 1811), vol. 2, p. 166.
615 William Ogilvie to Emily, Duchess of Leinster, 11 May 1786, N.L.I., Ms. 625.
616 Brian Fitzgerald (ed.), *Correspondence of Emily, Duchess of Leinster,* 3 vols., vol. 3, p. 82.
617 ibid., p. 236: L. Conolly to Emily, Dowager Duchess of Leinster, 8 November 1776, Castletown.
618 L. Conolly to S. Bunbury, née Lennox, 12 May 1774, I.A.A. The Irish Georgian Society's Uncatalogued Conolly Letters.
619 S. Bunbury, née Lennox to Emily, Dowager Duchess of Leinster, 10 September 1775, Castletown, N.L.I., Ms. 618.
620 Brian Fitzgerald (ed.), *Correspondence of Emily, Duchess of Leinster,* 3 vols., vol. 3, p. 145: L. Conolly to Emily, Dowager Duchess of Leinster, 6 August 1775.
621 ibid., p. 150: L. Conolly to Emily, Dowager Duchess of Leinster, 13 September 1775.
622 S. Bunbury, née Lennox to Emily, Dowager Duchess of Leinster, 10 September 1775, Castletown, N.L.I., Ms. 618.
623 Brian Fitzgerald (ed.), *Correspondence of Emily, Duchess of Leinster,* 3 vols., vol. 3, p. 236: L. Conolly to Emily, Dowager Duchess of Leinster, 26 July 1775, Castletown.
624 ibid., p. 139: L. Conolly to Emily, Dowager Duchess of Leinster, 25 June 1775, Castletown.
625 ibid., pp. 214–15: L. Conolly to Emily, Dowager Duchess of Leinster, 23 August 1776.
626 S. Bunbury, née Lennox to Emily, Dowager Duchess of Leinster, 10 September 1775, Castletown, N.L.I., Ms. 618.
627 Brian Fitzgerald (ed.), *Correspondence of Emily, Duchess of Leinster,* 3 vols., vol. 3, pp. 214–15: L. Conolly to Emily, Dowager Duchess of Leinster, 23 August 1776, Castletown.
628 ibid., p. 220: L. Conolly to Emily, Dowager Duchess of Leinster, 28 August 1776, Blackrock.
629 ibid., p. 298: L. Conolly to Emily, Dowager Duchess of Leinster, 26 June 1778, Castletown.
630 ibid., p. 314: L. Conolly to Emily, Dowager Duchess of Leinster, 6 September 1778, Castletown.
631 Joseph Addison, 'The Spectator', no. 414, 25 June 1712, from John Dixon Hunt and Peter Willis (eds), *The Genius of the Place, The English Landscape Garden 1620–1820,* p. 142.
632 D.C.C. Chambers, *The Planters of the English Landscape Garden,* p. 187.
633 ibid., pp. 156–63.
634 Brian Fitzgerald (ed.), *Correspondence of Emily, Duchess of Leinster,* 3 vols., vol. 1, p. 76: E. Kildare to J. Kildare, 9 May 1759, Brockley Park.
635 William Ogilvie to Emily Ogilvie, Dowager Duchess of Leinster, 29/30 November 1783, N.L.I., Ms. 624.
636 William Ogilvie to Emily Ogilvie, Dowager Duchess of Leinster, 10 February 1787, N.L.I., Ms. 624.
637 William Ogilvie to Emily Ogilvie, Dowager Duchess of Leinster, 23 September 1786, N.L.I., Ms. 625.
638 Thomas Whateley, *Observations on Modern Gardening,* p. 141.
639 ibid., p. 129.
640 William Ogilvie to Emily Ogilvie, Dowager Duchess of Leinster, 12 November 1783, N.L.I., Ms. 624.
641 Ann Lynch to Emily Ogilvie, Dowager Duchess of Leinster, 14 January 1791, N.L.I., Ms. 631.
642 William Ogilvie to Emily Ogilvie, Dowager Duchess of Leinster, 12 November 1783, N.L.I., Ms. 624.
643 William Ogilvie to Emily Ogilvie, Dowager Duchess of Leinster, 18 February 1787[?], N.L.I., Ms. 624.
644 William, second Duke of Leinster, to William Ogilvie, 13 October 1787, Carton, N.L.I., Ms. 631.
645 William Ogilvie to Emily Ogilvie, Dowager Duchess of Leinster, 2 October 1786, N.L.I., Ms. 625.
646 L. Conolly to S. Bunbury, née Lennox, 10 September 1774, I.A.A. Conolly Letters.
647 William Ogilvie to Emily Ogilvie, Dowager Duchess of Leinster, 18 February 1787, N.L.I., Ms. 624.
648 William Ogilvie to Emily Ogilvie, Dowager Duchess of Leinster, 5 March 1787, N.L.I., Ms. 624.
649 William Ogilvie to Emily Ogilvie, Dowager Duchess of Leinster, 8 October 1786, N.L.I., Ms. 624.
650 William Ogilvie to Emily Ogilvie, Dowager Duchess of Leinster, 5 March 1787, N.L.I., Ms. 624.
651 William Ogilvie to Emily Ogilvie, Dowager Duchess of Leinster, 19 May 1792, N.L.I., Ms. 626.
652 Jean-Jacques Rousseau, *Émile,* p. 369.
653 William Ogilvie to Emily Ogilvie, Dowager Duchess of Leinster, undated, N.L.I., Ms. 623, no. 16.
654 William Ogilvie to Emily Ogilvie, Dowager Duchess of Leinster, 26 July 1782, N.L.I., Ms. 624.
655 Sybil Rosenfeld, *Temples of Thespis, Some Private Theatres and Theatricals in England and Wales, 1700–1820* (London, 1978), p. 43.
656 L. Conolly to S. Bunbury, née Lennox, 13 August 1771, I.A.A. Conolly Letters.
657 Sybil Rosenfeld, *Temples of Thespis, Some Private Theatres and Theatricals in England and Wales, 1700–1820* (London, 1978), p. 171.
658 L. Conolly to S. Bunbury, née Lennox, 24 September 1771, I.A.A. Conolly Letters.
659 Brian Fitzgerald (ed.), *Correspondence of Emily, Duchess of Leinster,* 3 vols., vol. 3, p. 305: Lady Louisa Conolly to Emily, Dowager Duchess of Leinster, 24 July 1778.
660 Sybil Rosenfeld, *Temples of Thespis* (London, 1978), p. 44.
661 ibid., p. 169.
662 Louisa Conolly to Sarah Bunbury, née Lennox, 31 August 1777, I.A.A. The Irish Georgian Society's Uncatalogued Conolly Letters.
663 Brian Fitzgerald (ed.), *Correspondence of Emily, Duchess of Leinster,* 3 vols., vol. 3, p. 305: L. Conolly to Emily, Dowager Duchess of Leinster, 24 July 1778.
664 Dora Wiebenson, *The Picturesque Garden in France,* pp. 96–7.
665 L. Conolly to S. Napier, née Lennox, 10 June 1795, I.A.A. The Irish Georgian Society's Uncatalogued Conolly Letters.
666 L. Conolly to S. Bunbury, née Lennox, 7 January 1772, I.A.A. The Irish Georgian Society's Uncatalogued Conolly Letters.
667 L. Conolly to Thomas Conolly, 7 January 1772, I.A.A. The Irish Georgian Society's Uncatalogued Conolly Letters.
668 Arthur Young, *A Tour in Ireland,* p. 103.
669 Brian Fitzgerald (ed.), *Correspondence of Emily, Duchess of Leinster,* 3 vols., vol. 1, p. 156: Emily Kildare to James Kildare, 16 December 1762.
670 See R. Bentmann and M. Muller, *The Villa as Hegemonic Architecture* (Humanities Press, 1992), pp. 37–49.
671 Norman Bryson, *Looking at the Overlooked* (London, 1990). The chapter entitled 'Xenia' explores how such spatial manipulations were developed in Roman interior decoration schemes. The ideas developed in this chapter on the ambiguous possibilities of framing devices and theatrical space are indebted to Bryson's work in this area.
672 John Olley, '20 St James's Square, Part 2', *Architect's Journal,* 28 February 1990, p. 53. This analysis of Robert Adam's decorative scheme for 20 St James's Square has informed the discussion of the painted interiors at Lyons.
673 Marguerite Lillis, 'A Roman Landscape Painter in Ireland', *Apollo,* February 1982, pp. 114–15.
674 ibid., p. 115.

675 Patricia Cashen, 'Valentine, Lord Cloncurry, and his collection at Lyons' (unpublished M.A. thesis, U.C.D., 1986), p. 145.
676 Marguerite Lillis, 'A Roman Landscape Painter in Ireland', Apollo, February 1982, p. 144.
677 Denis Cosgrove, *The Palladian Landscape* (London, 1993), p. 109.
678 Emily Ogilvie, Dowager Duchess of Kildare, to William Ogilvie, 30 July 1788, N.L.I., Ms. 609.
679 Emily Ogilvie, Dowager Duchess of Kildare, to William Ogilvie, 11 June 1788, N.L.I., Ms. 609. I am indebted to Dr Michael Browne for his identification of the pamphlet Common Sense.
680 Brian Fitzgerald (ed.), *Correspondence of Emily, Duchess of Leinster,* 3 vols., vol. 2, p. 59: Lord Edward Fitzgerald to Emily, Dowager Duchess of Leinster, 21 November 1788, New Brunswick.
681 Jean-Jacques Rousseau, *Émile,* p. 200.
682 Dora Wiebenson, *The Picturesque Garden in France,* p. 100.
683 ibid., p. 104.
684 ibid., p. 93.
685 ibid., p. 77.
686 ibid., p. 77.
687 Brian Fitzgerald (ed.), *Correspondence of Emily, Duchess of Leinster,* 3 vols., vol. 1, p. 76: Emily Kildare to James Kildare, Brockley Park.
688 Dora Wiebenson, *The Picturesque Garden in France,* p. 13: 'One later French garden can be associated with the spirit, style, and possibly even the construction of Stanislaus's work [Lunéville] – Monceau, designed by Carmontelle, who surely referred to the earlier work of Stanislaus when he created the Duc de Chartres's Parisian park in the 1770s.'
689 Brian Fitzgerald (ed.), *Correspondence of Emily, Duchess of Leinster,* 3 vols., vol. 1, p. 535: Lady Caroline Fox to Emily, Duchess of Leinster, 12 May 1768, Nancy.
690 Dora Wiebenson, *The Picturesque Garden in France,* p. 12.
691 Mary, Dowager Countess of Kildare, to Emily Ogilvie, Dowager Duchess of Leinster, 10 May 1776, N.L.I., Ms. 629.
692 C.D.A. Leighton, *Catholics in a Protestant Kingdom,* p. 126.
693 Gerard Campbell, *Edward & Pamela Fitzgerald, Being some Account of their Lives. Compiled from the Letters of those who knew them* (London, 1904), p. 61: Lord Edward Fitzgerald to Emily Ogilvie, Dowager Duchess of Leinster, 6 May 1793.
694 ibid., p. 62: Lord Edward Fitzgerald to Emily Ogilvie, Dowager Duchess of Leinster, 6 May 1793.
695 ibid.
696 Mark Laird, 'James Maddock's Blooming Stage', *Journal of Garden History,* vol. 24, no. 1, p. 78.
697 Gerard Campbell, *Edward & Pamela Fitzgerald,* p. 63: Lord Edward Fitzgerald to his mother, Emily Ogilvie, Dowager Duchess of Leinster, 8 May 1793.
698 ibid., p. 64: Lord Edward Fitzgerald to Emily Ogilvie, Dowager Duchess of Leinster, 11 June 1793.
699 ibid., p. 67: Lord Edward Fitzgerald to Emily Ogilvie, Dowager Duchess of Leinster, 6 February 1794.
700 ibid.
701 ibid., p. 129: Lord Edward Fitzgerald to Emily Ogilvie, Dowager Duchess of Leinster, February, 1797.
702 Valentine Lawless, Lord Cloncurry, *Personal Recollections of the Life and Times, with extracts from the correspondence of Valentine, Lord Cloncurry* (Dublin, 1849), p. 38.
703 Marianne Elliot, *Partners in Revolution: The United Irishmen and France* (New Haven and London, 1982), p. 175
704 ibid., p. 253.
705 Valentine Lawless, Lord Cloncurry, *Personal Recollections* (Dublin, 1849), p. 154.
706 Patricia Cashen, 'Valentine, Lord Cloncurry and his collection at Lyons' (unpublished M.A. thesis, U.C.D., 1986), p. 129.
707 Dora Wiebenson, *The Picturesque Garden in France,* p. 104.
708 Valentine Lawless, Lord Cloncurry, *Personal Recollections* (Dublin, 1849), p. 159.
709 Patricia Cashen, 'Valentine, Lord Cloncurry and his collection at Lyons' (unpublished M.A. thesis, University College Dublin, 1986), p. 31.
710 Valentine Lawless to Thomas Ryan, 16 April 1803, Rome, N.L.I., Ms. 8492.
711 Valentine Lawless to Thomas Ryan, 10 May 1803, Naples, N.L.I., Ms. 8492.
712 Valentine Lawless to Thomas Ryan, 25 May 1804, Rome, N.L.I., Ms. 8492.
713 Valentine Lawless to Thomas Ryan, 28 January 1805, Rome, N.L.I., Ms. 8492.
714 Valentine Lawless to Thomas Ryan, 23 April 1806, N.L.I., Ms. 8492.
715 Valentine Lawless, Lord Cloncurry, *Personal Recollections* (Dublin, 1849), p. 216.
716 Dora Wiebenson, *The Picturesque Garden in France,* p. 104.
717 Valentine Lawless, Lord Cloncurry, *Personal Recollections* (Dublin, 1849), p. 157.
718 ibid., p. 157.
719 ibid., p. 40.
720 Gerard Campbell, *Edward & Pamela Fitzgerald,* p. 66: Lord Edward Fitzgerald to Emily Ogilvie, Dowager Duchess of Leinster, 23 January 1794.
721 Brian Fitzgerald (ed.), Correspondence of Emily, Duchess of Leinster, 3 vols., vol. 3, p. 220: L. Conolly to Emily, Duchess of Leinster, 28 August 1776.
722 Gerard Campbell, *Edward & Pamela Fitzgerald,* p. 69: Lord Edward Fitzgerald to Emily Ogilvie, Dowager Duchess of Leinster, 4 March 1794.
723 ibid., p. 71: Lord Edward Fitzgerald to Emily Ogilvie, Dowager Duchess of Leinster, 23 June 1794.
724 ibid., p. 107: Lord Edward Fitzgerald to Emily Ogilvie, Dowager Duchess of Leinster, 29 July 1796.
725 ibid., p. 77: Lord Edward Fitzgerald to Emily Ogilvie, Dowager Duchess of Leinster, November 1794, Kildare.
726 ibid., p. 73: Lord Edward Fitzgerald to Emily Ogilvie, Dowager Duchess of Leinster, 23 June 1794.
727 Lynn Hunt, *Politics, Culture and Class in the French Revolution* (London, 1984), p. 94.
728 Jean-Jacques Rousseau, *Émile,* p. 23.
729 Gerard Campbell, *Edward & Pamela Fitzgerald,* p. 99: Letter of Sarah Napier.
730 ibid., p. 99: Lady Pamela Fitzgerald to Lady Lucy Fitzgerald: ' *Il est toute la journée à l'air et se bêgne tous les matins dans l'eau froide aussi il a une santé parfaite.'*
731 ibid., p. 57.
732 ibid., p. 101.
733 Mona Ozouf, *Festivals and the French Revolution* (Harvard, 1988), pp. 131–2.
734 ibid., p. 198.
735 ibid., p. 165.
736 ibid., p. 200.
737 Campbell, *Edward & Pamela* (1904), p. 16.
738 ibid., p. 105.
739 ibid., p. 110.
740 Mona Ozouf, *Festivals and the French Revolution* (Harvard, 1988), p. 143.
741 John Brewer, *The Pleasures of the Imagination* (London, 1997), pp. 377–8.
742 ibid., p. 50.
743 L. Conolly to S. Bunbury, née Lennox, 2 August 1768, I.A.A. The Irish Georgian Society's Uncatalogued Conolly Letters.
744 William Ogilvie to Emily, Duchess of Leinster, undated, N.L.I., Ms. 623, no. 15.
745 Mary Pat O'Malley, 'Lios an Uisce', *Blackrock Society Proceedings,* vol. 4, 1996, p. 36.
746 ibid., p. 38: from John Wesley, *Journal* (1783).
747 ibid., p. 44.
748 Weston St John Joyce, *The Neighbourhood of Dublin* (Dublin, 1971), pp. 35–6.
749 ibid.
750 Simon Schama, *Citizens* (London, 1989), pp. 134–7.

751 Linda Lunney, 'The Celebrated Mr Dinwiddie: An Eighteenth-Century Scientist in Ireland', *Eighteenth-Century Ireland / Iris an dá chultúr,* vol. 3, 1988, p. 78.

752 John Olley, '20 St James's Square, Part 1', *Architect's Journal,* 21 February 1990. This article has informed my reading of Merrion Square's development.

753 Liam Mac Cóil, *The Book of Blackrock* (Blackrock, Co. Dublin, 1981), p. 41.

754 John d'Alton, *The History of County Dublin* (1976), p. 433.

755 Louisa Conolly to George Napier, 3 October 1820, I.A.A. The Irish Georgian Society's Uncatalogued Conolly Letters.

756 Louisa Conolly, undated, I.A.A. The Irish Georgian Society's Uncatalogued Conolly Letters.

757 Louisa Conolly to George Napier, 3 October 1820, I.A.A. The Irish Georgian Society's Uncatalogued Conolly Letters.

## Chapter 5

758 David Coffin, *The English Garden: Meditation and Memorial* (Chichester, 1994).

759 William R. Chetwood, *A Tour Thru Ireland* (Dublin, 1746), p. 233.

760 ibid., p. 239.

761 Malcohm Kelsall, 'The Iconography of Stourhead', *Journal of Warburg and Courtauld Institutes,* no. 46, 1983, pp. 133–43.

762 Johnathan Fisher, *Scenery of Ireland* (London, 1795): from text accompanying the plate 'The Wooden Bridge at Hermitage on the river Liffey'.

763 *The Copper Plate Magazine,* vol. 1, London, late eighteenth century.

764 See Malcolm Andrews, *The Search for the Picturesque* (Aldershot, 1989), for the development of the picturesque tour in England, Scotland and Wales.

765 Johnathan Fisher, *Scenery of Ireland,* Introduction.

766 ibid., text accompanying the plate 'View on approaching Luttrellstown Park'.

767 ibid.

768 ibid., text accompanying the plate 'Poula Pooka, on the River Liffey'.

769 The discussion of touring and tourism contained in this chapter is indebted to: Malcolm Andrews, *The Search for the Picturesque* (Aldershot, 1989), John Dixon Hunt, *Gardens and the Picturesque* (M.I.T., 1992), and Sidney K. Robinson, *Inquiry into the Picturesque* (London, 1991).

770 Brian Fitzgerald (ed.), *Correspondence of Emily, Duchess of Leinster,* 3 vols., vol. 3, p. 538: William, Marquess of Kildare, to Emily Kildare, 24 September 1768, Milan.

771 ibid., p. 526: William, Marquess of Kildare, to Emily Kildare, 11 December 1768, Vienna.

772 William, second Duke of Leinster, to Emily Dowager Duchess of Leinster, 29 September 1775, N.L.I., Ms. 616.

773 William, second Duke of Leinster, to Emily Dowager Duchess of Leinster, 6 August 1775, N.L.I., Ms. 616.

774 William, second Duke of Leinster, to Emily Dowager Duchess of Leinster, 15 December 1776, N.L.I., Ms. 616.

775 *Sketch of the Glen and Part of the Park, at Carton with the Farm at Kellystown,* Carton House. Horner states that it is marked at the rear of the frame: 'Plan of the New Road from Kellystown to Carton by Lieut. Browne' 1788[?].

776 William, second Duke of Leinster, to Emily Dowager Duchess of Leinster, 20 April 1777, ., Ms. 616.

777 William, second Duke of Leinster, to Emily Dowager Duchess of Leinster, 23 June 1776, N.L.I., Ms. 616.

778 William, second Duke of Leinster, to Emily Dowager Duchess of Leinster, 26 June 1777, N.L.I., Ms. 616.

779 William, second Duke of Leinster, to Emily Dowager Duchess of Kildare, 5 October 1777, N.L.I., Ms. 616.

780 Henry D. Inglis, *A Journey throughout Ireland* (London, 1834), p. 344.

781 Prince Pückler-Müskau, *Tour in England, Ireland and France in the years 1828 and 1829,* 2 vols. (London, 1832), vol. 1, p. 171.

782 Marianne Elliot, *Partners in Revolution: The United Irishmen and France,* p. 6: Memoirs of Miles Byrne, edited by his widow, 2 vols. (Dublin, 1906), vol. 1, p. 3: 'How often had he shown me the lands that belonged to our ancestors now in the hands of the descendants of the sanguinary followers of Cromwell.'

783 ibid., p. 7.

784 *Journal of Horticulture and Cottage Gardener,* vol. 29, 17 February 1863, pp. 130–1.

785 ibid., p. 131.

786 ibid., pp. 130–1.

787 John Barrow, *Tour around Ireland* (London, 1836), pp. 159, 180, 146.

788 ibid., Preface.

789 Prince Pückler-Müskau, *Tour in England, Ireland and France* (London, 1832), p. viii. The question was that of Catholic Emancipation.

790 Henry D. Inglis, *A Journey throughout Ireland* (London, 1834), p. 341.

791 ibid., p. 348.

792 *Journal of Horticulture and Cottage Gardener,* vol. 29, 10 February 1863, p. 117.

793 ibid., p. 118.

794 ibid., pp. 131–2.

795 Diary of Gerald Fitzgerald, subsequently fifth Duke of Leinster, 1862–1863 (b. 1851, d. 1893), N.L.I., Ms. 18,852: 16 November 1862.

796 Diary of Gerald Fitzgerald, subsequently fifth Duke of Leinster, 1862–1863 (b. 1851, d. 1893), N.L.I., Ms. 18,852: 1 October 1862.

797 *Journal of Horticulture and Cottage Gardener,* vol. 29, 17 February 1863, pp. 278–9.

798 Brian Fitzgerald (ed.), *Correspondence of Emily, Duchess of Leinster,* 3 vols., vol. 1, p. 139: Emily Kildare to James Kildare, 20 November 1762.

799 Lord Clarendon to the third Duke and Duchess of Leinster, 1849, P.R.O.N.I., D 3078/3/36/1–26.

800 *Journal of Horticulture and Cottage Gardener,* vol. 29, 10 February 1863, p. 131.

801 *Journal of Horticulture and Cottage Gardener,* 6 May 1872, p. 407.

802 George Eliot, *Middlemarch* (London, 1994), p. 326.

803 W.E. Vaughan, *Landlords and Tenants in Ireland 1848–1904* (1994), pp. 40–1.

804 ibid.

## Epilogue

805 Finola O'Kane, 'Nurturing a Revolution – Patrick Pearse's School Garden at St Enda's, Rathfarnham, Co. Dublin, Ireland', *The Journal of Garden History,* vol. 28, no. 1, 2000.

806 Diary of Gerald Fitzgerald, subsequently fifth Duke of Leinster, 1862–1863 (b. 1851, d. 1893), N.L.I., Ms. 18,852.

# Bibliography


## Manuscript Sources

### The National Library of Ireland (N.L.I.)

Barker, Johnathan, *A Map of Booterstown and all its subdenominations surveyed in 1762,* Ms. 16.G.18.

Castle, Richard, *Essay on Artificial Navigation,* Ms. 2737.

Carton Library Catalogue, Ms. 14,923.

Carton Maps, Mss. 22, 004, 22,503.

Cloncurry Papers, Mss. 3147, 5657–5660, 5665–5667, 5693–5694, 8492, 12,818–12,909.

Cloncurry Estate Maps, Ms. 21. F. 50 (1–36).

Conolly Papers, Mss. 14,338–43 and P. 6796.

Donacumper Library Catalogue, Ms. 19737.

Dublin Maps, Ms. 16. G. 50.

Heron Papers, Mss. 13,047–13,056.

Inchiquin Mss.

Kildare Maps, Ms. 16. H .14.

Leinster Papers, Ms. 606–635, Brit. Mus. Add. Mss. 30,990 P743, Ms. 13,828, Ms. 16,156, Ms. 18862, 19,689–19,693.

Molesworth Papers, P3752, 3753.

Molesworth Estate Map 1822, Ms. 16. G. 41 (25).

Smythe and Barbavilla Papers, P.C. 434, 445.

Strafford Papers, P527–528 (Brit. Mus. Add. Mss. 22,228).

St Wolstan's Library Catolague, Ms. 16253.

Walker, John, *Essay on Plantations of Trees presented to Lady Louisa Conolly,* 1809, Ms. 15,397.

### The Library of Trinity College Dublin (T.C.D.)

Conolly Papers, Mss. 3931–3984.

Ordnance Survey Maps.

### Irish Architectural Archive (I.A.A.)

Uncatalogued Castletown Papers.

Irish Georgian Society's Conolly Letters.

O'Rourke, Mona, Transcript of Extracts from the Bolger Papers Relating to Building Work at Carton House 1815–1825.

### Public Record Office of Northern Ireland (P.R.O.N.I.)

Castletown papers, T.2825.

Strutt Papers, T.3092.

Leinster Papers, D.3078, T.3092.

### National Archives, Dublin

Conolly-Carew Papers, Ms. 6917.

### British Library

Holland House Papers, Add. Ms. 51426.

## Published Manuscript Sources

Chart, D.A. (ed.), Clements Mss., *Historical Manuscripts Commission Report on Various Collections,* vol. 8 (1913).

Cooper, Anthony Ashley, 3rd Earl of Shaftesbury, *Letters from (him) to Robert Molesworth with two written by Sir John Cropley and intro.* (London, 1721).

Day, Angélique (ed.), *Letters from Georgian Ireland, Mary Delaney 1731–1768* (Belfast, 1991).

Fitzgerald, Brian (ed.), *Correspondence of Emily, Duchess of Leinster,* 3 vols.,

Irish Manuscripts Commission (Dublin, 1947, 1953, 1957).

Lewis, W.S. (ed.), *Horace Walpole's Correspondence,* 48 vols. (London, 1939–1974).

## Contemporary Works and Pamphlets

Austen, Jane, *Mansfield Park* (London, 1966).

Barrow, John, *Tour around Ireland* (London, 1836).

Bowden, Charles, T., A *Tour Thro' Ireland* (Dublin, 1791).

Brewer, J.N., and Neale, J.P., *The Beauties of Ireland,* 2 vols. (London, 1825).

Burke, Edmund, *A Philosophic Enquiry into the Origin of our Ideas of the Sublime and Beautiful* (London, 1757).

Chambers, William, *A Dissertation on Oriental Gardening* (London, 1972).

Chetwood, William R., *A Tour Thru Ireland* (Dublin, 1746).

Edgeworth, Maria and Richard Lovell, *Essays on Practical Education,* 2 vols. (London, 1811).

Eliot, George, *Middlemarch* (London, 1994).

Fisher, Johnathan, *Scenery of Ireland* (London, 1795).

Fraser, James, *Handbook for Travellers in Ireland* (Dublin, 1854).

Gilpin, William, *Observations on Several Parts of Great Britain, particularly the Mountains and Lakes of Cumberland and Westmoreland, relative chiefly to Picturesque Beauty made in the Year 1772,* 2 vols. (London, 1808).

–, *Three Essays: On Picturesque Beauty; On Picturesque Travel; On Sketching Landscape* (London, 1792).

Girardin, René, *An Essay on Landscape and a Tour to Ermenonville* (London, 1982).

Hall, Samuel Carter and Anna Maria, *Ireland: Its Scenery, Character etc.* (London, 1853).

Hoare, Richard, Colt, *Journal of a Tour in Ireland, A.D. 1806* (London, 1807).

Inglis, Henry D., *A Journey throughout Ireland* (London, 1834).

Knight, R.P., *An Analytical Enquiry into the Principles of Taste* (London, 1805).

Langley, Batty, *New Principles of Gardening* (London, 1728).

–, *Gothic Architecture Restored and Improved* (London, 1747).

Lawless, Valentine, Lord Cloncurry, P*ersonal Recollections of the Life and Times of* (Dublin, 1849).

Lewis, Samuel, *A Topographical Dictionary of Ireland* (London, 1837).

Loudon, J.H., *Arboretum et Fruticetum Britannicum* (London, 1842).

Mc Intosh, Charles, *The Book of the Garden* (London, 1853).

Milton, Thomas, *Views of Different Seats of the Nobility and Gentry* (London and Dublin, 1783).

Miller, Philip, *The Gardeners Dictionary* (London, 1737).

Molesworth, Robert, *Some Considerations for the Promoting of Agriculture and Employing the Poor* (Dublin, 1723).

Neale, J.P., *Views of the Seats of Noblemen and Gentlemen in England, Wales, Scotland and Ireland* (London, 1825).

Pearse, P.H., *The Story of a Success, being a record of St. Enda's College, Sept. 1908–Easter 1916,* ed. Desmond Ryan (Dublin and London, 1917).

Price, Uvedale, *A Dialogue on the Distinct Characters of the Picturesque and the Beautiful* (Hereford, 1801).
–, *An Essay on the Picturesque* (London, 1794–1798).
–, *Sir Uvedale Price on the Picturesque: with an essay on the origin of taste, and much original matter, by Sir Thomas Dick Lauder* (London, 1846).
Pückler-Müskau, Prince, *Tour in England, Ireland and France in the years 1828 and 1829,* 2 vols. (London, 1832).
Robinson, William, *The English Flower Garden* (London, 1986).
Rousseau, Jean-Jacques, *Émile* (London, 1995).
–, *The Social Contract and Discourses* (London, 1993).
Shaftesbury, Lord, *Characteristicks of Men, Manners, Opinions, Times* (London, 1711).
Swift, Jonathan, *The Drapier's Letters to the People of Ireland against rec. Wood's Halfpence* (Oxford, 1935).
Switzer, Stephen, *The Practical Kitchen Gardiner* (London, 1727).
Switzer, Stephen, *An Introduction to a General System of Hydrostaticks and Hydraulics, Philosophical and Practical* (London, 1729).
Walpole, *The History of the Modern Taste in Gardening* (New York, 1995).
Whateley, *Thomas, Observations on Modern Gardening* (Dublin, 1770).
Young, Arthur, *A Tour in Ireland, 1776–1779,* vol. 1/2 (Shannon, 1970).

## Periodicals

*The Copper Plate Magazine*
*The Gardener's Chronicle*
*The Gardener's Magazine*
*Irish Gardening*
*Journal of Horticulture and Cottage Gardener*

## Exhibition Catalogues

*Irish Houses and Landscapes,* 1963 Exhibition Catalogue, Ulster Museum, Belfast, 20–17 July 1963, Municipal Gallery, Dublin, 2 Aug–22 Sept. 1963

## Secondary Sources

Aalen, F.H.A., Whelan, K., and Stout, M., *Atlas of the Irish Rural Landscape* (Cork, 1997).
Ackerman, James S., *The Villa, Form and Ideology of Country Houses* (London, 1990).
Andrews, J.H., *Plantation Acres* (Omagh, 1985).
Andrews, Malcohm, *The Search for the Picturesque* (Aldershot, 1989).
Barnard, T.C., *'Gardening, Diet and "Improvement" in Later Seventeenth-Century Ireland', Journal of Garden History,* 1990, vol. 10, no. 1, pp. 71–85.
Barnard, Toby, *The Abduction of a Limerick Heiress: Social and political relations in mid-eighteenth-century Ireland* (Dublin, 1996).
–, *'Public and private uses of wealth in Ireland,* c. 1660–1760', in Jacqueline Hill and Colm Lennon (eds.), *Luxury and Austerity* (Dublin, 1999).
–, and Clark, June (eds), *Lord Burlington, Architecture, Art and Life* (London, 1995).
Barrell, John, The Idea of Landscape and the Sense of Place: An Approach to the Poetry of John Clare (Cambridge, 1972).
–, *The Dark Side of the Landscape: The Rural Poor in English Painting,* 1730–1840 (Cambridge, 1980).
Batey, Mavis, *Regency Gardens* (Buckinghamshire, 1995).
–, Buttery, H., Wilkie, K., and Lambert, D., *Arcadian Thames* (London, 1984).
Bence-Jones, Mark, *A Guide to Irish Country Houses* (London, 1988).
Bentmann, R., and Muller, M., *The Villa as Hegemonic Architecture* (Humanities Press, 1992).
Bermingham, Ann, *Landscape and Ideology* (Berkeley, 1986).
Black, Eileen, *A Catalogue of the Permanent Collection 3: Irish Oil Paintings, 1572–c.1830* (Belfast, 1991).
Boylan, Lena, *Castletown and Its Owners,* Irish Georgian Society Guidebook, Parts 1 and 2, Irish Georgian Society, 1968.
–, *'The Conollys of Castletown',* Bulletin of the Irish Georgian Society, 1968.
–, *'Skeaghgutta or Thornhill',* The Celbridge Charter, no. 141, May 1985.
Bowe, Patrick, and Lamb, Keith, *A History of Gardening in Ireland* (Dublin, 1995).
Braudel, F., *The Identity of France,* vols. 1 and 2 (London, 1990).
Brewer, John, *The Pleasures of the Imagination* (London, 1997).
Brickell, C. (ed.), *The R.H.S. A–Z Encyclopedia of Garden Plants* (London, 1996).
Brown, Michael, *Francis Hutcheson in Dublin, 1719–1730* (Dublin, 2002).
Bryson, Norman, *Looking at the Overlooked* (London, 1990).
Campbell, Gerard, Edward and Pamela Fitzgerald, *Being some Account of their Lives. Compiled from the Letters of those who knew them* (London, 1904).
Casey, Christine, 'Books and Builders: A Bibliographical Approach to Irish Eighteenth-Century Architecture' (unpublished Ph.D. thesis, Trinity College Dublin, 1992).
Cashen, Patricia,Valentine, Ld. *Cloncurry and his collection at Lyons* (unpublished M.A. thesis, University College Dublin, 1986).
Chambers, D.D.S., *The Planters of the English Landscape Garden* (Yale, 1993).
Charlesworth, M.J., 'The Wentworths: Family and Political Rivalry in the English Landscape Garden', *Garden History,* vol. 14, no. 2, pp.120–37.
Clark, J.C.D., *English Society 1688–1832: Ideology, social structure and political practice during the ancien régime* (Cambridge, 1985).
–, *Revolution and Rebellion: State and Society in the Seventeenth and Eighteenth centuries* (Cambridge, 1985).
Coffin, David, *The English Garden, Meditation and Memorial* (Chichester, 1994).
Collette, F., and Péricard-Méa, Denise, *Le Temps des Jardins* (Seine et Marne, 1992).
Connolly, S.J., *Religion, Law and Power, The Making of Protestant Ireland, 1660–1760* (Oxford, 1992).
Conway, Hazel, *People's Parks: The Design and Development of Victorian Parks in Britain* (Cambridge, 1991).
Copley, S., and Garside, P. (eds), *The Politics of the Picturesque, Literature, Landscape and Aesthetics since 1770* (Cambridge).
Corkery, Daniel, *The Hidden Ireland* (Dublin, 1967).
Cosgrove, Denis, *The Palladian Landscape* (London, 1993).
–, *Social Formation and the Symbolic Landscape* (London, 1984).
–, and Daniels, Stephen (eds), *The Iconography of the Landscape* (Cambridge, 1995).
Craig, Maurice, *The Architecture of Ireland* (Dublin, 1982).
Curl, James Stephens, *A Dictionary of Architecture* (Oxford, 1999).
d'Alton, John, *The History of County Dublin* (Cork, 1976).
de Jong, E., and Domenicus-van Soest, *Aardse Paradijzen, De Tuin in de Nederlandse kunst 15de tot 18de eeuw* (Amsterdam, 1996).

Doubleday, H.A., and De Walden, Lord Howard, *The Complete Peerage of England, Scotland, Ireland, Great Britain and the United Kingdom* (Gloucester, 1984).
Eagleton, Terry, *Ideology* (London, 1994).
Elliott, Marianne, *Partners in Revolution: The United Irishmen and France* (New Haven and London, 1982).
Everett, Nigel, *The Tory View of Landscape* (London, 1994).
–, *Wild Gardens: The Lost Demesnes of Bantry Bay* (Bantry, 2001).
Eyres, Patrick (ed.), 'Hearts of Oak, Commerce, Empire and the Landscape Garden, Parts 1 and 2', *New Arcadian Journal,* nos. 35/36 (New Arcadian Press, 1993).
Fabricant, Carol, *Swift's Landscape* (London, 1995).
Ferguson, Oliver, *Jonathan Swift and Ireland* (Urbana, 1962).
Fitzgerald, Lord Walter, 'Carton', *Journal of the County Kildare Archaeological Society,* vol. 4, no. 1, 1903.
Foster, R.F., *Modern Ireland 1600–1972* (London, 1988).
Girouard, Mark, *The Victorian Country House* (London, 1979).
–, *Life in the English Country House: A Social and Architectural History* (Penguin, 1978).
Guinness, Desmond, and the Knight of Glin, 'The Conolly Folly: A Case for Richard Castle', *Bulletin of the Irish Georgian Society,* vol. 6, no. 4, October–December 1963, pp. 61–73.
–, and Ryan, W., *Irish Houses and Castles,* 1971.
Headley, G., and Meulenkamp, W., *Follies: A National Trust Guide* (London, 1986).
Hinde, Thomas, *Capability Brown: The Story of a Master Gardener* (London, 1986).
Hobhouse, Penelope, *Plants in Garden History* (London, 1994).
Hoog, S. (ed.), *Les Jardins de Versailles et de Trianon d'André le Nôtre à Richard Mique* (Paris, 1992).
Horner, Arnold, 'Carton, Co. Kildare, A Case Study in the Making of an Irish Demesne', *Quarterly Bulletin of the Irish Georgian Society,* vol. 18, nos. 2 and 3, April–September 1975, pp. 45–101.
Howley, James, *The Follies and Garden Buildings of Ireland* (Yale, 1993).
Hunt, John Dixon, and Willis, Peter (eds), *The Genius of the Place: The English Landscape Garden 1620–1820* (London, 1975).
–, *Gardens and the Picturesque* (MIT Press, 1992).
–, *Garden and Grove: The Italian Renaissance Garden in the English Imagination: 1600–1750* (Princeton, 1986).
–, 'Reckoning with Dutch Gardens', in 'The Anglo-Dutch Garden in the Age of William and Mary', *Journal of Garden History,* vol. 8, nos. 2 and 3, April–September 1988.
Hunt, Lynn, *Politics, Culture and Class in the French Revolution* (London, 1984).
Jacob, Margaret C., *The Radical Enlightenment* (London, 1987).
Jacques, David, and van der Horst, Jan, *The Gardens of William and Mary* (London, 1988).
Johnston-Liik, Edith Mary (ed.), *History of the Irish Parliament 1692–1800,* 6 vols. (Belfast, 2002).
Jones, Barbara, *Follies and Grottoes* (London, 1989).
Joyce, Weston St John, *The Neighbourhood of Dublin* (Dublin 1971).
Kavanagh, M.V., *A Bibliography of the History of County Kildare in Printed Books* (Kildare, 1976).
Kelleher, Ann Margaret, 'The Long Gallery of Castletown House', *Bulletin of the Irish Georgian Society,* vol. 22, 1979, pp. 133–43.
Kelsall, Malcolm, 'The Iconography of Stourhead', *Journal of Warburg and Courthauld Institutes,* no. 46, 1983.
Laird, Mark, 'James Maddock's "Blooming Stage", *Garden History,* vol. 24, no. 1, pp. 71–254.
Lawrence, E. Klein, *Shaftesbury and the Culture of Politeness: Moral Discourse and Cultural Politics in Early Eighteenth-Century England* (Cambridge, 1994).
Leatherbarrow, David, 'Character Geometry and Perspective: The Third Earl of Shaftesbury's Principles of Garden Design', *Journal of Garden History,* vol. 4, no. 4, 1984.
Leighton, C.D.A., *Catholics in a Protestant Kingdom: A Study of the Irish Ancien Regime* (Dublin, 1994).
Leith, J.A., *Space and Revolution: Projects for Monuments, Squares and Public Buildings in France, 1789–1799* (London, 1991).
Lillis, Marguerite, 'A Roman Landscape painter in Ireland', *Apollo,* February 1982, pp. 114–15.
Louis XIV, *Manière de Montrer les Jardins de Versailles* (Paris, 1992).
Lunney, Linda, 'The Celebrated Mr. Dinwiddie: An Eighteenth-Century Scientist in Ireland', *Eighteenth-Century Ireland, Iris an dá chultúr,* vol. 3, 1988, pp. 69–83.
Mac Cóil, Liam, *The Book of Blackrock* (Blackrock, 1981).
Mc Cullough, Niall, *Dublin, an Urban History* (Dublin, 1989).
–, and Mulvin, Valerie, *A Lost Tradition* (Dublin, 1987).
Mac Curtain, M., 'Rural Society in post-Cromwellian Ireland', *Studies in Irish History: Presented to R. Dudley Edwards* (Dublin, 1979).
Mc Cutcheon, W.A, *The Industrial Archaeology of Northern Ireland* (New Jersey, 1984).
Mack, Maynard, *The Garden and The City* (Oxford, 1969).
Mc Parland, Edward, 'The New Junta for Architecture', in T. Barnard and J. Clark (eds), *Lord Burlington, Architecture, Art and Life* (London, 1995).
–, *Public Architecture in Ireland 1680-1760* (Yale, 2001)
Malcolmson, A.P.W., *John Foster and the Politics of the Anglo-Irish Ascendancy* (Oxford, 1978).
–, *The Pursuit of the Heiress: Aristocratic Marriage in Ireland 1750–1820* (Antrim, 1982).
Malins, E., and Bowe, P., *Irish Gardens and Demesnes from 1830* (London 1980).
Malins, E., and Fitzgerald, Desmond, *Lost Demesnes; Irish Landscape Gardening, 1660–1845* (London, 1976).
Mosser, M., and Teyssot, G. (eds), *The History of Garden Design: The Western Tradition from the Renaissance to the Present Day* (London, 1991).
Nelson, E. Charles, and Mc Cracken, Eileen M., *The Brightest Jewel: A History of the National Botanic Gardens Glasnevin, Dublin* (Kilkenny, 1987).
O'Brien, Conor Cruise, *The Great Melody: A Thematic Biography of Edmund Burke,* 1992.
O'Kane, Finola, 'Mixing Foreign Trees with the Natives: Irish Demesne Landscape in the Eighteenth Century', Ph.D. thesis, 2 vols., N.U.I., 1999.
–, 'Nurturing a Revolution: Patrick Pearse's School Garden at St Enda's, Rathfarnham, Co. Dublin, Ireland', *The Journal of Garden History,* vol. 28, no. 1, 2000.
Olley, John, '20 St. James's Square, Parts 1 and 2', *Architect's Journal,* 21 February 1990, pp. 34–57, and 28 February, 1990, pp. 34–53.
O'Malley, Mary Pat, 'Lios an Uisce', *Blackrock Society Proceedings,* vol. 4, 1996, pp. 34–50.
O'Sullivan, Peter, *Newcastle Lyons: A Parish of the Pale* (Dublin, 1986).
Ó Tuama, S., and Kinsella, T., *An Duanaire 1600–1900: Poems of the Dispossessed* (Portlaoise, 1981).
Ozouf, Mona, *Festivals and the French Revolution* (Harvard, 1988).
Pevsner, N., *The Buildings of England,* 46 vols. (Harmondsworth, 1951–74).
Pressley, W.L., *James Barry: The Artist as Hero* (London, 1983).
Pugh, Simon, *Garden-Nature-Language* (Manchester, 1988).
–, *Country-City-Capital* (Manchester, 1990).
Rackham, Oliver, *The History of the Countryside* (London, 1987).
Reeves-Smyth, Terence, 'Demesnes', in F.H.A. Aalen, K. Whelan and M. Stout, *Atlas of the Irish Rural Landscape* (Cork, 1997).
–, *Irish Gardens and Gardening before Cromwell* (Kinsale, 1999).
Robbins, Caroline, *The Eighteenth-Century Commonwealthman: Studies in the Transmission, Development and Circumstance of English Liberal Thought from the Restoration of Charles II until the War with the Thirteen Colonies* (Harvard, 1959).
Robinson, Sidney K., *Inquiry into the Picturesque* (London, 1991).

Rosenfeld, Sybil, *Temples of Thespis: Some Private Theatres and Theatricals in England and Wales, 1700–1820* (London, 1978).
Ross, Ian Campbell (ed.), *Public Virtue, Public Love: The Early Years of the Dublin Lying-in Hospital, The Rotunda* (Dublin, 1986).
Ryan, W.P., *The Pope's Green Island* (London, 1912).
Schama, Simon, *Landscape and Memory* (London, 1995).
–, *The Embarrassment of Riches* (London, 1987).
–, *Citizens* (London, 1989).
Shaffrey, P., *Castletown* (Castletown Foundation, 1990).
Simo, M.L., *Loudon and the Landscape: From Country Seat to Metropolis* (Yale, 1988).
Smyth, W.J., 'Estate Records and the Making of the Irish Landscape: An Example from County Tipperary', *Irish Geography,* vol. 9, 1976.
Stewart, David, 'Political Ruins: Gothic Sham Ruins and the "45"', *Journal of the Society of Architectural Historians,* vol. 55, no. 4, December 1996, pp. 400–11.
Stroud, Dorothy, *Capability Brown* (London, 1984).
Symes, Michael, *The English Rococo Garden* (Princes Risborough, Buckinghamshire, 1991).
–, 'The Hon. Charles Hamilton at Holland Park', *Journal of Garden History,* vol.3, no.2, pp. 129–33.
Thompson, E.P.,Whigs and Hunters: *The Origins of the Black Act* (London, 1975).
–, *The Making of the English Working Class* (Harmondsworth, 1968).
Tillyard, Stella, *Aristocrats: Caroline, Emily, Louisa and Sarah Lennox 1740–1832* (London, 1994).
Vaughan, W.E., *Landlords and Tenants in Ireland 1848–1904* (Dundalgan Press, 1994)
Watson, Ross, 'Francis Wheatley in Ireland', *Irish Georgian Society Bulletin,* vol. IX, no. 2.
Wiebenson, Dora, *The Picturesque Garden in France* (Princeton, 1978).
Wilkie, Kim, *Arcadian Thames* (London, 1994).
Williams, Raymond, *The Country and the City* (London, 1973).
Williamson, T., *Polite Landscapes: Gardens and Society in Eighteenth-Century England* (Stroud and Maryland, 1995).
Willis, Peter, *Charles Bridgeman and the English Landscape Garden* (London, 1977).
Wittkower, Rudolf, *Palladio and English Palladianism* (London, 1974).
Woodbridge, K., *Landscape and Antiquity* (Oxford, 1970).
–, *Princely Gardens: The Origins and Development of the French Formal Style* (London, 1986).
Woudstra, Jan, 'The Planting of the Privy Garden', in Simon Thurley (ed.), *The Privy Garden at Hampton Court Palace* (London, 1995), pp. 43–77.

# Index

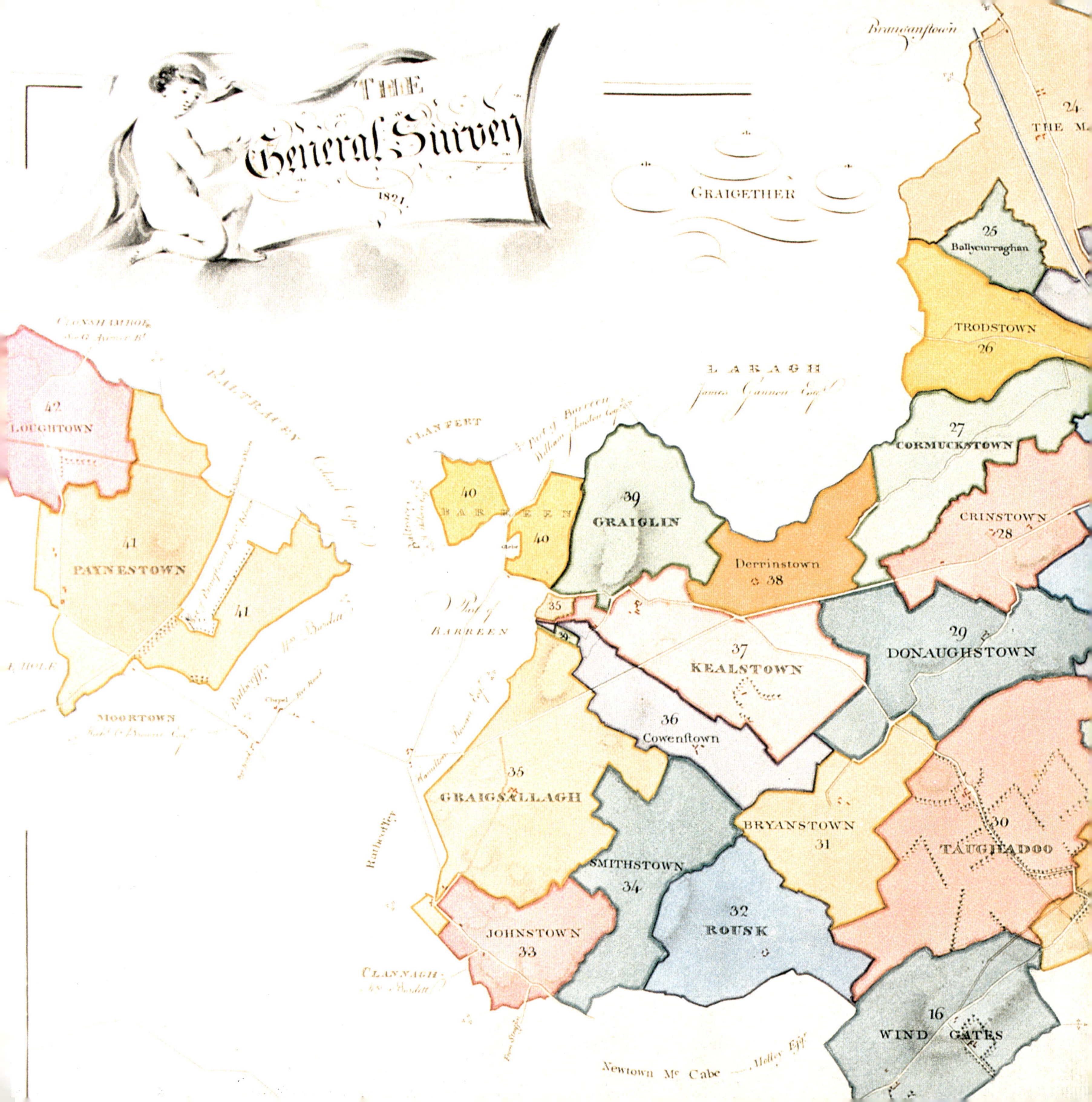
THE
General Survey
1821
GRAIGETHER
Brianganstown
24
THE M.
25
Ballycurraghan
TRODSTOWN
26
LARAGH
27
CORMUCKSTOWN
CRINSTOWN
28
42
LOUGHTOWN
CLANFERT
40
BARREEN
40
39
GRAIGLIN
Derrinstown
38
41
PAYNESTOWN
41
35
Part of
BARREEN
37
KEALSTOWN
29
DONAUGHSTOWN
MOORTOWN
36
Cowenstown
35
GRAIGSALLAGH
BRYANSTOWN
31
30
TAUGHADOO
Rathcoffey
SMITHSTOWN
34
32
ROUSK
JOHNSTOWN
33
CLANNAGH
16
WIND GATES
Newtown Mc Cabe